MOSES IS DEAD

MOSES IS DEAD

LARRY HERNDON

TATE PUBLISHING
AND ENTERPRISES, LLC

Published by Tate Publishing & Enterprises, LLC
127 E. Trade Center Terrace | Mustang, Oklahoma 73064 USA
1.888.361.9473 | www.tatepublishing.com

Tate Publishing is committed to excellence in the publishing industry. The company reflects the philosophy established by the founders, based on Psalm 68:11,
"The lord gave the word and great was the company of those who published it."

Book design copyright © 2012 by Tate Publishing, LLC. All rights reserved.
Cover design by Rodrigo Adolfo
Interior design by Errol Villamante

Published in the United States of America

ISBN 978-1-62147-805-8
1. Religion / Biblical Studies / Exegesis & Hermeneutics
2. Religion / Biblical Criticism & Interpretation / General
12.08.13

DEDICATION

I would like to dedicate this writing to my friend Phil who has already passed through this natural life and now is seated right next to Jesus. I only knew Phil for a short time on this earth, but somehow I have always known him. He is the first man I ever saw actually converted right in front of my eyes. I have seen many people accept salvation, but I have only seen a total conversion one time, and all at once. It was an earthquake; a shifting of identities, from a natural man born under the Mosaic Law freed from the law by a non-natural spiritual birth into his real identity—a son of God. It just took all of his days to see this happen. He was and always will be a son of God; he just had not yet accepted his new identity, and his entire life was a series of shakings or tremors, even in struggles and failures and in sins and in work and in relationships, a journey to a new identity in Jesus Christ, or rather, letting Jesus out, who was in him. It was a revelation of Jesus Christ to himself and then to the rest who would see this change, and then he was ready to go.

Phil had a religion-based knowledge of Jesus—he had been in and out of the church for years—not a personal inward knowing in the heart, until one day at church when the Holy Spirit convicted him, not of his sins but of not believing in Jesus, and somehow I knew it. Actually Jesus showed me through a supernatural experience. He did not *just* get saved or have his sins forgiven. He had an encounter with the risen Christ Jesus, and Phil knew it, as did we. Phil later declared as he was being baptized that Jesus leapt or jumped into his heart, which of course meant that Jesus had to be present to do just that! He found his identity in Jesus and lost his old one, and he is alive forevermore.

It is still one of the greatest things I have ever witnessed—a man being converted by the power of God, His grace, Christ in us, unto an eternal relationship of love. He was filled with a joy that passes carnal understanding. He was rejoicing even in his struggles. Phil has inspired me time and again because he did not have time to play act or be religious, he was facing the end of his days on this earth. He had lost all fear of death because he knew that he would not die. He was full of joy for he knew that his name was recorded in heaven. All fears were gone; "perfect love casteth out fear" (1John 4:18). He loved more than many do in a full lifetime with a love that is from above, with a love like God's love for him.

This statement comes from a teaching of Jesus' in Luke 7:47, "…her sins which are many, are forgiven; for she loved much…" However, Jesus did not say, "he who loves is forgiven…" No, love is a response to what Father God, through the cross of Jesus, has done for us. He loved us first, and how much we love is simply seeing and believing and then receiving how much we are truly loved and how much we are completely forgiven. If little, then you will love little, but if you have been forgiven of all sin, you will love much! I still remember Phil taking my hand and putting it under his face, holding me in his presence even as he slept. Love desires the presence of those loved. It is a God like love that only He can give to us, pouring His love into us by the Holy Ghost.

Love is the evidence of a changed life, as is the absence of fear. Jesus changes lives. Grace is living out that life in knowledge of being loved more than anyone could ever earn; it is a position, a new identity, no matter how long we live, of receiving love first from Father God through Jesus and then administering the same. Of being forgiven and so forgiving, of receiving His grace and then giving graciously. It is hard to give something you do not have or have not experienced first. It is harder to teach something you have never experienced firsthand. That is why Jesus is the love of God come down to the earth.

It is a greater love than we have ever known that breaks our hearts and causes us to love with no thought of ourselves—a total abandonment of self and of our past life before Jesus, of what others think or say. It just took Phil a little longer to finally see himself as Father God had always seen him. It was a revelation of Jesus to and in Phil, a mighty man of valor, a son in right standing, rich though poor, healed though sick, alive though dead, strong though weak, eternal in a temporal realm, loved and able to love, and love is eternal. I could see the light of God in Phil; it is the life of Jesus, who is light. Phil is living life to the full and so should we, here and now, life to the abundant.

Thank you Phil, my brother, for showing me this love in this life—a Jesus love—and for losing yourself in Him. My friend is experiencing that love face to face, and soon we who remain will as well. Phil, save a seat for us, we'll be right behind you. We love you in Jesus! And I'm still causing the sparks to fly: I'll bet you can see them, here comes some more.

ACKNOWLEDGEMENTS

I would like to acknowledge all of those who have helped me to grow and to learn. To those whom Father has sent to me and who have instructed me; to the One who has been so patient with me and now extends the same to you, thank you Jesus. To the Holy Spirit who has led me into truth, all truth. To the Word of God which will never end, not one word; to my heavenly Father who loves me more than words can form—thank you!

TABLE OF CONTENTS

FOREWORD

I love Moses. I love how he lived his life, how Father God used him. I love how Moses saw Father God, how he obeyed Him because he trusted Him. The Law was given by Moses, but grace and truth came by Jesus Christ. One sounds distant and one sounds very personal. I can still hear Moses speaking, but the Law no longer speaks to me. I want to hear Jesus alone. It was Jesus who taught a parable about a rich man and a beggar named Lazarus. The rich man and Lazarus both died in the same day and one was found held in Abraham's bosom and the rich man was in eternal torment. Somehow this rich man could see the beggar Lazarus across a chasm no one could cross over, and he asked for water, a single drop to cool his tongue.

Did you ever think about that? How many times in eternity will those who do not accept Jesus curse themselves and remind themselves of their refusal to accept Jesus? When Abraham refused to send Lazarus with the drop of water, the rich man then asked if someone, even Lazarus himself, could go back and warn his brothers. This sounds good doesn't it? Yet look at what Jesus said.

> "Abraham saith unto him, They have Moses and the prophets; let them hear them. And he said, Nay father Abraham, but if one went unto them from the dead, they will repent. And he said unto him, If they hear not Moses and the prophets, neither will they be persuaded, though one be raised from the dead."
>
> Luke 16:29-31

Did you know that Jesus then raised Lazarus from the dead? But did they listen? Look at how the religious leaders reacted to this miracle.

> 'Much people of the Jews therefore knew that he was there: and they came not for Jesus's sake only, but that they might see Lazarus also, who he had raised from the dead. But the chief priests consulted that they might put Lazarus also to death; because by reason of him many of the Jews went away, and believed Jesus.'
>
> John 12:9-11

It is still the same. If people won't hear Moses and the prophets, they will not be persuaded even though Jesus was raised from the dead. It was Jesus who said in Luke 24:44, "These are the words which I spake unto you, while I was yet with you, that all things must be fulfilled which were written in the law of Moses, and in the prophets, and in the Psalms concerning me." The next verse says that *then* he opened their understanding that they might understand the Scriptures.

You see the prophets only wrote what the Spirit of Christ that was in them told them to.

> 'Of which salvation the prophets have inquired and searched diligently, who prophesied of the grace that should come unto you; searching what, or what manner of time the Spirit of Christ which was in them did signify, when it testified beforehand the sufferings of Christ, and the glory that should follow.'
>
> 1 Peter 1:10-11

In other words, Moses wrote about One to come and of His grace for us, as did all of the prophets. Don't feel alone if you did not understand this, for the Bible tells us that the angels themselves desire to look into these things written about Jesus. It takes help to understand. We need the Holy Spirit.

I assure you, I am not against Moses. I love him. He fulfilled his life in serving Father God and prophesied of Jesus saying another one like him was coming. He saw Jesus afar off. But to us who believe Moses is silenced, Father said on the mount, "This is my beloved Son in whom I am well pleased, hear him." (Luke 9:35). If this was obeyed from the heart, I would not need to write another word. But here it is, *Moses Is Dead.*

As I began to write this book, I was warned of the journey and the effect of what I would share. It was to be a battle that does not end. I would much rather write a story you would enjoy or perhaps even share some doctrine that you would like but this is not so with this writing. It will in fact bring many of you to places that will cause your hearts turmoil, for it is the sword of the Spirit I will bring and as it is written, "Yea, a sword shall pierce through thy own soul also, that the thoughts of many hearts may be revealed." (Luke 2:35).

This was so spoken to the mother of Jesus by an old man named Simeon, and so it was to be. All revelations of Jesus cause this, first in those who have experienced this truth and in those to whom the same is shared. But know that I write this because of what the Lord has shown me by the Spirit of how He sees His church today. It is a blended church, a bride who wears two rings, who Paul called a spiritual adulteress, being married to two different men.

But I do not write to condemn—I myself walked here with you for years—but to bring light to a truth I pray you will see and believe. For of a truth beloved, Moses is dead. Father so told Joshua these very words before he was to lead Israel into the Promised Land. The journey of Moses, the law, was to stay behind, for the law is not of faith. Faith comes with the Holy Spirit and not with the law. The law demands and strikes the rock while faith speaks to the rock, and life comes out freely. Only in faith are the Promises of God accessed. It is this journey I want to take you on, to a higher place, a come up thither place, and when you reach this place, His great and precious promises will be there waiting for you. It will be a long and difficult journey, and there are many who will oppose you. They have me. But know that everything in this life is a journey from one place to another. There are many choices along the journey, and this is one you may not have known existed. It is for this reason I offer you *Moses is Dead, A Journey of Life and Death*.

Preface

Iknow this is hard for us to accept but if I do not share this with you, the entire writing of this book is without any purpose. There are so many who teach things because that is the way they have been taught themselves. It is the way things have always been—traditions of men. But with the Lord and with the Holy Spirit, it is not as men always say. There is much debate over the Holy Spirit or Holy Ghost, and, in fact, many see any discussions about the Holy Spirit as divisive or disruptive.

This is not nor ever has been the purpose of the Holy Spirit. Jesus said that it would be better for us that He go away for He would send the Holy Spirit to us. (John 16:7). How could this be better than seeing Jesus? Faith! It is to be by faith alone! The Holy Spirit was to be sent to lead us into all truth. Grace and truth came by Jesus Christ, not by Moses. Some say one thing, some another. But the word of God says that the Holy Spirit came when the fullness of time had come and when those ordained to receive Him were praying and waiting for this promise to come from God, just as Jesus had so said. It was to be with power that He came, and when He came, those who awaited His coming were filled with boldness and a faith that they did not have before. 'But before faith came, we were kept under the law, shut up unto the faith which should afterwards be revealed' (Galatians 3:23). They came out of hiding and boldly spoke of Jesus and the resurrection of the dead, knowing full well of the outcome of such speech.

There was no order of service for the Spirit to come. Just read Acts and see for yourself, but He did come and signs and wonders followed. Some say that He came when they had prayed long enough, when they had remained long enough. Maybe this is a truth because they were too tired to still resist Him, but the Bible says that when the time was fulfilled He came. He is still coming today. The Bible tells us in 1 Corinthians 2:12 that the Holy Spirit is given that we might understand those things Father God has *freely given* to us—the freely given is referencing His grace and favor—things we cannot understand in the natural realm.

Grace is a hard thing to fully understand, and this is why He was sent, why He came—to help us understand grace and all that Jesus did before He left, testifying to us of Jesus and everything that He said, taking from Jesus and making that which was Jesus's known to us. We cannot receive what we do not understand! He would lead us into all truth. He would convict the world of not believing in Jesus. He would teach us what it means to be righteous by faith alone. He would inform us of Satan's judgment being a fact. He would help us to understand that Father has forgotten our sins and iniquities and that our sins He would remember no more. He would impart gifts to the church, to His bride. He would send supernatural gifts to men that we might know Him and help the world to better see Him who is unseen. He would help us to understand that Father and Jesus and the Holy Spirit live in us and will never leave us nor forsake us. In fact, Jesus said that He, the Holy Spirit, would be in us and we would know it.

This is not a word-of-mouth thing where someone else just says it is so. He said we would know it by experience. Do you? The Spirit of God is sent to help us to receive what we cannot see with the natural eye and to hear what is not heard with natural ears—"He who has an ear let him hear what the Spirit says"—(Revelation 2:7)-and to understand all that Jesus has done for us already. It will be an awakening to a inner voice all believers in Jesus should have. "My sheep will hear My voice." (John 10:3.)

   LARRY HERNDON

I need Him, I desire everything He has for me. You will never fully understand grace, what is freely given us by Father, without the Holy Ghost or Spirit. He is sent to bring glory to Jesus… 'Christ in us the hope of glory' Colossians 1:27….His glory and not ours! But He will not be received through any efforts of the flesh. In fact, He is silenced by human efforts. He comes to those who have yielded control, all control to Jesus. He comes to those who are tired of leading and seek to be led, tired of doing and want to rest in His finished works. As long as we try to be good enough, we will never fully understand that Father already sees us this way. We will wear ourselves out!

He comes by faith into a broken vessel, a vessel willing to yield to One greater. You cannot be saved without the Holy Spirit, but you can continue living your life in charge, in control, in your own power. Or you can give up and receive Him and with Him the power Jesus promised. But not through the law, for the law is not of faith!

For example I took our little dog out into the yard this morning to do her business. She is very old, and I carried her out. After she was finished, I reached down to pick her up to carry her back into the house. She is nearly blind and cannot hear very well, and as I placed my hands under her belly to pick her up she squatted and then pushed herself up. But was it her strength or power that pulled her up into my arms, or was she simply doing what she believed was needed to propel her just as she always had? Was there any real power in her efforts? She was going to be picked up by me no matter what, but as long as she can help, she will try. You will never convince her that her efforts did not make the difference. It is the same thing with the Holy Spirit. He is simply waiting for us to be unable to do for ourselves.

Until we grow tired and give up and recognize that we too are blind and nearly deaf, we will not receive Him and everything He brings to us in fullness. Do we need this power? Not as long as you can see and do for yourself, not as long as you are still able.

You will never need and desire His power! How tired are you beloved? How long will the trials and tests continue for you? And just who is testing who? When will you finally yield to Him and receive Him? The power of the Holy Spirit is to serve, but by His leading, not our efforts. The preface for everything I share must be for this purpose or it is for nothing at all. It is all about Jesus!

As I read the words Jesus spoke to the religious leaders of His day I wondered at what He truly was trying to show them. Why could they not see the truth that He was bringing to them? Power and prestige are places where many fall and fail. They denied both Jesus and the truth *for envy* the Bible says. Why? Was it the loss of fleshly controls they had? The law speaks only to the flesh, the outward aspects of mankind, and it is understood in the natural realm. But Jesus came to reveal this Law to men, did He not? Yes! So Jesus magnified the Law of His Father to a place where no man could say, "I keep the law." Not one!

But let me share with you something so wonderful that without this truth your journey in this book will be like the bridge built that leads to nowhere. In Matthew 12:41-42 Jesus is speaking these truths to us as well as to the religious leaders of that day:

> 'But I say unto you, That in this place is one greater than the temple…the men of Nineveh shall rise in judgment with this generation, and shall condemn it: because they repented at the preaching of Jonah: and, behold, a greater than Jonah is here…The queen of the south shall rise up in judgment with this generation, and shall condemn it; for she came from the uttermost parts of the earth to hear the wisdom of Solomon, and, behold, a greater than Solomon is here…'

Can you see this? It is the place of beginnings and it is the place where we must finally come to see. Someone greater than everything else in our lives has come. He is greater than the Law, greater than all of our sin and our doubt and our cares for our families and for our health and prosperity. He has overcome death and sin. He has overcome the whole world! He is greater than all things! I will not magnify sin above the One who vanquished it on the cross. I will never preach sin when I can preach Jesus and Him crucified. I will never use the law as a tool to save the lost when in fact salvation is from faith in Jesus's name and by the law is the knowledge of sin. They already know they are condemned. They are not seeking someone to point at them but someone who will point them to someone!

The key is the hearts of men. These religious leaders of Jesus's day even said that Jesus had cast out devils by the devil. Imagine that! One greater than the enemy came and cast him out yet those God placed to show forth His mercy and grace called His works of the devil. What is it that is in the hearts of men? If all we see is evil, is our heart filled with the wrong knowledge? If all we see is condemnation, is not our heart filled with the wrong doctrine? What fruit do we share with the world? Is it a sin message or a message of His amazing grace and mercy? Do we bind Satan in order to praise God? Or do we praise God and in so doing bind the enemy? Who do we empower with our words beloved? Do we see everything in this world greater than the One who came down? Do we violate His words? Do we blend the law with grace in order to make it more palatable to those who still live under the rule of Mosaic laws? *One greater than…*Moses is dead, beloved. To quote the Father from heaven again, "This is My beloved Son, hear Him…" Who will we listen to?

In seeing this truth of grace alone, we then allow a place for the fleshly man to be replaced by a new creation, a new heart that is tuned into Jesus and hears the Holy Spirit who leads us into all truth. We do not know the truth without Him! Jesus taught those Jews who held the words of God as sacred that they would "know the truth and the truth would set them free." (John 8:32.) They did not know the truth for Jesus is the truth. They knew the law and the traditions and the rituals, but they did not know the

One sent down; whose truths they could not hear because they were deaf and dead because of the law and its power to condemn. They could not see through the eyes of love what Father was saying to us with the law. They were deaf. Is what you are being taught freeing you or binding you to the Law of Moses again? It is a matter of life and death I bring beloved. "Is the law then against the promises of God? God forbid: for if there had been a law which could have given life, verily righteousness should have been by the law" (Galatians 3:21). But the Bible says that all righteousness is of faith alone; the law brings death! Jesus is the way, He is the truth, He is the life, and Moses is dead. Who and what is alive in your hearts?

This journey will begin in Egypt, from a place called Goshen, or nearness. It was a place where Father God desired to be near His people even though they were in the power of human bondage. This place of nearness protected them even as the plagues destroyed those who held Israel in bondage. But there they did not know Father God, so He led them by His Spirit on a journey to His Promised Land, to His promises, but only two of the original made it. They, Joshua and Caleb, were of another spirit. They trusted God completely. They saw the promises of God as theirs, even if they had to fight for them. The question then arises, will you?

Introduction

How would you like a bowl of ice cream with a big pile of sour kraut on it? How about a new string bikini for your trip to the North Pole? These things do not go together do they? The question arises in my heart as I consider those who blend law, the commandments of God, with grace which is the work of God for us. Is blending law and grace something we can eat and enjoy? Can we live in this mixture? Is it wrong to blend them? You know, a little law helps to keep the flock under control. A little guilt goes a long way in curbing sinfulness in mankind. Is it good to put new wine in an old wine skin?

Law reveals man's sinfulness while grace reveals God's mercy. Law reveals our unrighteousness, and grace His righteousness. Law reveals our inability to love God enough, and grace reveals His perfect love for us. Law reveals what we lack, and grace reveals all that Father has for us in Christ Jesus. Law reveals what we must do, and grace what Jesus has already done for us. Law reveals to us that we are dead, and grace reveals a greater truth—we are alive by faith to Father God through Jesus and the cross. The law reveals our nakedness and shame and guilt, and grace reveals the One who covers us and who bore our shame and guilt. Law reveals our inability, and grace His ability. The law reveals our inability to be good enough, and grace reveals the One who gave us His Son because He knew we could not be. These are direct opposites. One brings us to death and the other into life eternal; one to the end of ourselves and the other to Jesus; one works on the fleshly man to bring him to see the truth, the other brings forth life by the Spirit who reveals all truth to us. Jesus is the truth!

The greatest journey you will ever undertake is the journey from bondage to freedom, from Egypt in the place of nearness or Goshen to the Promised Land, a place where milk and honey flow, where promises are ours for the taking, where inheritance is already assigned to a place no one could have ever imagined we would end up—Christ in us, even closer than a place called nearness. It is a journey that will take us from bondage into rebellion and into places in our hearts we did not know existed, places where Jesus is revealed to us in ways we did not know Him, places to stop and see but not to stay forever—epiphanies I believe they are called—and we will have many as we go through life and on this journey.

It will be through the sea and around the hills to a river we cannot cross over, to a place where our reproach and shame are removed, at Gigal, the place of rolling away. And there we will move into our inheritance, the Promised Land or His great and precious promises, where we know His Presence is not just with us, but in us. A journey from the fear of not knowing to the assurance of His finished works, from rejection to total acceptance through the works of another. Jesus is the revealer of all truth by the Holy Spirit. He is the fulfiller of all prophecies. He is our all in all. He is the land of fruitfulness in our barrenness. He is the cross in the place we cross over. He is the bridge that takes us across the river we cannot cross over. He is the Passover feast and the Passover Lamb. It is His unveiling or revealing or revelations that we need to see and believe, for in Him is life. In Him is our nearness even when we are far away. In Him is our peace even as the storm blows. It is a journey from nearness to in us. Won't you join me?

THE KING OF SODOM

In the book of beginnings or Genesis we see a story told of Abram going into the city of Sodom to save his nephew Lot from the hands of those who had plundered the city and had taken Lot and his family. The story is told from a place where Lot and Abram separated due to strife, both were very successful through the blessing God had spoken over Abram. Lot went to Sodom and Abram remained in the hill country. As soon as Lot left, Abram heard again from the Lord God of the promise to come to him. It was the promise of many people and much land to contain them in. In fact, Father promised Abram everything that he could see was his.

What was it Abram saw? He saw that he had no descendants to pass everything to. So God promised Abram a son, Isaac. It was what Jesus saw as well and Father promised Him descendants, and just as Abram saw them afar off, so did Jesus. He saw us—people, family, those he could call His own. What good is land if no one lives in it? What good is money or inheritance if there is no one to share or leave it with? What good is love if there is no one to love?

It later became a part of the Abrahamic covenant of faith and promise. It was to be a gift from Father God to Abram. However, Lot fell victim to a war over servitude to another king named Chedorlaomer. One man escaped from this battle and ran to Abram who was the first to be called a Hebrew, which means to cross over. Many will debate on the meaning of this, but for us it is those chosen of God to believe by faith and not through some physical manifestation. Yes, God manifested Himself to Abram in many ways, but first, Abraham believed God, and God reckoned his faith as righteousness.

Abraham is the father of faith, he is hewn from the Rock we of faith are all hewn from- (Isaiah 51:1-2). Abram rallied 318 men who were in a covenant with Abram. Three hundred eighteen men then attacked these mighty armies of Chedorlamer and defeated him. The Bible tells us that 'Abram brought back all the goods, and also again his brother (nephew) Lot, and his goods, and the women also, and the people.' (Genesis 14:15). This is most significant to all that I will share in the book you are reading. Something we seldom see is seen here: we (ordinary everyday people) are the focus of Father God. After the great victory, we see a type and a shadow of Christ Jesus come to Abram in the person of Melchizedek, the priest of the most high God. He blessed Abram—the greater blessing the lesser—and Abram gave a tithe of everything to him. But look with me at what this defeated king of Sodom wanted: "And the king of Sodom said unto Abram, 'Give me the persons, and take the goods to thyself'" (Genesis 14:21). Abram responded that he would take nothing from this king saying that he had raised his hand in pledge to the Lord God who owned heaven and earth. Immediately, the Lord responded to Abram telling him to fear not, "I am your shield and you very great reward," (Genesis15:1) and promised Abram a seed from within himself, and they made a covenant in blood.

But note that the king of Sodom did not ask for the wealth but for the people God had rescued through Abram and his confederates. He sought out people to control. The people have always been the source of envy for the enemy of God. When Jesus was tempted in the wilderness for forty days and nights, the enemy Satan appeared and tempted Jesus with food and with power over kingdoms to prove himself as the Son of God, but he did not tempt Jesus with people. Even the enemy of God knows that the real battle for control is not one of goods for what good are goods in a physical realm if no one will follow or worship you. No, the real temptation was to keep the Seed from freeing the people from a fear that was born into their flesh—controlling and being controlled by death—and to see life past the physical to life in Jesus—resurrected life, life by the Spirit.

The Pharisees and Sadducees and Herodians and the religious leaders of Jesus's time were afraid of losing control of people they controlled with fear, even using God's laws against them while they placed themselves above the same laws using the laws for gain and control. Did you ever wonder why the Pharisees and law-givers brought the woman caught in adultery to Jesus? They in fact declared that she was guilty of adultery, having been caught in the act. They did not need Jesus's approval to stone her. The truth is this, they did not care about her or her acts of sin nor the law itself. They wanted to remain in control of the people using the law for their own gains and power. They wanted Jesus to be crucified because they were envious of the people who flocked to Him. They feared no one would follow them—"if we don't stop Him the whole world will follow Him." (John 12:19).

The battle is the same today, friends. It is for the souls of men the battles exist. One side seeks to control mankind with physical things and desires, blinding them to this truth. The other has come to free them from all fears into eternal vision through no external controls or anything of the flesh. Anything of the flesh is corrupted and will not pass through the fire. Only those things born again of God will survive, because they are born of His Spirit. And those born of the Spirit are no longer under the laws of Moses. They are under a new and living way, a covenant between Father and Son, in His blood—grace! This is the battle beloved, and the victory has been won for us by Jesus who overcame physical death for us and who has vanquished sin on the cross, enabling all who will to *come up thither* or to a higher place called grace. We can now live out our lives not bound in death, but risen in Christ Jesus, and all by grace. Jesus was promised an inheritance, and it was not things or wealth or power that He came down for, for He already had everything. It was for us that He came. We are the focus of His battles and victory, even as we walk out the free will He purchased for all, including those who will reject Him.

The Lord awoke me just the other night and placed this verse in my heart and reminded me the next day to look at it again and again. "Arise O God, judge the earth; for thou shalt inherit all nations" (Psalm 82:8). Who shall inherit all nations? Jesus! Look at this Messianic prophecy Psalm 2:7-8, "I will declare the decree; the Lord hath said unto me, 'Thou art my Son; this day have I begotten thee. Ask of me, and I shall give thee the heathen for thine inheritance; and the uttermost parts of the earth for thy possession.'" Can you see this? When John looked into the heavens in a vision we call the Revelation of Jesus Christ, we see Jesus revealing to John and then to us from 10:7-11 that when the seventh angel "begins to sound" and time should be accomplished, John was to take the little book, the new covenant, and go to many peoples and nations and tongues and kings.

Why? Revelation 11:15, "And the seventh angel sounded; and there were great voices in heaven, saying, 'The kingdoms of this world are become the kingdoms of our Lord, and of His Christ; and He shall reign forever and ever.'" It is exactly what Jesus taught us to pray: "Thy kingdom come, thy will be done in earth as it is in heaven…" We are to be going and establishing His kingdom by freeing those bound and telling of His inheritance to all heathens or Gentiles and the seventh angel cannot finish until they become His. It is the message of grace. Jesus is resting until everything has become his footstool, including the enemies of the cross as Paul calls them, those who try to blend law and grace as one covenant. Even the battles we fight, and there will be many who oppose us, we are secured with this word. Victory is assured. It was Father God's promise to Jesus. People are His inheritance. And as Jesus began His earthly ministry, He shared how this was to be from the Word, showing His spiritual DNA, His rights of inheritance, and even though no one understood this truth, including His own disciples, in the strength of the Word of God, Jesus finished the race for us. He won for us the victory over sin, over death, and over the laws (Mosaic) that were used against us by the enemy, nailing them (the Laws) to His cross.

How? One greater is come! It is from this place of victory (the Cross) we fight, and all we have to do is to believe and receive. We are here to bring those chosen and called to the awareness of their heritage and of who it is that purchased them. It sheds a new light on why we are chosen, called, placed where we are and when we are, and who we are here for. If we have this vision, this truth, in our hearts there is nothing Father will not do for us, having prepared in advance the good works we are called to do. Oh, the battles will rage, but just as Abram beat up several kings of powerful armies with plowshares and 318 men, so shall Father give to us everything we need to fulfill His plan. But our efforts are not to get victory, but from victory over death, sickness, poverty, and even the law, but for the people we fight, for the souls of mankind, for they are Jesus's inheritance. Victory is won, yet battles will continue for the greatest prizes, people- the creation Father made and has declared "very good" (Genesis 2:31). Just as Abram turned away from the things of this world in view of the Promises of God, so must we! For Him we go and do, and by Him we exist and are held together as are all things—all! The journey begins here and it will not end until the seventh angel sounds the victory. This will be a battle to let go of the old and take hold of the new, but you must grasp the little book and hold it fast. It is the Seed that is incorruptible and it will accomplish all that Father wants it to. Jesus is the Seed, He is the Word of God made flesh, and we who have been with Him from the beginning must tell. It is time to grow up and move forth. The seventh angel is beginning to sound the call. It is for the souls of men, not things. Can you hear it?

I Did Not Know Him This Way

A Place of Nearness

Once Jesus spoke with some of His closest friends, and he told them that if they believed they would see the glory of God, and they did. Jesus was revealing who He was and who His Father was to them even in the midst of death itself saying, "I am the resurrection and the life." (John 11:25). Jesus wasn't quoting a verse but He was telling them He was about to reveal Himself to them in a greater way. He was about to resurrect the dead—Lazarus. It was a new way, a way in which they had not seen Him before. They knew Him as Lord and as Teacher or Rabbi. They knew Him as a friend, a miracle worker, but they did not know Him as *the* resurrection and *the* life. They later would see Him as the suffering Messiah and Christ, but they had not seen or known Him in this way yet. It is how Jesus reveals Himself to us that will determine how we see Him, not how we have seen Him based on what others say of Him. Jesus later told John to come up here or thither and it was from there that John was to see more revelations or unveilings or revealings of Jesus, in ways we had not known Him before.

Again the Spirit of the Lord awakened me with another verse of Scripture for this journey. "I will bring you in unto the land, concerning the which I did swear to give it to Abraham, to Isaac, and to Jacob; and I will give it to you for an heritage; I am the Lord" (Exodus 6:8).

Now this may not seem to fit what is coming up after this, on this journey, but believe me it does belong right here. We must look at what is happening in the lives of the Hebrews as Father God begins to deliver them from the bondage they were enslaved in while in the land of Egypt. You see, He led them to Egypt to save them and to prepare a place for them, Canaan, a land flowing with milk and honey. But first He had to see the end of those who inhabited the land, the Gentile world. Father had led Israel to Egypt and had saved the heritage of Abraham and Isaac and Jacob from dying in starvation during a drought and famine that lasted seven years.

The enemy will do anything he can to stop the plan from coming to fruition. Father God saved them by sending in one of their own, a brother born of another mother, of Rachel. Joseph, a type of Jesus a type of savior to come if you will, brought them into a place called "Goshen" or nearness. It is the heart of Jesus, and of Father, to be near us, even in us, "I want them to be where I am…" (John 17:24).

Oh that we might believe this truth! It is for us to see that even in our enslavement to the things of this world, even in our bondage to the things and circumstances that hold us and keep us from seeing Jesus and Father as they truly are—the bondages of life, even religion itself—we are in a place where Father desires to be near to us through Jesus. It is also the place of deliverance once the time is fulfilled for us to come forth. "But when the fullness of time was come, God sent forth his Son, made of a woman, made under the law, to redeem them that were under the law, that we might receive the adoption of sons…" (Galatians 4:4-5).

Remember that in Goshen, nearness to Father, the same things that happened to Egypt did not happen in Goshen to the Hebrews; no plagues or diseases or pestilences or darkness or hailstones hit them. In His Presence, there can be nothing greater than He is! But Father God promised in covenant to bring those from the bondage of Egypt into the Promised Land, Canaan. Four hundred thirty years later, this became a reality. Moses led them from Egypt into the wilderness, a place where faith was to be the way. They were led by the Spirit, learning to trust in a God they did not know in this way, having only seen the gods of Egypt. They had forgotten their heritage and the power of their God who loved them and chose them, and He had always been with them!

But Moses could not take them in. It was Joshua that took them in. It was Jesus who came to set us free from bondage— all of them! The law can bring you to the place of crossing over Jordan, to death—the baptism of faith. But only Jesus can lead us across by His grace, and in each step it is to be by grace through faith, what He did by what we believe and trust. It is the place of all assurance, secured by His efforts alone. It is a step of unveiling Jesus in us, and we must simply follow. We must in fact see Jesus in a way we did not know Him before, a new and living way. "For ye have not received the spirit of bondage again to fear, but you have received the Spirit of sonship whereby we cry, Abba Father" (Romans 8:15). He came to set us free from bondage to the law that condemns us, and only a child can receive this truth. Did you know that the law is bondage to those born again of God? Fear is not of faith. Faith works by love. Love is displayed on a cross, not in human efforts to do in order to receive. The promises (Promised Land) are only accessed by grace through faith, and the law is not of faith!

It is clearly seen in Exodus 6:2-3, "And God spake unto Moses, saying, 'I am the Lord, JEHOVAH and I appeared unto Abraham, unto Isaac, and unto Jacob, by the name of God Almighty, but by My Name JEHOVAH was I not known to them.'" In other words, these who Father God had made covenant with did not know Him except by God Almighty. El Shaddai was His name to those that He mentioned in these verses. But now, to those in bondage, to those He is about to deliver, He announces His name is Jehovah, a new revelation of Himself, but they did not know Him in that way. It is a combination of Hebrew words that Father God told Moses earlier at the burning bush. "I AM that I AM. tell them I AM sent you." (Exodus 3:14). It is literally, Jah plus Havah—God being revealed as or through communications as what you need—I AM.

The revelation of Father God to us has always been by Him to us, for no one can see what He does not want them to see. This truth is then clearly seen in Exodus 6:6-8 (verses 6-8) take out where we see the words "I will" repeated many times. This is of course before the Law was given to Moses. There were no *ifs* attached to these words linking His promises to their performance. It was how the people were to see Him, God. He had always been the Creator God, God Almighty, but even in the name He chose to reveal Himself through, He identified many things, including His own Son Jesus. Jah saves or Jaweh is salvation—Jesus...Jeshua. The Great I AM reveals His heart to save saying, "I will..."

But look at these words from Exodus 6, "I will bring you out...I will rid you out of their bondage...I will redeem you...I will take you to Me for a people...I will be to you a God...I will bring you in unto the land...I will give it unto you..." Notice that there are no *thou shalts* in this revelation from Father God to those about to be redeemed and delivered...none! It was grace being revealed to them, but would they see it? The law reveals what we must do, and grace always reveals what God has done or is doing for us. There was no performance tied to His promises, none! Grace is a work of God. He would do it for them...but would they simply accept, receive, and believe it? Say you see this beloved.

But because of the damage done to their spirits, "they hearkened not to Moses for anguish of spirit, and for cruel bondage..." (Exodus 6:9). They did not see or hear. What bondage is it in our lives that blinds us from seeing this truth? Isn't it the bondage of fear caused by condemnation? Isn't it because we have lived in the land of sin or Egypt so long we fail to see the greatness of His grace. We see ourselves and not Him who desires to be near us and now even in us? Did not Paul write that we should not be again in the bondage of fear, but by the Spirit that indwells us, cry out Abba or Daddy or Papa or Father? Isn't this what Jesus came to reveal to us all? This bondage again is being reyoked to the Law beloved, and it produces in us the fear of punishment. It, in fact, condemns sin and those who are under it. That is its job. The sacrificial system set up in the law even reminded those under the law of their sinfulness. They never could have a clear conscience toward God.

It was the same for those delivered from Egypt by God's right arm, Jesus! They looked back and were reminded of Egypt, a place they were all too familiar with. Don't ever look back beloved! Jesus came to set us free, to remove the yoke of bondage, but are we truly free if we are afraid of all that is coming upon this world, still being condemned or feeling condemned? It takes a change in how we view Father God for this to occur in our hearts. We will never be who He says we are until we quit identifying ourselves with this world, with the flesh, with the carnal nature. Not only was Father revealing Himself to them as Jehovah but He was revealing something else to them, but only two could see this. "I have called you out as My own, and I will do it!" His call was not so that He could be seen, for everything reveals to us that He exists, but rather, that with great patience, Father is trying to show us how much we are loved and cared for. But will you dare to believe this, even fight the battles of faith to receive this? It is still the same today beloved. Nothing is new under the sun.

None of all who left Egypt with Moses entered into the Promised Land, God's promises, except for Joshua and Caleb, men God called, men of "another spirit" (Numbers 14:24). There was nothing personal for them to see and believe from their old revelation as slaves. There was to them nothing new under the sun. There was nothing for them to do but believe and receive, but they would not! They were slaves, in their hearts and bondservants, and from that place they could not see I AM, nor would they hear what He was saying to them. "I have chosen you, I Am near you!"

In fact, despite the truth that they could not see His hand, His strength, even in the miraculous, Exodus 14:8 tells us that "the children of Israel went out with a high hand." The Hebrew word here is *yad* or open hand. Literally in the Hebrew language, in their alphabet, the "hand" is the picture that identifies the letter. If interpreted correctly Jaweh is spelled without any vowels or as JHVH (only backwards or from right to left in Hebrew HWHY—the *y* being transliterated as a *j* and the *w* as a *v*) each letter identified with pictures—the open hand of God Jah *y* or *j* (grace) nailed in (grace.) The *h* being seen as a window or a portal to grace (a place to see through, a revelation), the *v* a nail, a picture of God's right hand being nailed. It is Jesus being revealed, even there, even now. Can you see it?

It did not come to them, because their hearts were hardened. They mixed no faith with the Words of God. (Hebrews 4:2). Jesus is the Word. They could not enter into the Promised Land. For you cannot enter without the revelation of grace. We did not know Him this way—Christ Jesus in us! They did not know God Almighty in this way, and they all perished despite the great deliverance by the hand of God. He is God, but now we call Him Father—Abba Father if you will—Daddy.

How do you see Him, and how do you know Him? And can you even perceive to accept what He speaks of you? Can you see your identity revealed by His Word and receive this as a truth? Is it by the hearing of the ear as Job once did to his own demise? Will you rely on what others say about Father God and Jesus and the Holy Spirit or will you seek them face to face, every day, in every way, and through what Jesus has done for us? Is He the Way or just a way? Or is He still God Almighty? Is He the One who came down to be with us and free us because He desired us, desired to be "near" us? Is it you seeking Him or do you see Him seeking you? Is He who He is because of what you do or because of what He has done, is doing and will do? Is He in fact a gracious and loving Father? Are we truly who He has declared us to be, and do we walk in that truth? Is He truly righteous in calling the sinner righteous? Do we dare approach Him in this way?

This journey won't be easy if you have a mind already set to seeing Him through a covenant with the Jews—the Law—for the covenant has surely come to an end as a way to see Him and be with Him and Him in us. But sadly, to their own demise, many, even most, mix law and grace as if this were the way it was supposed to be, never seeing "I will give it to you for a heritage" as it really is—all by grace or not at all. So many still see themselves under a performance contract: do good, get good; do bad, get burned. They never see that Father God no longer sees us except through the finished works of Jesus. As Jesus is, so are we in this world. It is a journey of seeing things from His perspective, a "come up here and see what I see" journey. This journey is not for you if you are satisfied with what you can do for Him, with works of the flesh plus grace, which is nothing. Look closely as you begin this journey. Look with eyes that have not already been closed. Hear with ears hoping to hear from Father a truth that frees. Look fresh and pray over the Scriptures Father has given to me. Let Jesus explain them to you by the Holy Spirit. He will lead you into all truth; it is His job. Will you let Him? Don't shut out the truth in order to keep your traditions alive just to stay in the place of bondage, of human efforts, for He has made known to me by the Spirit, that you are His. And His desire is for you to be with Him and to see Him in us, revealing Himself through us and to us, not as you see Him, but as He is—the alpha and the omega, the beginning and the end, the first and the last, the all in all, the God who saves, Jesus is the I AM.

"Rejoice, again I say rejoice."(Philippians 4:4). Paul declared this from a prison cell. He and Silas once sang as they sat in stocks. Peter told us, "wherein ye greatly rejoice though now for a season, if need be, ye are in heaviness through manifold temptations…"(1Peter 1:6). Do we rejoice as we are in heaviness through manifold or many trials and tests?

Jesus told His disciples that "whither I go, ye cannot come…" (John 13:33). He had been with them face to face every day for over three years- but now He was going away- it would no longer be face to face but by faith- it was a time of change. It was to be a time of testing for them. He had prayed for them and asked them to pray that they fall not into temptation, but it fell upon them. Jesus was going to the cross to die for all sin, and He taught them this, "And ye now have sorrow; but I will see you again, and your heart shall rejoice, and your joy no man taketh from you" (John 16:22). It was later, on the road to Emmaus that Jesus hid Himself from His disciples who were walking away from where He told them to go. Why were they leaving? "But we trusted or hoped that it had been He which should have redeemed Israel; and beside all this, today is the third day since these things were done…" (Luke 24:41).

The temptation was to not see Jesus as the suffering Christ spoken of in the Scriptures, and He had been teaching them this truth for some time. But they were blinded by what they expected or hoped or trusted—natural or physical remedies to their plight—blinded by the cruel bondage of the law and hurting spirit. They went on to say that the women had gone to the tomb where Jesus's body was placed and found He was not there. The stone was rolled away, and He was gone. Jesus corrected them with this: "Ought not Christ to have suffered these things and to enter into his glory?" Jesus called them "slow of heart and fools not to believe all the prophets have spoken."(Luke 24:25-26). They had never seen Him this way, but then, Jesus broke bread— communion, a reminder of his body broken for them—and they "knew" Him. Their eyes were opened, and He vanished right before them. A place of remembrance and revelation came forth.

Their hearts began to burn from within as Jesus opened up the Scriptures to them and then later to the rest of the disciples and apostles saying, "these are the words which I spake to you while I was yet with you, that all things must be fulfilled which were written in the law, in the prophets, and in the psalms concerning me."(Luke 24:44). In other words, Jesus came to fulfill what was written of Him. He is the fulfiller and the fulfillment of all prophecy. (Revelation 19:10).

The question is not if this is truth, for He did fulfill all prophecies concerning Himself, but will He not also now fulfill all that He promised to us? Are we still slow of heart to believe *all* the Scriptures and *all* that He said? Are we foolish and dull in our hearts? You see, Jesus is easily seen in the Scriptures for they are written of Him. "And beginning at Moses and all the prophets, he expounded unto them in all the scriptures the things concerning himself" (Luke 24:27). Just as He so revealed Himself to them, we also can experience this unveiling or revelation of Jesus Christ in the Scriptures by the Spirit sent to bear witness to us of everything Jesus said.

The battle is for and over the Word of God, for people who will know Him by the Word. It always was and always will be until it is settled within our own hearts. Look at what Mark says of this: "And He began to teach them that the Son of Man must suffer many things, and be rejected of the elders, and of the chief priests, and scribes, and be killed, and after three days rise again" (Mark 8:31). "And how it is written of the Son of Man, that He must suffer many things, and be set at nought…" (Mark 9:12). "For He taught His disciples and said unto them, The Son of Man is delivered into the hands of men, and they shall kill Him, and after He is killed, He shall rise the third day" (Mark 9:31) But look at their response from verse 32: "But they understood not that saying, and were afraid to ask him."

How does this tie in to everything else? Remember the rejoicing? Remember John 16:22? "And ye now therefore have sorrow; but I will see you again, and your heart shall rejoice, and your joy no man taketh from you." How is this possible, to see Jesus in the Scriptures, in Moses, in the prophets, in the Psalms, in the New Covenant, in the Revelations, and in the Gospels. But look at John 16:24: "Hitherto have ye asked nothing in my name; ask, and ye shall receive, that your joy may be full." We no longer have to be dull or foolish in our thinking. We do not have to be slow to believe. All we have to do is ask, and He will answer us that we might have a joy no man can take from us, an inner joy of hearing His voice from within by the Spirit of Christ within us even as Jesus is revealed to us in the Scriptures.

But have you known Him in this way? What sorrows have withheld this truth from your eyes? What veil or cruel bondage is pulled over your eyes? Is it the Law that blinds you to the gospel of grace? Are you afraid to ask Him what the Scriptures mean? It is in the Scriptures that we will see Jesus revealed through His revelations to us, and our hearts will be set on fire by the Holy Spirit. Will you rely on human abilities? No, we need the Holy Spirit to help us. Ask Him to help you now, for this is just the beginning of our journey, and you will need Him to understand. Don't be afraid; ask Him. He will not let you fail. You must know Him in this way. The Scriptures must be fulfilled. "If you being evil know how to give good gifts to your children, how much more shall your heavenly Father give the Holy Spirit to them that ask him?" (Luke 11:13). A friend on a journey will have need of a guide.

Won't you ask Him now? He will not come until you ask. Receive the Holy Ghost, Jesus said. The Scriptures must be fulfilled! We can never see Jesus as He is being revealed without His help. Do you know Him this way?

The Fear of Failure

I wonder how many of us will sit on the side line never entering into the arena we were called to enter after being reborn of Father God? I was bound in that place for many years seeing what I had done wrong as the reason for being a bench-sitter. It also suited my need to never do anything except attend church and throw a little money in the plate, sing two or three songs, and run out the back. Oh, don't be foolish. They want you to serve but only under the qualifications they have set upon you. These may be good, but they also may cause you to serve for a little while, become frustrated, and no longer serve, or maybe even quit coming at all. You will never find your place if you are afraid to fail.

It sounds something like this: What if, when I lay my hands on that person and pray for them, they don't get any better? What if, when I give this, I don't have enough? What if I tell them about Jesus, they become angry with me and no longer want to be my friend? What if I run them away by telling them I don't want to do that because I am a Christian? What if they ask me to teach or to sing? I had better not try that. It is not a good time to invest in that or this! He won't use me; I don't have any talents at all. I can't teach anyone, I don't know the Bible well enough. I can't stand in front of people and speak about Jesus. They all know what I have done in the past! And sometimes, even in serving, we face those who want to see limitations placed on us because of what we have done wrong in the past! I once even had a preacher tell me that by spreading a little guilt and shame on the people, they could be more easily controlled. It is true, but it is still based in fear.

If we teach grace alone, the whole bunch will just sin all they want to using grace as a way out! This same fear causes us to yield ourselves into ritualistic services that never bear any fruit for God, because we are afraid to do those things Jesus called us to do. If we step out in faith we might be seen, maybe even rejected- better to just go along and never rock the boat- this is still being controlled by fear. Fear! It was this very fear of losing control that caused the religious ones of Jesus's days to say, "If we don't stop Him, the whole world will follow Him." (John 12:19). Pilate even said that he knew that they, the Jewish religious leaders, had brought Jesus before him because of their envy of Him. That is what fear produces—envy, jealousy, anger, and rage. All of them are seeking to control "others" or even themselves. It is a fleshly function, not a spiritual gifting. It is literally trying to make others like us and not letting them be formed by the Spirit as they behold Jesus and become like Christ. Being led by the Spirit is a walk of not being able to see exactly where we are being led. We walk by faith and not by sight! But do we? Aren't most of us afraid if we follow the Spirit blindly we might be led by the anti-christ? What if I tell others I speak in tongues, and they cast me out? What if I tell them that Father miraculously lifted me over a bad situation, picking me up and moving me to another place? What if, when I go to my pastor and tell him I do not agree with him about some things he is teaching, he casts me out? Fear, fear, fear!

God did not give us the spirit of fear but gave us a spirit of power and of love and of a sound mind. (2 Timothy 1:7). These were the words of the Apostle Paul to his beloved son Timothy from prison. He was encouraging a timid young man to become who God had called him to be, not by what he could do, but by who God had made him and into what he was

> Who hath saved us, and called us with an holy calling, not according to our works, but according to His own purpose and grace, which was given us in Christ Jesus before the world began…(2 Timothy 1:9).

Not according to our works! Can you see this? Oh brethren, do we dare to believe such words? Will we receive such an exhortation and encouragement from a man who was imprisoned and beaten and abused for his walk of faith? Isn't it just easier to sit in the pew and be there? Or will we hear the heavenly call to "go ye therefore" and not just "come ye into and sit down"?

Circled in my Bible are these words spoken by Caleb, a man with a different spirit: "Only rebel not ye against the Lord, neither fear ye the people of the land; for they are bread for us; their defence is departed from them; and the Lord is with us; fear them not!" (Numbers 14:9). See for your own selves that rebellion broke out in the camp because of fear. They are linked together, and rebellion does not occur where fear is vanquished. The word *defence* here means "shadow or covering." It implies an unveiling of our enemies even as we walk through the shadows of death. But see that Caleb called this trouble or trial or test "bread for us." Caleb saw what the others feared as bread or as a source of strengthening. The others saw giants in the land as those they were unable to conquer or move, because they saw themselves as grasshoppers. Their words imaged their fears, and they spoke fear amongst themselves.

What they saw with their natural eyes went into their hearts and fear came out of their mouths. They spoke fear and not words of God-given faith. Numbers 14:2 says they murmured against Moses and Aaron and even said they wished that God would have let them die in the wilderness and even that their children would be a prey to the giants in verse 3.

So what did Father God do and say to this rebellion? "As you have spoken in mine ears, so will I do to you" (Numbers 14:28). In verse 31, we see these children who were spoken of as prey in fear. "But your little ones, which ye said should become a prey, them will I bring in, and they shall know the land which ye have despised." They fell in the wilderness and the children did enter in. Why? Because instead of seeing the greatness of our Father, they saw the greatness of their enemies. Instead of seeing His provision, they saw only what they did not have. Instead of seeing with spiritual eyes, they saw the natural greater than the spiritual, and they disdained, despised, or loathed the land God had so promised to give them on oath and in covenant with Abraham so many years before. Instead of mixing faith with His Word, they mixed in their own abilities, what they could do, and they all died. They had no remembrance of God and saw only by the natural eye. But He was always near to them.

What promises are ours that we despise and disdain and even loathe? Do we see them as ours to inherit but not see our need of them? Oh, beloved, I fear many of us have fallen here, including myself once. The promises of God are *yes and amen* for us in Christ Jesus, through what He did for us. But they come with battles, even resistance, and oppositions as Paul called his light and momentary struggles. This he spoke of being stoned, flogged, beaten, imprisoned, rejected, brought up before leaders to be tried as a conspirator against God, even by the church. And Paul said we are to rejoice, "again I say rejoice!" Why? How? Because we know of grace and have been given faith and have peace with Father God through Jesus. "By whom also we have access by faith into this grace wherein we stand, and rejoice in hope of the glory of God. And not only so, but we glory in tribulations also; knowing that tribulation worketh patience; and patience, experience; and experience, hope…" (Romans 5:2-4). Yes, we rejoice in troubles, not at the troubles, but in the knowing that these work for us. They are even our bread, our strengthening, and we will need it if we are to stand in the evil day that comes upon all of us sooner or later. It is how we see the trials of this life—either through eyes of the spirit or with natural vision. One causes faith to rise up knowing we are loved of God and that He will deliver us; the other causes us to wither and wilt back in fear, seeing the natural bigger than our Father, seeing our circumstances bigger than our God and Father, seeing our sins as reasons He won't do for us even despising His promises and gifts. It is a tough road we are called to walk, but it can be done.

It is a road not seen with the natural eye. It is a road He prepared, a walk of faith, one of believing in what is not yet, seen knowing that what is not will be manifested from the realm of God, who is a Spirit, into the natural realm we now abide in. It is a road all of the Old Testament saints walked—Abram, Isaac, Jacob, Moses, Joshua—it included Jesus as well as all who will follow after Him. It is the road few will travel, for on it there will be battles and trials; trials and tests sent to stop us but used by our Father to strengthen us in the faith. It is a faith that says He will never leave us. He is near to us, even in us, seeing the heavenly vision above the fleshly battles we face.

It was the call to John from Jesus: "Come up thither…" Dare we go there? Dare we walk the high road, the King's highway? Dare we focus on Jesus to the point of becoming blind to this life, seeing ourselves walking on water, raising the dead, healing the sick, operating the gifts as He so desires them to be? Preaching the gospel in love? Yes, we can just go and sit in the church once a week and eat the food meant for the starving ourselves. I, too, have done this. We can hear this good news gospel of grace every week and keep it all for ourselves, and it will enter into us like honey that is sweet to taste but exit us as nothing more than waste. The Seed meant for life becomes nothing more than waste! Will we fear to invest all that Jesus has gifted us with and be like the man of one talent who knew Jesus was an angry man who reaped where he did not sow, and do nothing? I would rather sow the one talent and fail than to do nothing in fear of what Jesus will say when I see Him face to face. This is a higher road beloved, a road kings are called to walk upon and no one but a king dare.

The challenge is laid, the call has been made, the response is our choice, and the results are eternal. Will you journey with me a ways? It is His call to come, is it not? Come up thither!

Compare and Contrast

I am not going to say that the law of God is dead, but rather that we, the believers in Jesus Christ, are to be dead to the law. This will be a journey to a place of rest if you will but allow His Words to enter into your hearts. It will be painful at certain locations, but the fruit of this journey will take you to places you did not even know existed and into freedoms you had never seen before. The children of Israel were free from Egypt, sin if you will, but they could never enter into rest and His divine provisions because, despite having been freed from bondage, their minds remained in Egypt. A short journey ended up costing all but two their lives, dying in the wilderness of their own minds. They never renewed their thinking from the bondage, even looking back with lust for the fleshly things they did not have. With natural eyes only, they looked over the grace of God from Heaven, the manna, the bread, even coming to loathe His provision and promises for them. They never saw the land flowing with milk and honey and homes they did not build, eating from trees they did not plant, for their eyes were closed, their imaginations darkened. They never desired what they could not see. They were carnally minded, saved but bound, alive but wrapped in death.

So many of us are at this place today—bound with the clothing of death, the law, hoping to receive grace while looking backwards, never adding faith to the Word, never finding this place of rest, at least in this life. It is a new and living way in which we have never known Him before. You will either hate this journey or you will love it. You must decide. It will be, as I said, filled with pain and will require many thoughts to be reviewed and minds to be renewed if you are to come forth a new creation. It is a journey to a new identification, a new name so to speak, one that Jesus alone can give you, but the new name is written up there, in the *come up thither* place of grace through faith.

But before we can begin this journey we must first see with the spiritual eyes Father has given to us through Jesus Christ's finished works on the cross. It takes the Holy Spirit to enable us to understand what Jesus has done and to be able to receive from Him what He wants us to have. You do not need the Holy Spirit to understand the law! It is do and do not when dealing with the flesh! Jesus said that everything Father had was His, and then He said that everything that was His the Holy Spirit would take from Him and give to us, make it known to us. (John 16:15).

This is why we must first receive the ministry of the Holy Spirit. Jesus taught in parables that were used to conceal truths for those who continued with Him, the Word. Often His disciples would ask Jesus to explain the parables because they did not understand them. Without the Helper it is still the same today. In many parables Jesus would teach in a way where many see with physical eyes, comparison, and not see with the eye of the Spirit, contrast. Jesus often used men not as comparisons to Father God but as contrasts. "If you being evil know how to give good gifts to your children how much more Father God will give you the gift of the Holy Ghost to them that ask." (Luke 11:13). Jesus is contrasting men and Father God, not comparing.

He once taught of a judge who did not even know God and how he gave in to a certain woman's constant requests and then He spoke of how quickly Father God would answer our requests. Jesus certainly was not comparing this godless judge to Father, and yet this is how this parable is often taught. Just keep asking from God until you make Him give to us—wrong! Contrast! Jesus taught the Apostle Paul this truth:

> For what man knoweth the things of a man, saveth the
> spirit of man which is in him? Even so the things of God
> knoweth no man, but the Spirit of God. Now we have
> received, not the spirit of the world, but the Spirit which
> is of God; that we might know the things that are freely
> given to us of God. Which things we speak, not in words
> which man's wisdom teacheth, but which the Holy Ghost
> teacheth; comparing spiritual things with spiritual. But
> the natural man receiveth not the things of the Spirit of
> God; for they are foolishness unto him; neither can he
> know them, because they are spiritually discerned.
>
> 1 Corinthians 2:11-14

The things that are freely given are righteousness of faith in what Jesus has already done for us. This is called grace or gifts, and they are never naturally discerned. This is why we need the Holy Spirit to understand them. You cannot compare the spiritual things, the unseen, with natural things, those things that are seen. Even the apostles themselves did not understand the parables of Jesus unless He told them what they meant until Pentecost had fully come. And so Jesus was resurrected from the dead and the Holy Ghost was sent down to help us understand a new covenant, written in His blood, grace through faith, knowing Him in a way we had not known Him before.

And so I offer up to you *Moses Is Dead: A Matter of Life and Death*, not to take away God's Word, but to contrast law and grace, for it must be one or the other. In so doing, you might think that I am endorsing sin, but I am not. However, I will never compare what Satan did in man with what Jesus did upon the cross. I will never compare the power of sinful flesh with the amazing grace of Father God through Jesus Christ and the cross of His finished works, never! Where sin abounds, grace super abounds! In fact I offer this truth from Father's own Word as a foundation for this teaching:

But not as the offence, so also is the free gift. For if through the offence of one many be dead, much more the grace of God, and the gift by grace, which is by one man, Jesus Christ, hath abounded unto many. And not as it was by one that sinned, so is the gift; for the judgment was by one to condemnation, but the free gift is of many offenses unto justification.

Romans 5:15-16

This is a faith thing beloved. It is received by faith alone, and it is free. A gift must be received. Have you received it? Righteousness or justification must be by grace alone, a free gift that is simply and humbly received apart from anything we do. This may not be easily seen as comparison and contrast but clearly the Apostle Paul is contrasting sin through Adam, the flesh in which all fell as one, with the free gift of God's grace through the righteousness of Jesus's sinless life and His blood, shed for all who will but accept this by faith. Look at this in the Amplified version:

> But God's free gift is not at all to be compared to the trespass (His grace is out of all proportion to the fall of man), for if many died through one man's falling away (his lapse, his offense), much more profusely did God's grace and the free gift (that comes) through the undeserved favor of the one Man Jesus Christ abound and overflow to and for (the benefit of) many. Nor is the free gift at all to be compared to the effect of that one (man's) sin. For the sentence (following the trespass) of one (man) brought condemnation, whereas the free gift (following) many transgressions brings justification (an act of righteousness.) Romans 5:15-16, amplified.

Can you see this? You will never see this truth if you place all of our sins as equal with the sacrifice of Jesus and His blood shed for us. For what Jesus did on the cross was a gross overpayment for us, one drop of His blood would have been enough- but Jesus gave His all! What can compare to His gift? Grace is an overpayment for what we have done! Achieving in order to become worthy and simply believing is the contrast! One requires receiving and believing this gospel of grace to receive freely, while the other requires something we cannot achieve to, setting demands through our own efforts. One brings forgiveness of sin through an act of love that draws us, while one requires payment through efforts brought on by condemnation and controls and produces fear and separation.

Don't be deceived beloved, for God is not condemning us and we must see this contrast if we are to receive all that He has for us in this life. Eternity does not begin at death but at rebirth. All that Jesus purchased for us is a gross overpayment when it is contrasted with the fall of mankind.

There is so much more for us, but first we must see Moses, the law to us, dead and buried in our hearts and lives. It is like Egypt, a place we can never look back to. You cannot receive the ministry of the Holy Spirit while under the law. He came to help those under grace understand grace, to help us stay free, to help us see spiritual truths manifesting the spiritual life in us and to us. This is why I write these things to you. Let me help you to see the contrast between the Law of sin and death and the law of life by the Spirit. That is the only law we can keep in Christ Jesus, for we are led by the Spirit and not by external rules that point out right and wrong! Do not compare grace with law, but contrast them. "For what the law could not do, in that it was weak through the flesh, God sending his own Son in the likeness of sinful flesh, and for sin, condemned sin in the flesh" (Romans 8:3) Contrast! Now all that remains is to believe on Jesus. "There is therefore now no condemnation to them which are in Christ Jesus!" (Romans 8:1). Contrast!

I will not magnify sin over grace, nor compare them and I pray Father opens your eyes of the Spirit to see His truth! Only in this can you see into heaven and call down "on earth as it is in heaven." (Matthew 6:10). We will be looking into many of Jesus's revelations of heaven from the Book of Revelations. I believe He will open up your hearts to see! Nothing and no one compares to His grace and love! No physical or carnal life can compare with the life of freedom by the Spirit. It can only be seen in contrast.

It Is All For Us

What I write I write to those who have already accepted Jesus into their lives. Here are three things Jesus has given to me to help you continue in this book. Receive these, and you can go on.

1. The Law is against us.

    "Take this book of the law, and put it in the ark of the covenant of the Lord your God, that it may be there for a witness against you" (Deuteronomy 31:26).

    "Blotting out the handwriting of ordinances that was against us, which was contrary to us, and took it out of the way, nailing it to his cross…" (Colossians 2:14).

    "Therefore by the deeds of the law there shall no flesh be justified in his sight; for by the law is the knowledge of sin" (Romans 3:20).

2. Jesus is for us.

    "For Christ is not entered into the holy places made with hands, which are figures of the true, but into heaven itself, now to appear in the presence of God for us…" (Hebrews 9:24).

    "Wherefore he is able also to save them to the uttermost that come unto God by him, seeing he liveth forever to make intercession for them…" (Hebrews 7:25).

"What shall we then say to these things? If God be for us, who can be against us? He that spared not His own Son, but delivered Him up for us all, how shall He not with Him freely give us all things? Who shall lay anything to the charge of God's elect? It is God that justifieth. Who is he then that condemneth? It is Christ that died, yea rather, that is risen again, who is even at the right hand of God, who also maketh intercession for us." (Romans 8:31-34).

3. The Holy Spirit is sent to us.

"Whereof the Holy Ghost also is a witness to us; for after that he had said before, This is the covenant that I will make with them after those days, saith the Lord, I will put My laws into their hearts, and in their minds will I write them; and their sins and iniquities will I remember no more." (Hebrews 10:15-17).

"But he Comforter, which is the Holy Ghost, whom the Father will send in My name, he shall teach you all things, and bring all things to your remembrance, whatsoever I have said unto you" (John 14:26).

Think about these truths before you go any further....selah..... let the Holy Ghost comfort your hearts and believe.

Remember Lot's Wife

They gathered themselves together and asked Him when the kingdom of God would be set up in the earth and Jesus's reply was somewhat confusing to them for He said, "The kingdom of God is within you."(Luke17:21). It is just like that for us as well as we often fail to recognize those changes that have been made around us and even in us. We relate to what we see physically and often fail to see the reality of God's kingdom in us. I must speak the truth in love. Moses is dead! We must see Moses as gone and buried, no longer in effect. Have you ever eaten something sweet and then later felt sick once you had consumed it? So is this truth for it is sweet in my mouth but it makes my stomach bitter or sickly. I know what I share will hurt some and even provoke many to anger, but it is my prayer and hope that what I share will help to move you from one place to another one- one that is higher and more sure.

As Jesus described the kingdom of God to these Pharisees, He spoke of them not being able to see what was already there just like Sodom and Gomorrah and the people in the days of Noah. Then he added in the story of Lot's wife looking backwards at what was once her home, the place she had come from, and as it was being destroyed she herself was likewise destroyed.

Change can occur quickly, and often mankind yearns for something familiar in order to "feel" secure. In looking back at things or people that have hurt us, we often look past the hurt and see something there that does not exist. The onions and leaks and fish looked good to Israel as they ate the manna, even loathing it and despising it as we have seen. Being afraid to completely let go is still fear, and from it comes anger and controlling, bondage. The children of Israel looked back at Egypt, which held them in bondage for 430 years, seeing there as a better place to be than walking by faith through the wilderness with God leading them by the Spirit. They desired the food and the slavery over the unseen, which produced fear in them.

This is why I disagree with so many who teach fear as a way to Father God. We can never come close to someone we fear. In fact, if we fear Him, we do not and will not trust Him. You can never move closer to a person who is afraid to even be near to you. This is a place we must see often on this journey if we are to be free. It is always the same with man, we always look over our shoulders as we leave one place and go to the next. But the Lord has spoken to me that in order to be moved, we must first be able to leave one place, and not desire to return to it. For if we do, we might return, or even worse, we will live in regret of what we have done.

My earthly Dad once told me that until we were completely finished with bad relationships we should just stay in them until we could walk away without any emotions. This is of course from a physical perspective, but it is truth. We can never enjoy what is ahead if we always look back to the good old days. In them we tend to remember only what we want and neglect the remembrances of pains and hurts. Yet as Sarai and Abram left their country, we are told this: "And truly, if they had been mindful of that country from whence they came out, they might have had opportunity to have returned" (Hebrews 11:15). Even Jesus Himself was tempted by the enemy to look back at His old physical life as a carpenter, as a physical man, after Jesus had heard His Father declare Jesus "My beloved Son in whom I am well pleased." (Luke 3:22). The Word tells us that after Jesus had been tempted by Satan, he left Jesus for a more opportune time.

He never quits trying to get us to lose focus on what lies ahead for us once we have been born again of God and have become the sons and daughters of God. He will always try to get us to stay where we once were and remain nothing but physical beings, never seeing who we are in Jesus Christ and what Father has declared over us. He will try, as he did Jesus, to get us to prove our relationship to Father and not just trust in it. The warning Jesus gave was to not look back, but be ready, for He is coming again, and soon! For us who have believed, He has come, for He is living in us. You will never move away from fleshly thoughts and actions until you see yourself as Father sees you—a son or a daughter born again of God Himself, made in His image, and God is Spirit! This failure is not related to sin for the believers because Jesus has dealt with sin in this age, but it relates to what we agree to and believe the Bible is saying to us and about us. For the Word is our inheritance; it is our identity, and it is sure. But to be a spiritual being we must see not through eyes of the flesh but through the eyes of Jesus who indwells us as does Father and the Holy Ghost.

This will shock most of us, but no matter what we see in the mirror each day, it is not who we are. For only in the word of God are we made manifest, and that all by faith. It is an act of faith to not look back at our old ways of thinking, at our old ways of living and being, at our old life. We must remain focused upon what Jesus has already accomplished for us and in us, looking at the works Father has prepared in advance for us to do and seeing ourselves through His eyes and not our own. We must see ourselves as He sees us through the finished works of Jesus and not our own abilities to do good and therefore become or remain accepted. We are either accepted in Jesus, the beloved Son of God, or we are not. I will share simple truths with you in order to help you walk by faith and not by sight, for if we walk by sight and if we remain under the law, under the altar, we will never see who Father says we are for the simple reason that the Law is not of faith. It will blind you to the truth of the new creation you are in Christ Jesus. If you have been justified by the blood of Christ

Jesus this must become a truth for you in your heart of hearts. "But that no man is justified by the law in the sight of God, it is evident; for, 'The just shall live by faith.' And the law is not of faith…" (Galatians 3:11-12a). Can you see it yet?

I Want to See Jesus

I cannot imagine a more painful experience than to speak a truth or to show a truth to those we love and care for and for their reply to be like this one: "Lord, show us the Father, and it sufficieth us."(John 14:8). In another version of this verse, the Amplified version, it says, "cause us to see the Father, that is all we ask; then we shall be satisfied." Jesus's response to that was this: "Have I been so long time with you, and yet hast thou not known me, Phillip? He that hast seen me hath seen the Father; and how sayest thou the, Show us the Father?" (John 14:9). Jesus went on to share with His disciples to simply look back at all that He had done as a testimony to who He truly was. "He doeth the works." (John 14:10b) Jesus was simply identifying the works that He had done were not of His own power but of the Father's working through Jesus. Jesus said this work was a response to something we need to see as a truth. "Believest thou not that I am in the Father and the Father in me? The words that I speak unto you I speak not of myself; but the Father that dwelleth in me, He doeth the works." (John 14:10). Jesus then said to believe that Father was in Him or believe in Jesus because of His works. Then He trumped all unbelief. "Verily, verily, I say unto you, He that believeth on me, the works that I do shall he do also; and greater works than these shall he do; because I go unto my Father." (John 14:12).

How painful would it be if we told our wives we loved them every day, but we had to go away for a long time, and they said, "If you really loved me, you would not go!" The "if you truly love me" then could be transferred to any number of requests: you would buy me a car, do what I asked you, anything you can imagine… and then she will believe that you love her. Jesus's response then to them was one of assurance: you can do anything that I have done. You get a blank and empty stare. Ouch! You might say, but look at how hard I have worked to provide for you, how many hours I have spent being with you, how many times I have been with you and held you, how many hours I have spent talking with you. But their 'look' was simply a blank and empty response that spoke without any words. A stare that said, "I don't and can't and won't hear you. Why are you looking at me this way?" You try to prove your love for them with bold statements like: if you need anything at all just call me and I will do whatever you ask of me. I have given you my name as your authority, and when you receive what you asked, I will be glorified in your receiving. You would say that this is stupid dialogue wouldn't you? But look at what Jesus said: "And whatsoever ye shall ask in my name, that will I do, that the Father may be glorified in the Son. If ye shall ask any thing in my name, I will do it."(John 14:13).

As I thought on this for a while, I decided that I too have done this to Jesus myself many times. In fact, if we are truthful, when we were taught that no one could do what Jesus did, we were glad and received that with thanksgiving. It set us free didn't it? But it was not the truth! It was received in the spirit of error. In other words, Jesus can't lie. He is the same yesterday, today, and forever, or He is not! Jesus's disciples had asked Jesus to reveal the Father to them and they would be satisfied but instead Jesus spoke the truth in love and pointed to all that Father had done through His ministry as evidence of the Presence of Father God in Him. They still did not yet understand! It was not until Jesus told them that they were loved that their faith came to believe. "At that day, ye shall ask in my name, and I say not that I shall pray the Father for you; for the Father himself loveth you, because ye have loved me, and have believed that I came out of God" (John 16:26-27).

Faith then works by love. It has action, not the faith, but the love. They believed that Jesus came from Father God, but the proof was not just with words alone. "Now are we sure that thou knowest all things, and needest not that any man should ask thee; by this we believe that thou camest forth from God" (John 16:30). This is straight talk beloved, simple and plain, easy to understand. But just in case:

> These things have I written unto you that believe on the name of the Son of God; that ye may know that have eternal life, and that ye may believe on the name of the Son of God. And this is the confidence that we have in him, that, if we ask anything according to his will, he heareth us; and if we know that he hear us, whatsoever we ask, we know that we have the petition that we desired of him.
>
> 1 John 5:13-15

It is hard to deny these truths unless you simply do not believe or you have been taught incorrectly. "Ask anything of me, and I will do it!" (John 14:14). This is an action motivated by love. But then we place the old hide and seek blanket over this truth with this: If we ask according to His will, He will do it. But how do we know for sure what we asked is His will? Matter settled, and we can just go on the way we have always gone on or along, right? Jesus said, "The works I do, and greater works than these shall you do because I go to the Father and when you ask in My name I will do it." (John 14:12). His will is to do it. Can you see this? The problem is not in our doing but in understanding exactly what Jesus is saying. Remember, words and works! If we are believers, then this is for us. We call it the great commission in other books of the Bible.

> Go ye into all the world, and preach the gospel to every creature. He that believeth and is baptized shall be saved; but he that believeth not shall be damned. And these signs shall follow them that believe; In my name shall they cast

out devils; they shall speak with new tongues; they shall take up serpents; and if they drink any deadly thing, it shall not hurt them; they shall lay hands on the sick, and they shall recover. (Mark 16:15-18).

There are those who wish this were not in the Bible at all because in so doing they are freed from the will of Jesus and of Father God. We simply do not see Jesus in this or we would not be afraid. The great fear is not is this His Great Commission, but can I do these things? No! You cannot! But Jesus can do them through you, if you believe Him.

Look at Mark 16:20: "And they went forth, and preached everywhere, the Lord working with them, and confirming the word with signs following, amen." Who was working with them? The Lord Jesus was. It was Him who did what they could not do but through them. They could do all things through Christ who strengthened them. Christ in us is the hope of glory. (Colossians 1:27). Remember that Jesus said He, Father God, would be glorified when we went and did these things. Our job is to tell; His is to confirm! Look at Acts 4:29-31:

> And now Lord, behold their threatening; and grant unto thy servants, that with all boldness they may speak thy word, by stretching forth thine hand to heal; and that signs and wonders may be done by the name of thy holy child, Jesus. And when they had prayed, the place was shaken where they assembled together, and they were all filled with the Holy Ghost, and they spoke the word of God with boldness.

This is not too hard to see and understand is it? But Father needs our hands and feet and mouths to work through. He cannot work apart from His own will. It is Him in us that Father may be glorified through the Son.

The world has never needed to see Jesus more than right now, beloved. The great darkness that is upon this world is the greatest opportunity the church has ever had. A light is never brighter than when it shines in total darkness, a total eclipse of the heart. But first, we must see Jesus for ourselves. We have shown the world many religions and many ways, but Jesus is the Way. They need to see Jesus! They do not need to see church. They need to see Jesus. They do not need to see rules and regulations and traditions. They need to see Jesus! They do not need to see order of service bulletins or meeting times. They need to see Jesus! It is our job to help them see Him, and it is the will of the Father for Him to be seen! If they cannot see Jesus, they cannot see the Father!

But look at what the Apostle Paul said:

> For I determined not to know anything among you, save Jesus Christ, and him crucified. And I was with you in weakness, and in fear, and in much trembling. And my speech and my preaching was not with enticing words of man's wisdom, but in demonstration of the Spirit and of power; that your faith should not stand in the wisdom of men, but in the power of God.
>
> 1 Corinthians 2:2-5

Never has this been more needed than in this hour! People need to see Jesus! If we were to look at this correctly we would need to see this same Paul in prison with Silas for preaching the word and demonstrating the power of God to those who needed to see Jesus. They were beaten and stripped of clothes and placed in stocks, but at midnight they began to sing and praise God. And the Bible says that the prisoners heard them. "And suddenly there was a great earthquake, so that the foundations of the prison were shaken; and immediately all the doors were opened, and every one's hands were loosed" (Acts 16:26). Many could say that this wasn't the power of God, but if you were to look a little further ahead you would see many who wanted to remain in prison, even the very worst of the worst, saw Jesus. The jailer, fearing for his life, was about to kill himself with his own sword after seeing the doors opened. He feared all had fled from prison. This is logical is it not? Look at Acts 16:28: "But Paul cried with a loud voice, saying, Do thyself no harm; for we are all here."

Why didn't these convicts run? What if our prisons were to have an earthquake that set free all who were bound? Do you think for a moment any of them would just remain there? No! But they stayed because they wanted to see Jesus—this Jesus Paul and Silas were singing to even though they had been beaten and stripped and placed in stocks. In great weakness and fear and trembling, they praised God and Jesus with songs which the prisoners heard, and even the so called refuse of the world did not run! Why? They were seeing a Jesus that they all needed to see more than even their freedom. There would be no selling of Jesus to those men or to the jailer who himself and his entire household believed that night, and all Paul and Silas did was sing. The power display was Father's business! It was and is His desire that every man might be saved through His only begotten Son. Do you think there is anything He would not do to reveal this Son whom He loves to every person? If you do, you have not seen the Father either!

I wish I could make this clearer, plainer, easier, or simpler, but there is nothing I can do to convince you but to tell you. Ask the Father in His name, and He will do it! I can share the truth of the gospel of grace, but I cannot save you, nor can I do anything apart from Him. But through Him, I can do all things. There I am limited only by what I say. What do you say? What spiritual gifts do you not believe? Is your faith limited to being saved and going to church? Is it with words alone? Is there any power in your life for others to see Jesus in you? Which of His works are displayed in your life to the world around you? You may be the only "Christ" they ever see. Who are you revealing to them? Is it Jesus and Him crucified for their sin, and then is Father confirming His Word with acts of power? It is a world hungry to see the Father beloved.

"Show us the Father, and it will satisfy us!" But only through the Son can the Father be seen!

I called my wife today and told her that I loved her. She believes me. She always has. But it is also true that I love her when I am with her, in what I do with her and for her. Love has action, not faith! Faith is believing; love is action. Faith has works beloved, but faith is not the motivation. It is love! Faith that works by love does something. It is moved or compelled into action because knowing we are first loved by Father God, we love. What experience do you need to believe that He loves you, to compel you into action? I want to see Jesus is not a clinical analysis of the Scriptures but it is an act of receiving His love and then loving others in this world as we have been loved. On a recent vacation we had the chance to show Jesus to two people we have become frineds with over the past few years. Our friend had a shoulder that was hurting him badly and when we asked him if we could pray for him, he agreed. We laid our hands upon him and Father healed him in the Name of Jesus. In tears his reply was this one- "I didn't know…" Faith works by love. Jesus did because He knew He was loved, and He loved. Seeing Jesus is seeing His love for you. Faith is a response to that love. "For God so loved the world that He gave His only begotten Son, that whosoever believes in Him might not perish but have eternal life."(John 3:16). Can you see Jesus now? "Whom having not seen, ye love, in whom, though you see him not, yet believing, ye rejoice with joy unspeakable and full of glory" (1 Peter 1:8). Can you see Paul and Silas in prison, rejoicing, singing? "Receiving the end of your faith, the salvation of your souls…" (1 Peter 1:9).

Did God Change His Mind?

And the Lord spake unto Moses saying, "Command the children of Israel, that they put out of the camp every leper, and every one that hath an issue, and whatsoever is defiled by the dead. Both male and female shall ye put out, without the camps, in the midst whereof I dwell." And the children of Israel did so, and put them out without the camp; as the Lord spake unto Moses, so did the children of Israel.

Numbers 5:1-4

The first time I actually read this passage in Numbers and thought about it, I asked the Lord why He said this. It almost made me mad. They could not help it if these things happened to them, could they? His answer stood. "I want to be with My people." This is the law as given to Moses in Leviticus, and all of them who were defiled were considered unclean "until even" or evening. But look at the "unclean" persons once Jesus, the expressed image of God came down, having magnified the perfect laws of Father God past the outward keepings men professed. Jesus gave the so called Sermon on the Mount—"When Jesus came down from the mountain…" (Matthew 8:1). Jesus raised the standard of the Law to heights unable to be attained by flesh—"Be ye therefore perfect, even as your Father which is in heaven is perfect" (Matthew 5:48). Jesus's first encounter was with a leper. "And Jesus put forth his hand and touched him, saying, 'I will…be thou clean…'" and immediately his leprosy was healed and cleansed (Matthew 8:3). What about the woman with the issue of bleeding for twelve years? She touched Jesus, and she was healed and cleansed.(Luke 8:43-50). What about Jesus then going to the house of a dead girl and a young man's funeral and to Lazarus's grave and raising up the dead. Once all unclean and dead, now alive and clean.

The answer lies ahead for us as we go on this journey. God did not change His mind. His plans were always the same—to send Jesus in "for us." The Bible teaches us that Jesus was the exact image of God, and so He is and was and always will be doing the things that please the Father. The difference is how we relate to Him, how we see Him by the Law. What we do with what He has demanded, our performance, or by grace, what He has done for us, Jesus's performance, what He fulfilled that we could not? You see, Jesus hung on the cross from nine until three in the afternoon, six hours, and three in the afternoon was the time of the evening or even sacrifice. All were unclean until they were cleansed and the even sacrifice was made—a lamb in the morning and one in the even or evening—Jesus crucified at nine and Jesus's life surrendered at three. All that was damaged was repaired between the two evenings, a day with two darknesses, a day prophesied of in Exodus 12:6.

When Father gave the law to Moses, He spent forty days and nights speaking or communing with Moses directly. The laws or Ten Commandments were given to Moses just before he came down from the mountain to find the children of Israel already in violation. But for the first thirty-nine days and twenty-three hours and fifty minutes before Father wrote the laws in stone with His own finger, Father gave specific instructions to Moses. "And let them make Me a sanctuary that I may dwell among them. According to all I show thee, after the pattern of the tabernacle and the pattern of all the instruments thereof, even so shall ye make it" (Exodus 25:8-9). Father was painting a picture, a shadow, giving a type or pattern, a forerunner for His Son Jesus.

Every feature of the tabernacle speaks of Jesus. The sacrifices were His sacrifices for us. The instruments of service speaking of what Jesus would come and do in great detail. The high priests clothing describes Jesus. The pattern revealed to Moses was Jesus. And this that Father might dwell among us, with us. Look at Hebrews 8:5, speaking of Jesus being our high priest forever, "Who serve unto the example and shadow of heavenly things, as Moses was admonished of God when he was about to make the tabernacle, for, 'See,' saith He, 'that thou make all things according to the pattern showed thee on the mount.'" The laws and tabernacle were all designed and built for a pattern Father could easily see and describe—Jesus. These things were only types and shadows, patterns of the real to come. "Let no man therefore judge you in meat, or in drink, or in respect of an holy day, or of the new moon, or of the Sabbath days; which are a shadow of things to come; but the body is of Christ" (Colossians 2:16-17). Judgment then is to be based on what Jesus paid for in His own body, not on rituals either kept or not that were just shadows of the realities Jesus would do for us.

Father has not changed His mind, but He has changed covenants. The way He deals with us is now through the blood of Jesus speaking more than the blood of animals. You see, the Bible teaches us that Jesus was crucified before the foundation of the world. The law and the prophets, the tabernacle, the sacrifices, the tools of service are all pictures of the reality to come into the world—Jesus. And grace and truth came by Jesus Christ. So the journey has only begun for us at salvation as we die to the law and to the "self," or flesh or carnal ways of man, and awaken to the righteousness of faith in what Jesus has done for us already. He is waiting for us to enter into His rest, a place of salvation and promise, a place past salvation, a place of faith and seeing what is unseen by the eternal vision that replaces the temporal. We move from Mount Sinai to Mount Zion, from earthly Jerusalem to the heavenly Jerusalem, just outside the camp where Jesus died for the lepers, for those stricken and unclean with issues or flows, for those dead to Father God that they might be raised alive to the place where He was rejected. He was sent that we might be received by Father God.

What if Father God desired to speak with us, with you? Would Father God need to remind you of or mention your failures, your sins, each and every time? Did He mention to Moses his sins? I did not see it written as Moses stood in the very presence of God at the burning bush, "You killed an Egyptian, Moses! I can't use you! Even if you confess and are forgiven, how could a man like you ever carry My Laws down the mountain having already broken 'thou shalt not kill'?" If this was truth, and it is not, no one could ever serve Father God, for all have sinned. So then what would Father want to talk with us about? I can assure you on full authority of Scripture, Father would say, "This is My beloved Son in whom I am well pleased…. Hear Him!" (Luke 9:35). He is the payment for all sins, and not for our sins alone, but for the sins of the whole world. You can talk to Father about what you have done wrong if you wish to, but I will confess Jesus and Him crucified. I will hear what Father by His Spirit says concerning sin—"Your sins and iniquities I will remember no more…" and "Where remission of these (sins) is, there is no more payment of sin." (Hebrews 10:17-18). I will be one of many praising Father for His Son who took away my sin and gave me His righteousness. I will be beholding Jesus, and not looking at me, for if I look back at what I have done, I will freeze like a pillar of salt. I will die in the wilderness of my own mind, never to see the promises of God, always afraid to come near to the very place and the only One who has called me to come into His Presence. In His Presence is life. He did not come to make us good. He came to give us life!

Victory over Death

Did you know that we already have victory over death? Did you know that it was Jesus who experienced death "for us" and overcame death? Did you know that in so doing, Jesus defeated Satan and his minions forever?

> Forasmuch then as the children are partakers of flesh and blood, He also Himself likewise took part of the same; that through death He might destroy him that had the power of death, that is the devil. And deliver them who through fear of death were all *their lifetime* subject to bondage.
>
> Hebrews 2:14-15

Jesus has entered into the strongman's house and has plundered it for us! This is not to be but already is! It is as it is revealed in Jesus's Revelation to John, "I hold the keys of death and Hades."(Revelation 1:18). His place of vision, seeing down, calling us up there, death is beaten. The ruler of this world, the natural realm, Satan, is defeated and judged. This is what Jesus was saying to His own disciples and apostles before He went to the cross in John 16. Jesus told them and us that "of judgment, because the prince of this world, is judged." (John 16:11). This was one of three things Jesus was telling the disciples the Holy Spirit would do and reveal to them and to us.

You see, in the garden Father gave but one commandment and with it He gave a penalty, "eat of this fruit and you shall surely die."(Genesis 2:17). Death then entered into the earth realm not by God's hand but through man's disobedience. We empowered

Satan to control us through this fear of death because of our sins, something man was never created to know. Death has always "reigned" until Jesus drew all judgment to Himself on the cross. If we would but look afresh at John 12 we would see that Jesus was called by the Gentiles and He acknowledged that this call spelled the end for the Jews and an opening for the Gentiles saying, "Except a corn of wheat fall into the ground and die, it abideth alone; but if it die, it bringeth forth much fruit…" (John 12:24). Jesus was saying that He would have to die in order to return life to mankind and defeat death, which came in through sin.

If you recall, there was thunder from heaven as Jesus said for Father to glorify Himself through this act of obedience unto death, and Father confirmed this. It was heard for our sakes. But look at verses 31-32 in John 12, "Now is the judgment of this world; now is the prince of this world cast out. And I, if I be lifted up from the earth, will draw all men unto me." The word "men" was added by the interpreters because they did not understand this. Jesus was not speaking of His death drawing all men, for not all are drawn. He was speaking of all judgments for all sin, and to this the Scriptures bear witness. We know that Jesus went through death and won for us who believe a victory over death, which we shall never have to face, but simply pass through. Jesus has already done so "for us." The judgments of God were righteously met by a sinless life and sacrifice, and thus the ruler of this realm was cast out and made powerless to condemn us. Look at this truth from Colossians 2:13-15:

> And you, being dead in your sins and the un-circumcision of your flesh, hath he quickened together with him, having forgiven you all trespasses. Blotting out the handwriting of ordinances that was against us, which was contrary to us, and took it out of the way, nailing it to His cross; and having spoiled principalities and powers, he made a shew of them openly, triumphing over them in it.

These principalities and powers were Satan and his horde. Jesus defeated them by fulfilling the righteous requiem of the law with His own blood. In so doing, He took away the right of the law to condemn us, nailing it, the law, to His cross. Publicly Jesus took away the laws of God that Satan used to condemn us. Can you see why Satan would hate the teaching of grace? Look at this from 1 Corinthians 15:53-57:

> For this corruptible must put on incorruption, and this mortal must put on immortality, so when this corruptible shall have put on incorruption, and this mortal shall have put on immortality, then shall be brought to pass the saying that is written, "death is swallowed up in victory. O death, where is thy sting? O grave, where is thy victory?" The sting of death is sin; and the strength of sin is the law. But thanks be to God, which giveth us the victory through our Lord Jesus Christ.

If we could but see this as it is, I could stop right here, and you would be free of all bondages. Indeed we are free, although we still often wear the clothes of the dead, never seeing this truth and even rewrapping the strips of death about us with wrong doctrines. When Jesus died He made it possible for this to become a reality for us. When He died as a mortal man, came as a mortal man, he accepted a house of flesh to complete a plan Father had designed to trap sin in forever. Jesus died, sinless according to the law, not condemned of any sin, and He surrendered His life to death for us, for our sins, for sin itself. Only the victor can hold the spoils and Jesus has won the victory for us in that He now holds the keys of death, not the enemy of God, Satan. Satan still has limited power in the earth realm in that the worldly, those who do not know God, allow themselves to be used of him as do Christians who yield themselves back to him through ignorance, accepting condemnation as if it were a holy thing to do. But he cannot take us through death for it is no longer in his power to do so.

Of special note here for us on this journey is a revelation of a powerful truth: the strength of sin is the law. The sting of death is sin, but God gave us the victory over sin and death through the cross of Jesus. The laws that can only point out our shortcomings cannot be used against those who no longer are under the covenants of the law, now being married to Jesus. In other words Satan used God's laws against us to control us with fear and to bring us into bondage, fearing death. I do not believe any believer is afraid to die, but many still fear death because they have been taught that the Law is still in effect and one day they will still have to stand in judgment for sin before God. They are bound in clothes they are not to wear. Jesus said, "let him loose." This is why Romans 8:1 says, "There is now no condemnation for those in Christ Jesus," for through what Jesus did on the cross, He took away the power and strength of sin itself, the law, nailing it to His cross and stripping Satan of any power to condemn those "in" Him, in Jesus. But victory is not a victory unless you know this- have you experienced this freedom from the bondage of death? If you have you have been born alive again to Father God through the cross of Jesus- and you are no longer an old sinner saved by grace- you are in fact the righteousness of God in Christ Jesus- a son or daughter of God in right standing by faith- not by anything you have done or could do- keep the death clothes off- you are no longer under the law- but under grace, in Christ Jesus…isn't He beautiful? You will never stand before Father God to be judged for Jesus stood in your place- you are free! Can you begin to see yourself as Father sees you? Will you believe Him and trust in Him- the promises of God are for those who by faith believe and will receive them- standing not in any human efforts, but in grace alone! There will be many who oppose you as you go- pointing out who you once were- trying to yoke you with your pasts- but refuse them- stand in faith- for you are a child of the Most High, born again through the perfect Son of God come down for us, Jesus the Christ. Can you see this yet?

What Saith the Scriptures?

These are the words of the Apostle Paul to the church at Galatia as they were trying to stand in two covenants, mixing law and grace. "What saith the Scriptures? Cast out the bondwoman and her son; for the son of the bondwoman shall not be heir with the son of the freewoman." (Galatians 4:30). This sounds extremely harsh, and it is from a certain perspective. They are strong words Father gave Paul to say. They are words taken from the story of Abraham and Sarah and her bondwoman Hagar, the Egyptian. Abraham had two sons, one born of Hagar and one of Sarah, one of human efforts and one of the promise by the Spirit. Paul taught this as an allegory or a parable to help us contrast law and grace. He spoke of two different covenants— law and grace. Hagar was Mount Sinai, the law, and Sarah was Mount Zion, grace. Hagar was a bondservant to the law while Sarah was a woman of promise by grace. Their offspring then represent human efforts (law) and spiritual creation (grace.) In Galatians 4:29 we read this of Ishmael or the law, "But as then he that was born after the flesh persecuted him that was born after the Spirit, even so it is now." Father God's response to this persecution is the same now as then: "Cast out the bondwoman and her son." Why? Because they cannot receive what God has provided for the rightful heirs of promise by grace alone!

You will see on this journey by the Holy Spirit what He wants us to see and show us of what Jesus has for us by taking of what is Jesus's and making it known to us. (John 16:15). He, the Spirit, will not reveal this truth to those mixing law and grace, only to the children born of the promise to be heirs of the world. An heir simply receives what has been left for him or her as provided in advance with no human efforts.

I would that every believer could understand this truth, but often it is decided exactly opposite and the "bondservants" cast out the children born of promise. It is called religion or traditions and they have been in place so long that "they" have become a god to many. No! We must awaken to righteousness, His righteousness, for no one can receive inheritance based on good works or fleshly deeds or be refused by the lack there of. For it is of faith that it might be by grace to the end the promise might be sure to all the seed. (Romans 4:16). Our assurance of this heavenly provision will not come by human efforts to be good or removed by our shortcomings. For grace is what Father has already provided for us in Christ Jesus. Grace is much more than just salvation; grace can only be accessed "in" grace. "By whom also we have access by faith into this grace wherein we stand…" (Romans 5:2).

Can you see it yet? Father has already prepared in advance everything we need to live our lives here in this realm, but only in grace through faith, and faith is not of the law! It actually voids our faith according to Scripture. This is the journey, and we can either circle Mount Sinai for forty years or we can simply move to Mount Zion where Jesus has already opened the heavens to us through the cross to the throne of all grace. It is up to you, but nonetheless, Father has already spoken, "cast out the bondwoman and her son," for His inheritance, for and to those born of His Spirit is "free." No one can earn it or brag that it is owed to them, no one!

Are you an heir or a bondservant? Are you free or bound? Who is your mother? Law or grace? Same Father but two different covenants with two separate and distinct paths or roads or highways. The call of Jesus is to the higher road, a "come up hither call" to a highway He has prepared for us to walk upon. But the choice is yours—choose life! It is either life by the Spirit, faith, or it is not. Can you see yet?

A Whole Lot of Shaking

The Word tells us that Father would shake everything once again until everything that can be shaken "is shaken" leaving for us only that which cannot be shaken remaining. (Hebrews 12:26-27). I do not know about your life and how you see yourself, but of a truth, there are many things we identify with that are not our inheritance. Our identities or even our identification with the people and the things we are surrounded by, our pasts and present situations, the pains and hurts that helped to mold us, the rejections, the doctors reports, the proclamation by those in the know of our state of mind, our bank accounts, our debt, our possessions, our family heritages, our looks or size, our jobs, our educations, our religious affiliations—Baptist, Catholic, Methodist, Assembly of God—and so forth. Even what we have believed about Father and Jesus and the Holy Spirit, is prone to a lot of this shaking until everything that "can be" shaken is shaken. It is a journey of faith and is made in faith alone. The Law is not of faith; therefore, the shaking must begin.

It may feel like a form of death, and in fact it will be, and often quite painful, for our flesh identifies itself through natural controls. It likes the law because it understands it well. Do good, get good is easy to understand as is the opposite. But grace and love to an undeserving person who sees their own identity as the limit of God's power and as the end of the story—this will take a shifting of understanding. You will need a helper, the Holy Spirit, for only He can unveil Jesus to us and in us. It is a revelation of Christ in us that we need in order to be who we have become in the spiritual realm. I have been on this journey all of my life, never fully understanding that how others see me, what they say of me, even what they claim they know of me or about me, even what I have said of myself is not the end but simply where I once was. I never saw the journey as it is—a road to a higher view. *Come up thither* to a place where Jesus desires us to rise up to and identify ourselves with Him.

Eternity is not a destiny, but it is a person. His name is Jesus, and He is God. Jesus said it this way: "This is eternal life, that they know God and Jesus Christ whom He sent." (John 17:3). All that the believer needs is found not in looking at ourselves but at Him, beholding Him, and allowing the Holy Spirit to transform us from glory to glory or as we see His glory revealed to us and even through us. This is all—that we might lose our identity as natural beings and finally accept who He says we are. It is a journey beloved; don't judge the end until the end comes. Just because I am down and out, or others are, even our children or friends or brothers and sisters, it isn't over. Even in the rejection by those we believe love us, this too can be for our own good.

Even Jesus had to face the old, "Isn't this the carpenter or the son of Joseph?" Old identities cling until they are removed, hence the shaking! This new identity as family by faith will bring about a lot of trials. Jesus had to face His testing's from the moment His ministry began until He gave up His life on the cross. "If you are the Son of God…" The tests and trials are not for us to prove our identity but to believe it and stand in it. Jesus never proved who He was in order to be who Father called Him. The trials and tests are not always from Father God but He can use them to bring forth the new creation that is hidden in us. I am not sure why we must go through these things, but in them we who truly believe turn inward first and eventually upward. It has an ending; even faith has an ending—the salvation of our souls. Oh this can be painful. You will never enter into His promises while being led by Moses and the law, but the entrance into the kingdom is with great tribulation. These then become platforms for movement but always from a lower to a higher revelation. If it refocuses us on our pasts, on who we once were or where we were yesterday, it is not from Jesus. If you allow this you will find yourself standing alongside the rock Moses struck waiting for water to come forth which only comes by faith, speaking to the Rock, His name is Jesus. All external controls must cease before life by the Spirit can become a reality.

"Behold, all things are become new" is a statement written in 2 Corinthians 5:17 and this is followed by another statement, "And all things are of God." What does that mean to you? It speaks of the origin of "all things" does it not? The new things do not originate in the natural realm for they are natural and God is a Spirit according to His own Word. But the journey that prepares us for this new identity, this change of origination is preempted by another statement: "Therefore, if any man be in Christ, he is a new creature, old things are passed away…behold all things are become new." And I believe it is important for us to know that "all things" are ours in Jesus Christ. How can this be you ask? "According as his divine power hath given unto us all things that pertain unto life and godliness through the knowledge of him that hath called us to glory and virtue…" (2 Peter 1:3). Can you see this truth?

The words *hath given* speak of something already accomplished and this then identifies *all things* as the subject matter. But how does this come to us? Is it by doing something good or not doing something wrong? No! But by learning about Jesus, what He did for us on the cross and through the cross, we have this life. If we remain in the past, identifying ourselves with the natural realm, the realm of sin and death, we are subjecting this new creation reality to an identity that no longer exists. We do not believe what has happened and who Father says is in us. Jesus cannot come out of someone who does not believe Jesus is in them. The identity is still with the old.

I can help you identify this in yourself by simply asking you this one thing: do you receive any condemnation? If you do, you are still alive to your old self. The Bible says that there is *now* no condemnation for those in Christ Jesus, none! Yet as it is being hurled at you from every place natural, if we believe we are still just natural beings and not new creations in Christ Jesus, we will receive something we are no longer able to receive. It is a form of death, covering over the new creation called out of death into life by Jesus, by what He did for us; it is a form of bondage being bound in grave clothes while awakened in the Spirit. It is acceptance of this new identity to the full onslaught of those who wish to hold us where we once were or now are. They tried it in Jesus. They will try you as well. "Isn't this the carpenters' son?" But Jesus promised to give us a new name only He and you or I would know, a personal name that would identify us in the newness of life He gave us. It is a literal *seeing* Jesus in us brought forth from within us, His glory being revealed in and through our lives. This newness of life by the Spirit cannot begin unless you let go of the past, and if you do not let go, a whole lot of shaking will begin to occur in your life. Not a punishment, but Father trying to convince us of what He already sees in us. A reality not seen with natural vision, only by the Spirit.

Letting go of the Law is a very hard thing to do. For if we are truthful, we like it; it is a familiar subject, and the law applies to the whole "family" of mankind. But to those born of the Spirit of God, the law should be silent. What could be seen was addressed in the seen realm by laws to govern the flesh, the natural man. But if we are truly born again of God our Father by His will, He has birthed into us in fullness, a new creature, created in true holiness and righteousness according to Ephesians 4:24. I am not here to condemn you who still "try" to keep the laws of God but to simply inform you of the higher calling to come up here, to ascend to the higher ground, to grace alone. And many have fallen from this higher place back into laws and traditions, from a remembrance that Father first loved you, you have forgotten *your first love* and made it all about how much you can show your love for Him. The law sets demands. Many of you have "settled in" wherever you are, and you do not wish to be disturbed. I am not the One who will do the shaking beloved; I am just reporting the facts as He wrote them to us.

"Who do people say that I am?" Jesus asked His disciples and so we must ask ourselves this question. But then He asked them, "Who do you say that I am?" (Luke9:18-20). It was a revelation from Father God to Peter—not to Simon, but to Peter. God has always called out from the beginning to the end. You are Abraham when he was always Abram. He called Jacob Israel; Sarai He called Sarah. Saul became Paul, and to each of us who are born of God, He will call out our new identification to us. And it won't be you; it will be the you that He sees already, a reality before we even know who we are.

He called a small child in a wooden basket floating down a river, "one drawn out" or Moses. He called another to lead His people into His Promised Land, Joshua or Jehoshua, and his name was once Oshea. He called Gideon, who was in hiding, a mighty man of valor. He is in the business of calling those things that be not as though they are. I wonder what He has called you. I wonder who He sees you to be, even as you are still living as the old person you once were. I wonder what lie you still believe that you have heard spoken by others that violated what He has said of you, or are you one of those who believe and receive even before you see it appear in the natural realm, even if it never does? Are you of another Spirit as was Caleb and Joshua? How many fleeces will we need to believe the good news of the Gospel of grace? When will we no longer be hurt by what others say, by what they do, or by what they have done to us in the past because we see ourselves alive in Jesus who has already bore our shame and guilt and reproach?

I write to those of you who have been hurt by divorces, rejected by a spouse for another, maybe even multiple times; to those raped or molested and are held by those acts of violence; to those of you who have experienced rejections in work, even in play, and especially at church. Jesus is still anointed to heal the broken-hearted and as you are so I once was. Let Him touch your hearts; ask Him to do so, and believe in His anointing, in His power. "Who will believe our report?" Isaiah asked the Lord God. (Isaiah 53:1). I ask you? Can you see past your present situation? Can you believe that everything that is seen is subject to change? Can you declare yourself rich while you are poor, strong when you are weak, able to see when you are blind, free when in bondage, free when bound in your past or present, maybe even in a church pew you are bound in death, bound with words or in painful pasts that do not come from above? Oh the journey has begun, and it will be painful, it will bring about change of locations and identities- it will be a journey with a lot of shaking- but along the way a new creation will emerge if you will but let go of the law, for the law is not of faith, and this journey must be by faith and not by sight! Can you see yet? Will you dare to believe that this road is for you, that this is the plan of God for you?

Antinomians

This is what scholars called those who were antinomians, or against the law. Anti law was and is still seen by those under the law as wrong doctrine. But a careful examination of what those Antinomians really believed reveals that they believed grace was a license to do whatever they desired to do and that they were not subject to the results of willful sins and acts. Gnostics believed there was no sin and trusted in their fleshly ability. Paul said that he had no confidence in the flesh, and neither should we. Only the new creation matters. But can we sin all we want too? I am not of that belief.

Sin has consequences! It still produces death in many ways. It still allows access to our lives and we do not have to yield to it. I, however, am a sold-out, "grace" man, and in this journey, I want to share a better way to live a Christian life than by rules and regulations and traditions. I hate sin! And yet I still sin! Do you? The Bible tells us that "anyone born of God does not sin" but we all still sin. It might be better translated that anyone born again of God's Spirit does not sin. This is the new creation, the new creature, the born-again-to-God-Spirit man.

We were all dead to God in sin. Jesus died and made an access through His own flesh for us to come back to Father. We were fleshly creatures with a soul. But God birthed us in Christ Jesus alive by the Spirit, which died when sin entered into man. Father then sees us alive in Christ Jesus and dead to sin because Jesus has paid for them all. Can we then sin all we want? Paul was asked these questions, and I pray that as we go, you too will ask and seek the answers to these questions that grace must provoke if grace is being taught correctly. I am not against the law, for through it I came to know how great my sin was and how damaging it can be. But I am dead and deaf to the law because of grace, for I am not saved by the law, for the law is not of faith. I am saved by grace through faith, and faith is pleasing to my Father. He rewards those who seek Him in faith. This is the higher calling, a *come up here* place where believers are called to live life after salvation and past sin and death. It is a place from which some fall from but never out of, for Jesus's hands surround us, it is a place that once experienced, you cannot forget.

Jesus said, "remember therefore from whence thou art fallen…" (Revelation 2:5). Jesus was instructing the angel or pastor over the church to return to God's love, who loved him first. Trying to prove we love God can wear us out. Love is never measured with human efforts but by the cross of Jesus. Fallen away from His love is as Paul said, *you have fallen from grace*! Grace, then, is life to the new creature, and we are dead to sin through the cross of Jesus as Paul so said to those who asked if we could sin all we want. Grace is the highest standard the living God gave to man. It is a place where we identify with Him through His Son Jesus the Christ who died for all sin on a cross before the world was even formed in Father's mind. It is a place of relationship, of being loved and then loving as we have been so loved, and removed from religion and religious activities. It is a place where the cross of Jesus is ever before our eyes. His sacrifice for us is a place where sin is seen defeated through His obedience on a cross only He could carry. He fulfilled a righteous requiem set by Father God no man could ever attain to, and all of this so that we too might have hope of being forgiven "according to the riches of His grace."(Ephesians 1:7). It is in fact the Revelation of Jesus Christ to us, seeing from His perspective what He did for us who will but believe and receive. "Come up thither….and I will show you." It is a place higher than the natural realm, a spiritual reality accessed only through faith and by grace, or by and through what Jesus has already done for us.

Before you judge me I ask you to consider this: Do you know this fullness or the riches of grace? And just how rich is Father? Do you have peace? It is "according to the riches of His grace" that we are forgiven, is it not? Not *from* the richness of grace but *according to* the riches of His grace. There is a difference. Not a part of but from the total of His grace. This is what Ephesians 1:7 says. Call me an antinomian or anti-law teacher, and I will respond to that statement with these questions: Have you experienced the life He has called us to while still under the law, under the altar? Have you seen His face, heard His voice, witnessed His mighty hands, experienced His touch and favor, seen His miracles, received the Spirit, and experienced His love and believed in it? Father no longer sits on a seat of judgment but upon the throne of all grace, not part grace and part law but all grace. This grace He lavishes on His children with extravagances we would never have known, but only by grace through faith!

If you can measure grace according to Father's riches, then you are surely living a life of abundance. Are you? Are you reigning in this life? Or are you just waiting for that day up yonder? Grace will empower us to live *life* to the full in spite of the world and its problems and trials. Remember 2 Peter 1:3: He has already given to us all things that pertain to *life*. Grace will never leave you asking "why me, Lord?" but even in the trials you will find hope and see deliverance. It is a heart filled with judgment and law that looks or turns upon itself during trials and struggles and seeks to find out "What sin have I committed that brought this upon me?"

It is an ugly thing we do, believing it is good that we place ourselves in the center of our lives and beat ourselves and condemn ourselves, never seeing that Jesus is our righteousness. We hold a form of godliness and deny the true power of God, the gospel of His grace, Jesus crucified. We are either under grace, measured only by the limits we place upon Father ourselves, or under the law, measured according to our ability to be good, or even worse, under a law-and-grace mixture which leaves us torn into two camps. Are we experiencing life to the fullest, an abundance of life? Are we "reigning in life by one Jesus Christ…"? and defined "by the free gift of righteousness and the abundance of grace…" (Romans 5:17)? Have you known the richness of this grace Father has bestowed upon us? I too hate sin. I hate death. I have experienced both in my life as well. They are enemies of my Father and yours. I simply see grace as the higher way to travel this life in, a higher calling. Oh, you can get there by believing in His grace for eternal life but live like you were in hell here on earth if you wish. There is more to the life of the new creation, and it is not according to my ability to be good or removed by my failures. It is by grace through faith, and it takes both! Remember, faith is not of the law! But you must decide!

SEEING JESUS
IS DEATH TO SELF

Well then, as one man's trespass (one man's false step and falling away led) to condemnation for all men, so one Man's act of righteousness (leads) to acquittal and right standing with God and life for all men. For just as by one man's disobedience (failing to hear, heedlessness, and carelessness) the many were constituted sinners, so by one Man's obedience the many were constituted righteous (made acceptable to God, brought into right standing with Him).

Romans 5:18-19, Amplified Bible

What Jesus has done is greater than, more powerful than, abounds more than the sin of Adam whereby all men were made sinners. His act of love is overly done, lavished, poured out without any measure ! The difference is not in what we did wrong or right, but in what Jesus has already done for us and in our faith in what He did for us. This single truth will lead you to the end of you as you see Jesus revealed in the Word of God. What I mean is that a single focus is required, and that on Jesus and not on us. The question is not, did Jesus really do all of this or not? It is, what do you believe He did for you? If you believe He truly died for all of your sins, and actually became sin for you, then you have been restored to a relationship with Father God greater than the one Adam and Eve had in the beginning.

For this relationship is born of God's will and by Jesus's precious blood covenant. It is greater than all we could ever do, and all because Jesus said, "Not my will, but yours!" I pray that you will let this death to self come, for the law points its finger at you beloved and will continue to do so until you see Jesus alive and resurrected in your hearts. Christ in us is the hope of glory! Quit looking at what you are doing wrong and see what Jesus did for you as greater than all your sins, and you have begun to move away from the Port of Religious activity. Let the Spirit blow and guide and lead you into the Port of Peacefulness where you will rest in what Jesus has already done for you. Trust in Him, seek after His face, hear His voice, and walk in faith. And again, the law is not of faith! Death reigned from Adam to Moses. "For if by one man's offence death reigned by one; much more they which receive abundance of grace and of the gift of righteousness shall reign in life by one, Jesus Christ." (Romans 5:17) Who and what is reigning in your hearts? Is it life or death? Law or grace? Self efforts or His efforts? Who are you looking at beloved? Is it Jesus or is it you?

Mystery Babylon

Words have power. Paul taught that those who were being taught to return to the law had been dissimilated with wrong teaching—words! He also said that he was in travail as a woman in childbirth "until Christ be formed in you again." Jesus was formed with words. "Be it unto me according to Thy Word." Mary said this and received Jesus into her womb by the Holy Ghost, and so it is in us who believe in the heart; and just as He was formed or built, so was He torn down with words.

There is a journey in life whereby every believer is to move onward, forward, ahead, toward a goal, a place, and a time set in our hearts by Father God. It is eternity. Sometimes as we go, we are stopped or misdirected or misled by some false doctrine or teacher or even an event in our lives. Each of these can become a place of stopping and death or a launching pad from which we move further and higher and closer to this life. On this journey, even though it is a long one, are teachings of both life and of death. They are places I stopped to see, or was stopped at, that became a launching pad to more, to higher places. Some were bad, but they could not hold me there, for God meant even those for good to help others around me.

It is always a choice to see what we will do with what has been thrown at us—free choices. We are in a war, you know; the enemy is unseen. His plan is to get us to stop at some place or another and not to continue up the mountain, to stop just short of the higher road, the come up thither road. Some of us stopped at Moses, some are still there, waiting for Jesus to come. Some stopped at judgment and are waiting and even praying for Father God to judge the world with fire and destroy it, even as they stand in a grace they did not deserve and cannot earn. Some are bound with death, and fear controls them as they try to act out a life they cannot have, never being free from their own pasts. They are seeking freedoms from painful experiences only until they become powerful or strong enough or have the opportunity to render the same to others as it was done to them. Being rejected and then rejecting, having been abused and then abusing.

This is how King Saul fell, for he believed in what the sons of Belial said of him more than what Father God spoke over him through the prophet Samuel. Words have power once we accept them, but whose will we believe? Will we remain under a blanket, a covering, controlled by anger and motivated by fear of losing controls we never had, acting out and living out a past life, angry and then sorry and then angry and then sorry, never coming to a place where they are free. I saw these persons, believers mind you, in the Revelation of Jesus Christ to John. There they were crying out for this judgment for "their" blood upon the world.

Simply stop and consider that for a minute. How can we who are saved by grace cry out for judgment? Did not the blood of Jesus cleanse all? Who is being held under the altar here? Is it those who cry for vengeance or those they cry against that are under the altar? Words! They are powerful and they pave the way of the heart. How do we see Father God, how do we see what Jesus did for all on the cross, how do we see ourselves, and how do we then project Father God and Jesus and the Holy Ghost to this world, a world blinded to the truths of the gospel? These who cried out to God for judgment and vengeance were *given* clean robes, righteousness even, as they demanded justice and judgment and they were told to wait. Why? Because Father is still patiently waiting for the last one, the one He has ordained to receive His grace to come. I remind you that it is His longsuffering that brings salvation, not ours. Where have you stopped on your journey? Are you also waiting for the day of vengeance or are you busy searching the Words of God to know Him better and then live *life* as a testimony from your hearts as those saved by grace, not of yourselves, by a gift of God to one in need. What doctrine has held you and stopped you from seeing eternally? How can we the church reach the lost and hurting if we ourselves are sick and hurting, hiding under an altar, focused on sin, afraid to come out, and holding onto a past life, an old way, or an old covenant?

> And upon her forehead was a name written, MYSTERY BABYLON THE GREAT, THE MOTHER OF HARLOTS AND ABOMINATIONS OF THE EARTH.
>
> Revelation 17:5

Many have written about this in regards to the end of days prophecies, and I will not add to this, but I wish to use the mystery according to the leading of the Spirit as an allegory to help us see. The word *harlot* speaks of a fornicator—a harlot or whore, an idolater—and in reference to this truth that the Lord has given to me, this is a significant thing to consider. You see, the Apostle Paul wrote of this in Romans chapter 7 where he used the analogy of a marriage by a woman to her first husband (the Law) and to another man while the first one was still alive. He called her an adulteress. Paul went on to say "but if her husband be dead, she is free from that law; so that she is no adulteress, though she be married to another man." Paul of course is speaking of anyone who is married to Christ must be free from the law in order to not be a spiritual adulterer. It is a form of idol worship, replacing Jesus with someone or something else, your goodness.

The name Babylon literally means to be in confusion through mixture. Babel is the word used to describe what happened at the tower of Babel when Father confused the tongues or languages of those who were attempting to raise themselves up to heaven by their own efforts. The word Babel is derived from the word balal which means to mix or to mingle. Clearly, Father God does not like the mixing of those things He designed to remain separated and different. This is law and grace. Law requires what we must do and grace gives what He has done already. It is a mixture of Jesus on the cross plus what we also must do. The law sets a demand upon us for righteousness and grace gives righteousness by faith. The mixing of grace and law, even a little bit, causes confusion to those who were meant to live life by the Spirit leaving them to live a mixed life between law and grace. It is quite like mixing identities looks good to the world but in fact it divides us. For example, we call people of other heritages African-Americans and Japanese Americans and Mexican Americans: this sounds good but in fact it causes us to be divided, for we are all Americans. One nation under God, indivisible… but how great is the division because of mixing or mixtures. Jesus prayed for us all in John 17 that we might all be one- He was speaking of understanding that God loves us all equally just as He so loved Jesus. This is the unity- taking two and making it into one; not taking one and making it into many mixtures. But even worse is mixing law and grace, which ruins the power of both.

Paul reveals what happens in these unions, and perhaps he is showing us the results of this.

> Wherefore, my brethren, ye are also become dead to the law by the body of Christ; that ye should be married to another, even to him who is raised from the dead, that we should bring forth fruit unto God. For when we were in the flesh, the motions of sins, which were by the law, did work in our members to bring forth fruit unto death.

> Romans 7:4-5

Which fruit are we going to bear, life or death? It is the Spirit life Jesus gave us who believe, and He releases us from the former, the law, in order to become fruit bearers unto God— righteousness. All other fruit is death! Jesus said in John 15: 5,

"I am the vine, ye are the branches; he that abideth in me, and I in him, the same bringeth forth much fruit; for without me ye can do nothing." Abiding in Christ is a relationship, and it is not based upon our performance, but upon faith alone. Abide means to dwell with and remain with or in, in relationship with Jesus. We entered into this relationship by faith alone and only in faith can we abide. No kingdom fruit is born apart from the Spirit and through faith. All else is works, fleshly. I am not saying physical works are not to be done but that, because of them, we do not abide or bear fruit to Father, only through faith! The Law is not of faith!

Paul told the Galatians that "anyone under the works of the law is under a curse, for cursed is everyone who does not do all of the law." What we do for Father God cannot be seen as the motivation for coming into His Presence; it must come by faith in what Jesus has already done. Why? Because when we fail, and not if, for no one can keep the law, we find ourselves cursed by the very law we sought to uphold. You can only be under grace by faith. No law! The law deals with the carnal or fleshly man, and as we have already seen, Paul said he put no confidence in the flesh, including his own. For he knew all fleshly motivations both from within and from without will fail, all efforts of human flesh is destined to fail, no matter how strong you are in yourself. Only eternal motivations and callings will last by the Spirit.

It is a great mystery that will be exposed and is to be revealed to us how that which Father designed to be fruitful unto Him still is producing death under the law; a confusing mixture of two covenants never intended to be mixed. It was the Apostle Paul who called any other gospel "no gospel at all" and pronounced curses upon those who would mix in human efforts with the precious blood of Jesus Christ. (Galatians 1:6-9). Is this what you have been taught? A little guilt and shame, a little bit of grace? No wonder the church has yet to come forth as she was called to be. Who is this sitting on a horse, and why is she sitting? Is it not the church of confusion, holding both grace and judgment in her hands? Why is she not looking for Jesus to come? Why is she seated in power? Is it her ability that enables her? Why is this harlot called a great city divided into three parts in Revelation 16:19? Could this simply be three doctrines—law, grace, and a blending of the two and an addition of worldly doctrines? Isn't this a world religion any and all can accept? And isn't she sitting upon many waters which are peoples and multitudes and nations and tongues according to Revelation 17:15? And are not these the same ones Jesus sent His church to in Revelations 10:11, 'And he said unto me, Thou must prophesy again before many peoples, and nations, and tongues, and kings'? Could this be the church Jesus speaks of in Revelations 2:24, "But unto you I say, and unto the rest at Thyatira, as many as have not this doctrine, and which have not known the depths of Satan, as they speak: 'I will put upon you none other burden.'" And this statement Jesus makes is from Acts 15:28, 'for it seemed good to the Holy Ghost, and to us, to lay upon you no greater burden than these necessary things.' And what were the things? Abstaining from meats offered to idols, from things strangled, from blood, and from fornication. You see men came and attempted to add the Law back into the Gospel of grace. Read this whole chapter in Acts 15 and see what the Pharisees were trying to add in and make a mixed gospel, which is not the Gospel at all. And aren't these very things the indictment against this Harlot? Isn't she drunk with the blood of the saints and filled with the abominations of her fornications according to Revelation 17:4-6? Is not this dividing us today? I am not writing this to scare you but to share what the Lord has shown to me of these last days. Won't you at least consider the truth of the gospel of grace, look with your own eyes and quit just accepting what others say without any Scriptural backing? I pray for you to see.

Warning: May Be Hazardous to You

Have you ever wondered why anyone would put a warning such as this on a label? They put these types of warnings on everything anymore. Almost every toy and pill and food product and even fast foods, furniture, tools, and any and everything that we have contact with has a written warning to be careful because it may cause injury or problems. If we actually listened to these warnings we probably would never take any of the so called medications that are being sold today. But even still, people buy and consume those things that have warnings on them. I suppose they always just assume "it can't happen to me."

That being said, I also have so warned you. If you are a religious person, a person who still is trying to attain to goodness through his or her own efforts or is one who condemns others in the body seeing themselves above the laws they use to condemn others, you will become instantly angry, for I am about to breach the strength of religion—the law. That's right; I am going to bring a frontal assault upon the "big ten" written in stone, the Ten Commandments. I am not saying that they are not useful, nor am I going to say that they are not God's will, nor will I say that they are not spiritual and perfect, for they are. I will not say that they have no place in our lives, but I am going to ruin you as you read this if you believe you can keep even one of them perfectly. Let's just shoot you right in the heart with number one. "Thou shalt love the Lord thy God with all they heart, all thy mind, all thy soul and all of thy strength…and thy neighbor as thyself." (Mark 12:30-31). No one except Jesus has ever done this perfectly, and you will never attain to this. Even if you could it would not qualify you for eternity with God. The Word tells us that no flesh shall be justified by the law, none of it, including yours and mine. And this is the law- a commandment! The very second our thoughts drift away from Father and back onto our selfish little lives, we have fallen short of perfect, and therefore, we are guilty and sentenced to death. This is what the law does; it magnifies or points out sin in man. The Bible calls the law, written in stone, the ministration of death and condemnation (2 Corinthians 3:7), the power or strength of sin (1 Corinthians 15:56). This failing then leaves us afraid of ever approaching the very Father we all so desperately need to see and know in these last days. You will never see Him by self efforts or by self examinations, but by grace alone!

> Neither pray I for these alone, but for them also which believe on me through their word; that they all may be one, as thou, Father, art in me, and I in thee, that they also may be one in us; that the world may believe that thou hast sent me. And the glory which thou gavest me I have given them; that they may be one, even as we are one.

> John 17:20-22

I want to share this truth with you all, but first, I must establish you in this truth- we are all one in what Jesus has done for us, in His grace. Just as Father and Jesus and Holy Spirit are one, so are we with Them. This is a truth if, in fact, you have placed your faith *in* Jesus Christ alone. We are not one in our denominational traditions; we are not one in any physical resemblances, or in our nationalities or political opinions, or in financial equalities, or in any fleshly or carnal things. But to attain to the level Jesus just addressed to us in a recorded prayer to His Father and ours, is if we are in faith alone.

It seems often that the difference in us establishes us and not our common bond—Jesus Christ our Lord and Savior. Difference is good; division is bad. There is but one Jesus and one God and one Holy Spirit or Holy Ghost, there is not a different Father for each denomination, albeit we may have different mothers. What we disagree on is often seen as our faith, but in fact it is not. Faith is not what we believe but what the Word says. I could speak of these differences forever for in fact they exist and always will for in them is the power of division- pride. The Bible teaches us that "only by pride cometh contentions" (Proverbs 13:10a) and so it is with all denominational divisions. Oneness in Jesus is our common denominator, and it is where I wish for us to remain. I write this not to point out our differences, but because we have them already. Jesus spoke of His glory which is simply this: He was and is the Son of God. He was seated with the Father before any of us came to be, and He is now seated once more beside His Father—the glory of all of us is our children. To be called a son or a daughter of Father God is the highest identity we could ever have as human beings now made into His children by faith alone. No earthly efforts could ever raise us up into this position; we are and must be born of His will, not our own. One is law, works of the law, the other is by His hand, grace. Can you see this? It is my prayer as I address these truths that we see them as truths revealed to the least of the saints by the Holy Spirit to refocus us as One, seeing the glory we have as One, the glory Jesus gave to us. This will be a battle in your hearts, but resist the desire to put this down until you have finished this. For it is the heart of the Father and Jesus for us. I do not seek divisions based upon denominational traditions nor ethnic variations nor social positions nor places of birth.

I want to help remove a veil from your hearts, from your eyes that you might better see the truth. The veil that once kept us from seeing Father God has a hole in it and it is the torn flesh of Jesus. It is only through Him that we can see Father God as

He truthfully is. Hebrews 1:1-2 tells us that *now* through Jesus, God is being revealed to us, no longer through Moses and the prophets. In truth, if we are trying to see Father God through the law or Moses, we will remain blinded to Him. When the law was given, people ran away from Father God in fear, but in Jesus's finished works, all are drawn when He drew all judgment to Himself. Why would He do this for us? "Father I will that they also, whom Thou hast given me, be with me where I am, that they may behold my glory…" (John 17:24). "And he ordained twelve, that they should be with him…" (Mark 3:14).

It is Jesus's desire to have us near to Him, in Goshen, He wants you and me close to Him, and it is His desire for us to know His Father as our own. But the law leaves us standing afar off asking Moses to tell us what God is saying—fear! It therefore is through Jesus, His love for us, through the cross and His crucifixion that we can now see and hear Father clearly, personally. He has not actually changed any at all but it is how we relate to Him that has changed. We *now* approach Him boldly through the completed works of Jesus, by grace through faith, not of our selves, lest we should boast. The law sets a demand upon us before we can ever come, and it leaves us always just short and asking, "What else must I do to inherit eternal life?" (Mark 10:17) and we can never meet them or do enough. This is the law and its purpose. It is not nor ever was written as a way to create fellowship or relationship with God. It was given by Moses to reveal sin in man and our need for a Savior who could help us to see and understand someone we all know and all need.

I read once that "it is not all about you," but in truth, from God's perspective, this is not truth. It is all about us. Why else would He send His only Son to death for us unless we are the most important beings in the created universe? The problem is and always has been self focus. As long as we look at ourselves, be it in a mirror or through the law, we are still looking at *me*. Jesus has come and is come to reveal to us a Father who so loves us that we can finally trust in Him enough to forget about *me* knowing that His love is more than enough. In fact, it is an immeasurable love, and I can forget all about me and just fixate *me* on Him and His love. David saw this in Psalm 28:7, "…my heart trusted in Him, and I am helped…" As long as we try to see God through our performance, we will always be disappointed and ashamed, discouraged and never content; we will always fall just short of enough. Trying to see Him through our personal experiences is even worse. Only through Jesus, what He did for us, can we ever see this truth and believe it. God is love, and His love is focused on *me*. It is all about *me*. I can trust Him. In truth, everything He wrote is about *me* and about *you*. He sent Jesus to meet *our* needs, to wash *our* feet, to serve *us* because He so loves *us*. But it cannot be seen clearly through law or legalism or church traditions. Only through a tear in the flesh of a loving and faithful Son named Jesus will we ever see and know and believe the love wherewith God has loved *us*.

Get ready, for I know this will rock your boat, maybe even sink it, but look at the Scriptures with an open heart, and let Jesus show you the Father. For He is eternal life, and this is why He came.

A Precious Death

"Precious in the sight of the Lord is the death of His saints…"

This is from Psalm 116 of David. It is the focus of this part of this writing and all that will be shared in it. Father sees our deaths or dying as precious to Him. It, death, is His enemy, however. How does this go together?

Paul said it this way, "but what things were gain to me, those I counted for loss for Christ." (Philippians 3:7). Paul was saying that everything that he was in the natural man, the carnal man—his education, his position, his heritage, his personal righteousness according to the law, his works, everything he had done—he saw them dead to himself in order to better see who and what Father God and Jesus wanted him to be. Paul went on to call all these things nothing but dung or waste! Isaiah declared *our* righteousness as filthy rags or menstrual cloths. Paul said he counted all things loss for the excellence of the knowledge of Christ Jesus my Lord. He offered them up to death until he saw them as they were—death.

It is an amazing fact that we will often hang onto those things that hurt us the most, even unto death. Father said in His Word that some of His children had made a covenant with death, and this to His dismay. Many bad habits are exercised in our lives until we die from them; so are many of our good habits as long as we see them as our qualifications before Father God. Both can bring us to death. This is nothing but the knowledge of good and evil. We often even know the things we do to ourselves bring us closer to death, and still we continue in them.

But remember, Father called this death to the things of this world; it was death, but it was precious to Him. Let's look at what Peter came to know late in his own life:

> Wherefore ye greatly rejoice, though now for a season, if need be, ye are in heaviness through manifold temptations; that the trial of your faith, being more precious than of gold that perisheth, though it be tried by fire, might be found unto praise and honor and glory at the appearing of Jesus Christ; whom having not seen, ye love; in whom, though now ye see Him not, yet believing, ye rejoice with joy unspeakable and full of glory; receiving the end of your faith, even the salvation of your souls...
>
> 1 Peter 1:6-9

I want you to see the words, *if need be.* These will be important to you, so remember them. But first let's look at the verses in an overview. Father called this testing and trial of faith precious! This is the death of His saints, death to all fleshly dependence, all fleshly goodness and righteousness of works or efforts, death to any and all things that might be placed before Him. It is a dead person, one dead to everything, one seeing this in their own heart that brings forth and displays the greatness of God's love and power. Or as Paul declared, "I am crucified to the world and the world to me." (Galatians 6:14). Paul also declared "we felt the sentence of death in our hearts that we might not depend upon man but upon God." (2 Corinthians 1:9). Can you see it yet? Until we are dead to this life, this realm of the physical and our need to be accepted or approved or endorsed or supported by men, including self efforts- we still have a shroud of death clothing on us.

Paul wrote in Romans 14:17, "for the kingdom of God is not meat and drink; but righteousness, and peace, and joy in the Holy Ghost." In other words, it is not what we take into us or do from our own physical strength, but it is His righteousness imputed or given and received by faith that gives us the knowledge of peace with Father through the cross and our joy over all Jesus has done for us by the shedding forth of love into our hearts by the Holy Ghost. Paul wants us to see the stark contrast of what we take in—food and drink, the life we once held as life—and what is already in us, Christ Jesus. Paul is calling us to see what is coming forth from within us by faith and then released into the world through Christ in us, the hope of glory, an act of love for others, a new life, a new creation in Him. This magnifies what Jesus said, "Seek ye first the kingdom of God and His righteousness and all these things shall be added unto you." (Matthew 6:33). Right standing with God is not of the flesh but of the submission to the Spirit of God from within us. "The kingdom of God is within you…" (Luke 17:21).Can you see it yet?

"For in Christ Jesus neither circumcison availeth any thing, nor uncircumcision; but faith which worketh by love" (Galatians 5:6). Oh, to better understand this simple statement and to shed this forth into the darkness of this present evil age, for this is the Gospel of Jesus Christ. We have all taught or have been taught that this has to do with loving God and Jesus and in the displaying of *our* faith, but this is nothing but simple and ignorant human analogy. The truth is this: no one loves God enough to make faith come or work. If we depend on ourselves to do this, then we cannot say what Paul said and we cannot do what Father said. It is only when we die to our selves, to self, that this is possible.

Remember how in 1 Peter we just read of this trying of faith would come upon us, "if need be"? Then this is something we must see and admit. Is this something necessary for me? And why is it necessary? To get us off of human *faith* depending upon our own goodness or seeing our human lack or badness, even our own strengths must die and we must refocus on the only love by which the gift of faith can operate—His love for us. No, make it personal—His love for me! "Herein is love, not that we loved God, but that He loved us…" 1 John 4:10a. The Commandment 'to love God with all of our hearts and minds and souls' is trumped in His gracious love for us. All sin is a manifestation of not trusting in God and therein attempting to satisfy our own needs in the flesh. He does not love me as much as I love me! Our love of self keeps us from seeing His love for us!

Faith cannot survive the fire unless it is secured and succored in a love greater than any flesh or carnal or human love. It is the fiery trial Peter himself endured when he boasted of his love for Jesus as Jesus spoke of going to the cross. Of course Peter's human love boasted of its strength until the fiery trial came, and it was necessary for Peter, as well as for us, to bring Peter, and us, to the reality of death—failure in the fleshly strengths he had, and they were plentiful. He had faith enough to walk on the water at Jesus's bidding, but not enough to stay afloat in the storm. Many teach that Peter lost focus and fell but the truth is that there is no human love strong enough to make faith work, because it always depends upon us, and we will fall. Only a faith that is anchored in and empowered by another's love—a love that overcame death and the grave, that captured the keys of death and hell, that passed through rock, that vanquished all sin forever and ever, that calls out across all eternity, that is spoken of from the first book of the Bible until the end—only in this love can faith work. This faith can move mountains, heal the sick, raise the dead, bring sight to the blind, and comfort to the hurting—life to the spiritually dead.

It is in the Psalm 116 of David that we see this truth revealed concerning how precious death of human or physical trusting is. David was crying out to Father God for help as death surrounded him and as he proclaimed his love for Father God and his trust in Him, in His grace and righteousness and mercy. He was delivered. Verse 8 tells us that Father delivered David from death, his eyes from tears, and his feet from falling. Sounds like fail-proof living.

Look a little further with me and you will see truth concerning this death to our own abilities. "What shall I render unto the Lord for all his benefits toward me? I will take the cup of salvation and call upon the name of the Lord" (Psalm 116:12-13). Can you see this? David's gift was to "take the cup of salvation," or simply said, to receive from Father! Did you get that? The Hebrew word for "take" here is nasa or nasah which means to accept, to bring forth, to furnish, to take. The Hebrew word for salvation is Jeshua. Do you know who that is? It means to take or to receive from Jesus! This then is the death to self, to simply and humbly receive from Jesus that which we need. It is one verse before this is written, "precious in the sight of the Lord is the death of his saints."

It would appear that taking from His provision and denying our own abilities is a form of death that Father sees as pleasing to Him. It is precious to Him. It lends great stock to what is written in Acts 20:35 from the lips of Jesus, "It is more blessed to give than to receive." Receiving from Father is a most humbling experience for the human flesh, just ask Peter as Jesus washed His feet. This is the way to the death of human efforts; all of them. Jesus is never stronger than when we need Him the most and offer up nothing of our own power.

> I will offer to thee the sacrifice of thanksgiving, and will call upon the name of the Lord. I will pay my vows unto the Lord now in the presence of all his people, In the courts of the Lord's house, in the midst of thee, O Jerusalem. Praise ye the Lord.

> Psalm 116:17-19

It is our praise for His faithfulness and for His kindness and love and mercies and for His trustworthiness, for He is worthy of all praise, is He not? But He will not share with others, things or people! Remember that we have an altar no one under the law can approach! "We have an altar, whereof they have no right to eat which serve the tabernacle" (Hebrews 13:10).

> By Him therefore let us offer the sacrifice of praise to God continually, that is, the fruit of our lips giving thanks to his

name; but to do good and to communicate forget not; for
with such sacrifices God is well pleased.

Hebrews 13:15-16

Is this not the same thing? Those who try to approach God
through their own goodness or stay away because of their sin can
never come to this altar, for it is the cross and only Jesus lifted
up for our sin was and is and will be able to accomplish this
way. No human service can earn or remove what Jesus has done,
nothing can be added or taken away. It is by faith in what Jesus
did, period! How that hurts those who seek to approach Father
by works of the flesh, by what we tithe, what we do at church,
what we don't do away from the church, how often we pray or
fast or witness. "By the works of the law shall no flesh be justified"
(Galatians 3:16). Can you see this death of all human efforts yet?
It is painful to us for we need this to satisfy our fleshly efforts, to
help a little bit to qualify us, to keep us alive just a little bit at any
cost. The law speaks to the flesh alone, and in it there is no ability
to bring forth life, only death! Ouch!

This is my hope: to help you to see death, to help you die that
you might better see and receive this truth—God is love. There
are many imitators, many types and shadows, that claim to be
love—things, people, ideas, all human and all good…but they
cannot sustain faith that overcomes *all* things. Only a faith that
is grounded and believes the love of God can pass through death
without fear.

Mohamed is in the grave as is Buddha, and all other carnal
gods. There is no flesh that can overcome death, but Jesus is
risen. He has conquered the grave and death, He lives because
He believes in the all consuming love of His Father, the Creator
being greater than the things created, and through our faith in
Him, in Jesus, we too have access to this the greatest of all things,
the love of our amazing God and Father. Whatever else you read
from here forward will most likely challenge your faith and may
even raise questions you do not have answers for. But of a truth,

you will either die to your religious truths and to this world, or you will become most irritated by what is going to be shared.

This may be nothing more than your human understanding or education, both of which are nothing more than errors waiting to be exposed. It may be your religious background and traditions or seminary education, which also must die. But if you can, and I pray you will endure to the end, this death to everything fleshly will have at least begun a good work in you. And He will finish it in you. I will not cover any of you in a cloak given for you to hide under, for this is not my calling, this is not what this writing is for. It is to make us all aware of a single truth—we cannot depend upon anyone, no man, no denominational teaching, lest we fall from grace. But if we are secured to the Rock of all ages, those ages past, the present evil age we live in, and for the ages yet to be, it must be in the love of One who loved us so much that He gave His very best, His only Son, and our hope in Him, in Jesus, in what He did for us; and we must see this through the eyes of a father or a mother who is asked to surrender not their own life, but the precious life of their children. Precious in the sight of the Lord is the death of His saints, for in their death they are believing in His love. They are learning to walk by faith, to trust in a love that crosses all boundaries and is not measured by any human love. In Father's sacrifice of His Son Jesus, we know and believe in His love. Now let's let go and begin to see His truth.

If Need Be

As I watched my own father slowly die I became aware of something I did not understand very well in this life. You see, my dad was on his way to Father, but he had yet to pass through this fiery trial we call death, fleshly death. I know this because as he slowly passed, he often would say that he did not know for sure that God loved him. He was basing this upon his own circumstances and feelings and not upon what Jesus did for us. This will always leave us feeling less than loved. It will cause us to turn inward and often even upon our own selves searching for the root cause of our troubles or sicknesses. Is it some hidden sin or disgusting habits? Is it because I did not confess each and every infraction I have ever committed? Yeah, that must be it. And off we go never fully seeing what we have neglected to see.

It is a fleshly focus or fixation that causes us to say things like this: "I do not know why my dad or mom or brother or sister or friends are suffering like this. They were good people!" Is this not a true statement? I also said those things once in my own trials when our youngest son was killed in a boat crash many years ago. He too had just become a believer in Jesus Christ, had joined our church, his life was changing, and then he was taken. Was God insane? What was He doing? Was He punishing me or our son for sins yet to be confessed? The questions came from every angle of human reflections. I found myself lying in a bed of sweat for months trying to rid myself of any and everything I had ever done in an unfruitful attempt to make this about me. For that is what the law does; it deals with fleshly man, and it points out our failures, bringing us to see we need a Savior.

The problem is this: I already had one, His name is Jesus. To say that this is wrong is to simply say that having two wives or husbands is not adultery, and it is! It was not a testing of my faith in what Jesus did but a simple doctrinal correction we all must see and understand. There is no life in the law. It is a ministration of death and condemnation sent not to perfect man but to help him see his needs, and they are many. It is written not to attain to God by "keeping" the law but to reveal our sinful natures, which are often masked under religion and religious coverings. How could anyone in the church of Jesus condemn those held in the bondages of sin unless they believe that they are not also subject to the law? But if we use the law then we must also submit ourselves to it. It is only when the law is silent to us that we can begin to hear the Spirit of God from within the born again new creation. It will stop accusing us when we are dead to our fleshly lives and alive to God by the Spirit.

I experienced this in my own life to a point where I did not know for sure I would survive, for I was ablaze in my own fiery trials. I wrote all of this down and placed it into my first book, *In the Cool of the Day*. It was a monumental struggle between law and grace. I wrote of doctrinal teachings in denominations that still impose the law upon the redeemed while it is written for the unrighteous according to Paul in 1 Timothy. Here, Paul was instructing young Timothy to beware of teachers of the law. It starts in verse 3 where Paul tells Timothy to stay put and warn those who teach the law, "that thou mightest charge some that they teach no other doctrine…" It is by grace alone we are saved. Paul reveals these false teachers in verses 7-9:

> Desiring to be teachers of the law, understanding neither
> what they say, nor whereof they affirm. But we know that
> the law is good, if a man use it lawfully; knowing this, that

the law is not made for a righteous man, but for the lawless
and disobedient, for the ungodly and sinners."

Clearly Paul lays out the purpose of the law: to expose sin in those who are unrighteous or without faith in Jesus Christ. Outward corrections of our flesh are not what God was seeking when He sent His Son to the cross, nor was it His focus when He, Father God, met with Moses on the top of Mount Sinai and gave him the Ten Commandments. He was seeking inward heart transformation based on honesty. This battle rages in our fleshly minds until we clearly see this truth. If we do not accept Jesus's payment for our sins, all of them, He died in vain. Our vanity!

Each day I would go to see my dad, and I would ask him if he knew how much God loved him. And at each visit, he would look dismayed or even separated from the truth, and he would say, "I do not know for sure." He too, just like me, and just like you, if you are honest, was measuring God with human standards. He loves me, and He loves me not. I read a book called *He Loves Me* which greatly helped me to see this truth. Quit using fleshly standards as the way to see God's love for you! Wayne Jacobson's book is a revelation of truth that will help each of us continually remember that love is not measured by what we are going through or given by what we do or removed by what we do not do. For in so doing, we lessen the only true measurement of God's love—Jesus sent down to live His life as a man and then to die for our sins that we might have life again with the Father. The Scriptures say it this way, "Herein is love…" (1 John 4:10). The Word then declares to us that we did not love God but He loved us and sent His only Son Jesus to die for us. Nothing else can be used once this is established, nothing! Over a period of about two years, I would go almost every day and sit and share God's love with my own dad until one day he declared that he now knew and believed the love wherewith God had loved him. Jesus had slowly been grown again in him with the truths of God's Word, and shortly after this, he passed. But the mistake was this one: never use any standards here in this physical realm to measure the love of God, for there are none in this world.

There is much to share and say, but let me add this by the Spirit of God as shared with me this very day: "Like newborn babes you should crave (thirst for, earnestly desire) the pure (unadulterated) spiritual milk, that by it you may be nurtured and grow unto completed salvation" (1 Peter 2:2, Amplified Bible). Do you have this desire and craving? Do you cry after and desperately seek the nourishment of His Word? For here we see that a completed or mature believer grows into the completed salvation God desires for us. It is not completed at birth but as we eat and are being fed or nourished. Eternal salvation is a finished work of God through Jesus Christ acquired by faith, but completed salvation is a process of continual growth.

It is what John writes in 1 John where he speaks of us being little children, then young men, and finally fathers. It is also the parable of the sower that Jesus taught us seeing hearts as fields of dirt. Jesus said this in Matthew 13:19, "When anyone hears the word of the kingdom, and understands it not, then cometh the wicked one, and catcheth away that which was sown into his heart." Jesus then described different kinds of soils until He finally declared in verse 23, "He that received seed into the good ground is he that heareth the word, and understandeth it; which also beareth fruit, and bringeth forth; some a hundredfold, some sixty, some thirty." But all of these are persons who are hearing the Word of God.

It is a continual process in which believers are to grow and mature past basic doctrines of Christ Jesus and end up in the understanding of righteousness. Christ is formed in our hearts as we hear and receive and experience the Word of God. This is Hebrews 5, and in it the writer urges us to move past these basics and into this righteousness and the *understanding* that comes with maturity seeking solid food, strong meat: "But strong meat belongeth to them that are of full age, even those who by reason of use have their senses exercised to discern both good and evil." (Hebrews 5:14). If we see this correctly, we are each being told that this maturing or growth process should "by reason of use" or experience have our spiritual senses used enough to discern good and evil from the inside out and not from the outside in.

This is grace and law. One works from the inside out and the other from the outside in. The bearing of fruit comes not by efforts but by a natural process of having a relationship with Jesus. Look at what Paul teaches us about this move from law to grace concerning this fruit bearing Jesus spoke of in the parable of the sower: "Wherefore, my brethren, ye also are become dead to the law by the body of Christ; that ye should be married to another; even to him who is raised from the dead, that ye should bring forth fruit unto God" (Romans 7:4). Can you see it? If you can, you have attained spiritual understanding and you have just seen your salvation grow or increase as we read in 1 Peter 2:2. It is a process that is ever increasing and ever changing us into the image of God, Jesus Christ. It comes not by observing the laws or our own selves but by focusing upon Jesus in the Word as He reveals to us the true nature of Father God.

It is Jesus who by the Holy Ghost moves us from faith to faith away from self examinations and into a single focus upon Jesus and His completed works. As long as we hold to two doctrines we are double minded, and we should not ever expect our prayers to be heard or answered. The enemy will always try to rob the word of grace spoken in faith, because he knows that once we believe and have received this truth, we know both good and evil from within, and the law he uses to condemn us with has lost its power. We will no longer be spiritual adulterers.

This adultery word may be offensive to you as you think of your own relationship with Jesus, but consider this story. A friend of mine came to me one day and spoke of his marriage being an unproductive marriage. It was his second. His first wife had left him for another man, and she had been quite the complainer and nagger finding him less than adequate in her own eyes. Despite having been condemned by her in the marriage and even after his remarriage to another, he still said he had thoughts of affection for his first wife! As I wondered why he had shared this with me, the Lord showed me Romans 7:3: "So then if, while her husband liveth, she be married to another man, she be called an adulteress; but if her husband be dead, she is free from that law, so that she is no adulteress, though she be married to another man." Add in the first part of verse 4, "Wherefore my brethren, ye also are become dead to the law by the body of Christ…that ye should be married to another…" The law cannot die to us but in what Jesus did, dying for us, we are dead to the law and free to be married again. But if we still yearn for the old, look back at what was, forgetting how we were condemned and rejected by our first marriage partner, even still pining after them, are we not adulterers? Yes, and we must cease all conversations with the dead to us. All intercourse must cease.

They may still be talking, but we no longer have to listen! My friend and I talked of this until he could see how this defamed his current wife, and she is beautiful in every way. This is what we do to Jesus when we still try to approach Him through our own efforts. The Lord so spoke this to my heart one day as I struggled with law and grace. If you do not believe that I have forgiven you all of your sins, then My Son has died in vain. With human wisdom, we are all vain in our thinking. We lessen what Jesus did for us if we fail to believe what He accomplished for us on the cross. He died in vain. Paul said it this way, speaking of the power of the Gospel of Jesus Christ: "By which also are ye saved if ye keep what I preached unto you; unless ye have believed in vain" (1 Corinthians 15:2).

The simple question here is this: Did Jesus's death purchase anything for you in your life? Did He leave something unfinished that you must also do? If His death did not furnish you a completely clean slate with Father God, then even His resurrection will not assure you of the removal of all sins forever! He died in vain. His death is of no importance, of no effect. If His death did not make you rich, then His death was in vain for we are told in Scripture that "He became poor that we might be rich…" (2 Corinthians 8:9) and "He who knew no sin became sin that we might become the righteousness of God…" (2 Corinthians 5:21)and "He Himself surely bore our sicknesses and diseases"(Isaiah 53:4 and Matthew 8:17) and "by His wounds we are healed." (Isaiah 53:5) The Bible tells us that "He Himself….." indicating to us what things Jesus did for us, but if we do not believe this, then to us these things cannot be. He died in vain. Can you see this now?

I am a servant to the Lord Jesus Christ, a son of God in right standing, one whom He has so loved. I am of little importance nor are my personal points of view. I would be fishing or working if this were not what He had called me to do. Yet as I write down these things I have been given to write I feel the need to expound on my calling which is this: to strengthen the brethren. It was the calling of Jesus to Peter after he had been "sifted like wheat" by Satan. This does not sound like anything anyone would seek out for their own lives. However, having been likewise so sifted, I now know that this is my calling as well. It is also the calling for many who have been or are even now being sifted by Satan. It is a fiery trial or testing we all fear and hope and pray never comes. Know this "sifting" comes only upon us, "If need be…" This is what Peter writes of in 1 Peter 1:6, "Wherein ye greatly rejoice, though now for a season, if need be, ye are in heaviness through manifold temptations."

Surely Peter had seen this in his days after he had denied the Son of God in his own human fears and doubts. Yet if we see all of these days of testing as they are, from Father's perspective, they are but preparations for the service we are called into. These tests make our faces like flint, they remove fears of men and of the so called powers, they believe they have in their positions, our self focus and self love die, our reputations before men die, for they make us useable in the hands of another who has seen every day that we shall live. The very failures we see as the impetus of our falling away will become the callings through which we serve out our lives. I would never rob anyone of the failure Father sees useful and necessary for destruction of the flesh and carnal natures we hold to. It was in Luke 22:32 that Jesus spoke this to Peter, having already prophesied his denial and approaching sifting by Satan. "But I have prayed for thee, that thy faith fail not; and when thou art converted, strengthen thy brethren."

This terminology was probably devastating to Peter as it would have been to me had I personally heard Jesus say this to me. What about you? Jesus told His friend and confidant of the inner circle that he would be sifted by Satan. Was this Jesus's will for Peter? No! Jesus wanted Peter to move from self-dependence into Jesus's dependence and this was of course because of Peter's will and human strength. Why didn't Jesus just send him home to hide until after the crucifixion was finished? The truth is this, without being sifted, Peter was not able to be used of God.

The very thing we fear the most will surely come upon us even as we boast of our own human power and strength, as we try to cover or pay for our own sin, and all of this *if need be*. Remember Job's ordeals? These too were not God's will for Job but were because Job saw God through his own righteousness as a human being. Job 32:1, 'So these three men ceased to answer Job, because he was righteous in his own eyes.' No human effort is righteous apart from Father. No human sacrifice for sin can bring us before God. The debate will arise over this statement I made and so let me ask you this question- if you could stop your children from hurting themselves, would you? Of course you would. But what if you warned them and they still did not listen? You would then "allow" them to do it their way knowing in full this lesson would be used to move them into the truth. This is free choice and Father has granted unto each of us this ability. He always advises us to choose life but often we do not see this until we are in the midst of a trial. No one on earth would surrender their children to Satan for buffeting- would you? God is a better Father than any of us- He does not use sicknesses or diseases or tragedies to chasten us but He will use them to teach us- He is with us even in the fiery trials. This is the purpose of the trial then is it not? That we might see His presence is with us? How would you feel if you could see this before it was occurring in your life? Would you rejoice as Peter later wrote in 1 Peter 1:6? I'll bet you that he did not rejoice as this occurred in his life, but only as he looked backwards at those events in his life was he able to so record those words inspired by the Holy Ghost for us who are called to follow.

It is in the knowledge that Jesus is and has prayed for us, for our faith in Him and what He has done for us, a gift from God, to hold us fast in the trials and storms of life. Remember that, in Jesus, everything is *yes and amen*. But the conversion Jesus speaks of seems out of place for us who have lived out our lives believing in Jesus and in God. Wasn't Peter already saved? Yes and no. Jesus told them earlier in the gospel of Luke that they should not rejoice in the fact that demons were subject to them in His name but rather they should rejoice that "their names were written in heaven" (Luke 10:20). But until the Holy Ghost fell at Pentecost, forgiveness of sin was not yet fully accomplished for us. Jesus had not yet been resurrected in their hearts by faith. It is written in Galatians 3:23, 'But before faith came, we were kept under the law, shut up unto the faith which should afterwards be revealed.' This is why the Holy Spirit came-He came to unveil faith- the law blinded all to faith.

So what does this all mean to us who follow after those who have gone before us? If you are to be used by Father and Jesus, He must prepare you. You must die that Jesus might live through your life, at least to self-willed or self-focused efforts. It is the death Father God declares as "precious in His sight." Conversion in Peter is the same in us today, seeing our strengths, seeing our human faith, seeing our human will, and yes, even seeing our human weaknesses (including our need to be seen as good), all of them, just as they are—human. Paul called it "the sentence of death in our hearts that we might depend upon God and not men…" They are not super natural, they are not spirit, they are not the things Father wants nor are they the things He will work through.

"And when thou art converted…." Conversion is not believing that God exists or is, conversion is what the church calls repentance or a turning toward God, a change of mind concerning what Father says. This is better said in that true repentance is not saying to Father that we are sorry we sinned and got caught in them, but in seeing ourselves standing before Him naked and in full view of His majesty in our broken and weak human state, admitting we need Him. The end of this conversion is knowing that we are loved by Father God and it is His love for us that holds us, not our love for Him. It is literally me acknowledging the truth. He can see me fully, in every aspect of my life, totally exposed and in shame before him, and He loves me. It was in this state that Adam first hid himself from Father in the garden behind the prickly leaves of the fig tree as if they could obscure God's view. The cover up of all mankind is the blindness to see that we are seen clearly by Father, even in our sinful states.

Some say God will not look upon sin, but if this is truth, and it is not, He would never look upon any of mankind. Sin does not affect Father God, it hurts us, His children. He hates sin and loves His creation. It is an awareness of His line of sight being clearly upon us and our admission of this truth. You see, if you believe that He cannot see you, you believe the lie Satan told Adam and Eve, "you will be like gods." (Gensis3:5). Self-awareness causes spiritual blindness, and it produced death then and it still does this day. Religion or the knowledge of good and evil only makes it easier for us to see just how far we have fallen, be it into sin or into our own so-called goodness. Yes, the tree that points out sin and the knowledge of it also points out our "good," and, in so doing, often we become self-aware of our own good and fail to see the real goodness of our Father who loves us. Can you see this now? Any self focus, be it on our goodness or on our own self and sin and weakness is still self focus, and it is filled with human pride. It is all about me. "I won't leave You, Jesus, even if all the others do because I love You the most!"

Jesus's calling to Peter was this, then: "When Satan tears you up like an old sock you will lose sight of your strengths, you will see Mine and see that you are standing in front of the Father always. He will be your strength; I will be your strength. In seeing us (Father, Jesus, and Holy Spirit) as your strength your supply will be without measure whereas your own strength must be seen as it is, although strong with men, nothing before the enemy of this world and in his deceitfulness." Jesus did not allow Satan access to Peter nor was this God's plan, but through this event, Peter came to the end of himself.

This is the great conversion all of us must have and see for if we stand in our own goodness and strength, we are as nothing before the roaring lion who deceives. And what will he use to stop us cold in our tracks? The law! "Thou shalt love the Lord thy God with all thy heart and mind and soul and strength and thy neighbor as thyself." His accusations against us are in fact true. We cannot ever love Father perfectly, we can never love our neighbors as we love ourselves. Our minds wander off of Father God and into areas we are not proud of. This is why we must die to the laws for they demand perfection. Only Jesus kept them all perfectly. We do not need the law; we need Jesus! But once we see Jesus in us, the hope of glory, Father's perfect plan, we can do all things through Christ who strengthens us, and nothing shall be impossible for us. It is in this knowing or knowledge that we turn from the weak and beggarly elements of the law, which simply point out right and wrong, and turn to the power of His Spirit of empowerment through being baptized by Jesus into His Spirit by fire. This is the true change or conversion we all need, and in this strength, which is His, we are being made fit to strengthen the brethren.

This means that we who have been converted are to help others be turned resolutely toward one direction, forsaking all self-efforts, not only to get there but to remain there. We do this all by faith knowing of God's grace toward us, and in so doing this, we have an assurance beyond the natural realm of focus. We have attained to a spiritual plain where the vision is eternal and not temporal in nature. It is a *come up thither* vision. Here our eyes are fixed upon Jesus, who is Spirit, and seeing His hands finish His work in the life we have surrendered to His sure and loving hands. It is a state of total dependency, of weakness, of complete exposure, of honesty, and in this place is the freedom all of us are desperate to find in this life. It is the place Jesus revealed also to Paul, "My grace is sufficient for thee: for My strength is made perfect in weakness." (2 Corinthians 12:9).

When is our love made perfect? When we rely on Jesus! It is then His love for me that casts out fear, not mine. A man who knows he is loved by Father God needs no other love to sustain him. Peter finally admitted his love was only human on the beach one day when Jesus asked him three times if he still loved Jesus— *more than these?* The mighty man broken, he was now able to be used by Jesus—feed my lambs, tend my sheep, and feed my flock. Only in a broken vessel can the strength of Jesus be revealed, not in our power or education, not in our physical or natural abilities, not in what we desire or want, and not in human faith, but in weaknesses. Here, then, in these states of honest evaluations being exposed naked and unashamed before God our Father we can once again see into the cool of the day past the flaming sword that kept us away and declare as did Paul, "Therefore, I take pleasure in infirmities, in reproaches, in necessities, in persecutions, in distresses for Christ's sake: for when I am weak, then I am strong." (2 Corinthians 12:10). These infirmities Paul alludes to are not physical sicknesses but his trials for sharing the gospel of grace.

Look at the previous chapter, "If I must needs glory, I will glory in the things which concern mine infirmities" (2 Corinthians 11:30). Paul had just listed his infirmities in verse 23-29, and they were fiery trials that helped bring him to death to self dependence. In fact Paul called these beatings and shipwrecks and stonings and perils from within and without, even of the Jews, his hunger and neglect, "in deaths oft" (verse 23). Death then is anything that moves us away from the fleshly life into the knowledge of a greater source of life, the Spirit of God within us. It is a fiery trial, a trial by fire, a consuming fire, the fire of God, not even sent by God but used to destroy pride and self sufficiency, to redeem, and even to deliver us. Just as Shadrach and Meshach and Abednego went through the fiery furnace, they went not by themselves. The same fire that destroyed those who tossed them into the fire delivered them to the place of service God called them into. It was Father speaking through the prophets who promised to deliver us through the fire and through the flood. The flood that consumed the world and Egypt delivered God's people. It is redemption Father is seeking for us, releasing us from the world and the world from us. The faith that condemned the known world delivered Noah and his family in the ark.

The second matter I would like to expose in this writing is this truth that brought me to tears as I saw what the Lord wanted me to see. "If need be…" "For whatsoever things were written aforetime were written for our learning, that we through patience and comfort of the scriptures might have hope…" (Romans 15:4). Have you ever been told by a parent or a friend or even a boss to do something a certain way and you did not listen to them? It is the old saying "do it my way or the highway;" not a literal going away if you do not do what they say, but a warning to listen to what they have to say. I am reminded today of the nation of Israel as the Lord God led them out of captivity into the desert. He led them out of bondage into a place where their hearts were exposed or what was revealed in them. They were but a little over 100 miles from their destination, and yet in forty years they never made it to the promise of God, a land flowing with milk and honey. In fact, only two made it in of the original group, Joshua and Caleb, representatives or foreshadows of Jesus, and through Him to the Gentile world, men of a different spirit who wholly followed the Lord.

The question is not did Father God lead them out, but why did He lead them there? Could He not have taken them on an easier pathway? He did it to show them what was in their own hearts. Was it to see if they had any faith? No. He knew before that they were a stubborn and stiff necked people and filled with unbelief. So why lead them out? It makes no sense unless this was a place of "if need be." It was not that He was testing or trying them, but they Him. That's right; the people were trying and testing God to see if they could trust Him. Look at what Hebrews 3:8-12 says of them,

> Harden not your hearts, as in the provocation, in the day of temptation in the wilderness; when your fathers tempted Me, proved Me, and saw My works forty years. Wherefore I was grieved with that generation, and said, They do always err in their heart; and they have not known My ways. So I sware in My wrath, They shall not enter into My rest. Take heed, brethren, lest there be in any of you an evil heart of unbelief, in departing from the living God.

This departing from God is literally an apostasy or leaving from Him—*tempting Me!* Notice the Holy Spirit is telling us that these people "have not known My ways." Even as Father God split the Red Sea and swallowed up their enemies, fed them with manna from heaven and water from a rock, even as He bore their doubts and rebellion, He was showing or revealing to them how much He cared for them. But at each revelation of His ways, His true nature, the people would demand another proving or temptation. They were filled with the spirit of error or *err*. They literally provoked Father God into anger or wrath because they did not trust Him. They did not know how much He loved them. The days in the wilderness were not days of God testing them but them trying or testing, "tempting Me…"

I had never seen this before, but Jesus held me in these verses in 1 Peter 1:4-9 for almost a year until I came to see this truth. We also then remain in our desert experiences not because Father is testing us, *if need be*, but rather because we continue to need proof He can be trusted. That He, in fact, loves me more than I do. Look at how this is revealed in Psalm 78:41, "Yea, they turned back and tempted God, and limited the Holy One of Israel." I urge you to read all of Psalm 78 looking not at the failures of Israel but to see if there is any truth in this for you. For in this truth, my heart was broken as I could see why I too often spend so much time not going ahead and receiving His precious promises. Despite His deliverance, and a mighty one it was from Egypt, through signs and wonders, despite feeding them and clothing them and keeping them all from death and sickness, they could never fully see a truth we too fail to see when we do not come into a trusting love of our heavenly Father.

God is love and He chose us, not the other way around. How does our faith then work? Isn't it by love? Not by how much we love Him, but the rather, seeing how much He loves us! And so it is. We fail to see His love for us in Jesus on the cross for our sins, for our failures, for our mistakes and lacks! As Father once told Abraham as he offered up his son Isaac. "Now I know that you love me because you did not withhold your son, your only son!" The problem with this is that Abraham had two sons. Father was prophesying of His own Son, and what then should be our response to so great a love? Isn't it: "And we have known and believed the love that God hath to us…God is love." (1 John 4:16). Why? Because He did not withhold His Son, His Son Jesus, the only begotten Son of God. Faith worketh by love, His for us! We can trust the One who loves us enough to die for us. This period of time or testing, *if need be,* is simply not trusting the very One who is worthy of our trust, and it takes time to learn this.

It is why Paul prayed for the church at Ephesus for a revelation of His love for us. Have you had one? Or do you still yet not know Him in this way? It is in these times of *if need be* that Father is trying to coax us out of the fears we have experienced in our own lives and of many failures dealing with mortal men. It will come to us all suddenly, all at once, in an instant. We come to the truth that we are safer in His care in a storm or trial, actually thanking Him in the trials, glorying in His presence in the tests we go through, than we ever could be without Him and by ourselves. We all must grow into this precious knowledge of our Father's worthiness of being trusted. Anything less says exactly what it has implied, "I do not think You are worthy to be trusted. I am not truly convinced You love me yet." It is then in vain to us. Can you see this now? Brothers and sisters, any time we hold to a wrong doctrine we are subject to the "if need be" trials and tests until we see the truth, God is love and He is worthy of all trust. You will never trust anyone you fear. If you are in this place of trials and testing's ask Father to reveal to you any areas you may be holding in your hearts as wrong doctrines about Him.

These teachings may be hard for us to accept, but when we do we become fruitful vines for Him to work through in this world, and it is a world desperate to see God as He is—faithful, worthy, righteous, holy, loving, and kind and mercy-filled, not waiting to judge or condemn but to embrace and love. The message must go out, and often, until all have at least heard. We can trust Him always and in all things, because He did not withhold His Son!

Moving Past the Old Way, Therefore Leaving

In the book of Hebrews is written for us who have began our journey away from Moses and the law and into a new and living way with Jesus our Lord, a single truth I feel many have simply overlooked in their "new life." Look with me now at Hebrews 6:1-6:

> Therefore leaving the principles of the doctrine of Christ, let us go on unto perfection; not laying again the foundation of repentance from dead works, and of faith toward God, of the doctrine of baptisms, and of laying on of hands, and of resurrection of the dead, and of eternal judgment. And this we will do, if God permits. For it is impossible for those who were once enlightened, and have tasted of the heavenly gift, and were made partakers of the Holy Ghost, and have tasted the good word of God, and the powers of the world to come, if they fall away, to renew them again unto repentance; seeing they crucify to themselves the Son of God afresh, and put him to an open shame.

Let me again bring you to see that the *therefore* that began these verses is there for a reason. The writer of Hebrews wants us to see that in chapter 5 he had just called the Hebrews "dull of hearing" or unable to hear despite what was being spoken. This should first call to our remembrance to 2 Corinthians 3 where Paul said that in the reading of the law of Moses, a veil is pulled over the eyes and hearts of those who still look to the law (what we must do) blinding them to the truths of Christ Jesus (what He has done for us). We must see that only in Christ can this veil be taken away, and concluding that change is not made from the outside in but the inside out, not by what we do but the rather, by whom we look at, who is in us, and His image becomes our image. 2 Corinthians 3:18, 'But we all we open faces beholding as in a glass the glory of the Lord, are changed into the same image from glory to glory, even as by the spirit of the Lord.' This is not a change of behaviors, but a change of focus, a heart transformation and not a behavior renovation. You see, the law is given to babies, little children who need milk and are unable to eat strong meats. We are God's children, but we do not know that we are also His heirs. This is what Paul conveyed in Galatians 4:1, "That the heir, as long as he is a child, differeth nothing from a servant, though he be lord of all…" But Paul concluded in this from verses 3-5,

> Even so we, when we were children, were in bondage under the elements of the world. But when the fullness of the time was come, God sent forth his Son, made of a woman, made under the law, to redeem them that were under the law, that we might receive the adoption of sons…

Paul then concludes that those who know this have the Spirit of the Son of God in them and call unto their Father, Abba, Father, Papa or Daddy, and in so doing acknowledge a new lineage by the Spirit of their Father and speak an end to the lineage of Adam.

For most of my adult life, and I was a saved, born again believer. However I lived as a child, under the law of Moses to some degree or another. In all of my years as a believer, I never heard anyone preach or teach this truth, never! We are not to remain under the first principles of Christ forever. No, we are to move onward into perfection and righteousness, into understanding who we are, our Spiritual DNA so to speak.

Be honest, how many of you are still sitting under teachers who control with the law or guilt or shame and preach sin and death? I have often heard it said that a little guilt goes a long way. But these believers in Jesus being written to in Hebrews 5 and 6 were facing a lot of trials and tests and were being assaulted by the Jewish factions who sought to return them to the controls of the law. Do good, get good; do bad, get bad! The writer of Hebrews isn't saying that these who have slipped back under the law have lost their salvation, but they have accepted a lesser position than Father God says they should be in.

He said, "by now you should be teachers…but instead you are in need of someone to tell you again just how saved you are." (Hebrews 5:12). You cannot lose salvation, but you can move away from faith and go back into works. "You have fallen from grace." Grace is a work of God loving us and never of any work that man does.

Remember Paul's instruction from Romans 11:6, "And if by grace, then it is no more of works; otherwise grace is no more grace. But if it be of works, then it is no more grace, otherwise work is no more work." It cannot be both. Salvation is a working of God, His grace, and our part is simply to receive and believe in what He has already done for us. Fruit can only be born from trees that are rooted in Jesus Christ, not Moses! This is the conclusion of Hebrews 6:19-20 concerning this matter, "Which hope we have as an anchor of the soul, both sure and steadfast, and which entereth into that within the veil; whither the forerunner is for us entered, even Jesus, made an high priest for ever after the order of Melchisedec." To this truth, Father God has so sworn on His own Name finding no one higher to swear by.

Wow! How can an anchor be sure and steadfast if it can be removed? How can a soul find assurance in eternal redemption if this is not truth? If Father's precious promises are not assured to us, why does He declare them promises? It is trust in a Father who is worthy! Can you see it yet? Only in the sure work of Jesus can this anchor of the soul truly be an anchor. I had a dream once about this in which our son who is already home in heaven came back down to me seeking to be anchored from the high winds that carried the hot air balloon he was riding in. He told me to anchor in the northwest corner and not to sell any rope to those of the circumcision or law. As I thought about this dream, this set of verses came into my heart and are a part of my understanding that in the law, which requires my obedience, perfect obedience, there is no assurance at all because it requires my ability to hold fast. No, only in the sure works of Jesus can we have this anchor of our souls and enter into the Holy of Holies and commune with Father God. It is a working of His grace, not our ability to perform under rules and laws. The thought of entering in based on our own goodness produces fear in itself.

Sadly, many still teach fear and doubts, using control and guilt and shame, and forsaking the truths of eternal salvation, leaving people unable to move past the salvation message, starving for the teaching of righteousness and perfection in Christ Jesus. I know this, for I have lived and walked this out in my life. Many teach and say that teachers of grace go too far and allow sin and unrighteousness into the lives of believers. To that I say hogwash! It is by grace alone we are saved and by grace alone we walk and exist.

I have yet to hear a teacher of grace encourage sin as a way to receive more grace. And so, rather than to accept grace alone, the blending of the gospel has became a most prevalent methodology of many denominations. Let me say this on the strength of the Word of God: how others view you is of little consequence until you have settled forever the issue of grace in your hearts. If you are still under the bondage of the law, you are a servant to the law, even though you are a full heir of this world, just as was Abraham; and Father God called Abraham His friend. It is grace that frees the hearts of men to move forward, not the laws of Moses and the keeping of said laws. Grace frees the hearts to love having experienced His love first, to see and understand the workings of Christ Jesus in our lives to the fullest extent. Love is the fulfillment of the law, and Jesus did this for us did He not?

"Therefore leaving…" Have you left yet? Have you pushed away from the dock and its security? I earnestly pray for you that as we leave and begin this journey you are beginning to move away, untying the ropes secured by your goodness and allowing for the wind of the Spirit to move and to lead you closer to Him, into the very Holy of Holies, and through the torn flesh of the Savior, for He has made you righteous brethren, and so you are in Him. Amen!

The Reality of This Life of Death

It is not then too hard for us to see how our hearts react to these words, "he or she or they are dead." Have you ever heard these words? Of course you have, and you will hear them over and over again in this world from almost every vehicle of communication. I want to tell you this: death is natural in this natural earth realm, but not in God's realm, it is a violation of creation and therefore it must be redeemed. Still, there is death! Man was not created to experience death. In fact it took mankind hundreds of years to learn how to die. Adam and Eve lived over nine hundred years and those who followed also lived long lives with each generation becoming more and more shortened. Sin was beginning to shorten lives, and so it is today. Death is not from God.

I have also faced these words many times but not until they became personal did I ever contemplate the power of words. In 2002 we lost our youngest son to a boating "accident" and this prompted a full scale depression like state in me for almost five or six months. It was at this time that this truth and the title of this writing came into my heart. I believe I was allowed to see this in order to help others who are facing this enemy of God each day. I was reading in my Bible from the book of new beginnings or of victory through faith, as it has been called, Joshua. It is a descriptive book given to detail the conquest of the lands promised by God to the Israelites or Hebrews or Jews after they had been held in Egypt as slaves for over 430 years.

The name Joshua means "Jehovah is salvation" in Hebrew but is translated in Greek as Jesus or Jeshua. In fact, in Hebrews 4:8 Joshua is called Jesus as the writer describes true rest. Rest was in a "place" for the Hebrews but is now found in a "person" today, that being of course Jesus, the Savior. Joshua had a father whose name was Nun which means to respout or propagate with shoots. It is like a stump bringing forth new life or shoots. This of course is descriptive of Jesus who was of the shoot of Jesse. His name, I mean Joshua, had been Oshea which means 'deliverer' which is a root of the word 'yasha' from which Jeshua comes and it means to be free or wide open, to bring salvation or victory. This was what Joshua was called to do, to bring a nation across a spiritual boundary which kept them from the Promised Land or rest. This story of deliverance is a wonderful type and shadow for today's believers for it is a parallel to Ephesians which describes the life Father wants His children to have because of our deliverer, Jesus. In Ephesians we can read and see three distinctive references to sitting, walking and standing. I declare to you that without understanding how well we are seated or at rest in the finished works of Jesus, we will never stand or walk worthy. This is why we see Joshua revealing the struggles of the Hebrews as they entered into the Promised Land. There were battles but every victory had already been secured before it was fought. The stories and battles along the Way are types and shadows of what Jesus has done for us at the cross where all was conquered by Him for us.

Yet it was in the first chapter of this book that Father God spoke these words to Joshua, "Moses is dead." It seems to be a frontal assault on Joshua in an attempt to get him to recognize what has just happened in order for him to become who Father had called him to be and to do what Father had already prepared for him. I wondered for a long time about these words for in fact Jesus so taught us and His own disciples that God is not the God of the dead but the God of the living and He mentioned how Father God called Himself the God of Abraham, Isaac and

Jacob. Simply spoken, they are not dead for Father has so stated. Yet Father declared death over Moses, or did He? Was not Moses seen on the mount of transfiguration with the prophet Elijah by the inner circle of Peter, James and John? Was not this the answer to Moses' request to enter into the Promised Land? Or was Moses only viewed dead because of the very laws he had carried down the mountain until the true Savior came into the world?

Have you ever wondered why Satan wanted Moses' body and why Michael the archangel came down to contest Satan over it? Maybe these thoughts never occur to you but to me they seem most logical questions. I believe these questions are for us to seek answers to in His Word that we might better understand all things Father has done for us through Jesus. First, Father did not want anyone to memorialize Moses' body or to enshrine it. He represented a time period in which God was dealing with man according to the laws of God. They were not given to correct sin but to point out just how sinful man was becoming. They were not given to bring life but to foreshadow or hide the greater revelation that was coming with grace and truth, His name is Jesus.

The enemy has always used what God gave to empower himself, in the fleshly realm, and this is where the laws are to be used. But for the born again spirit man the laws are dead and life is no longer found in the laws but in being led by the Spirit. The new creation is no longer seeking Father God through their own ability to obey the laws written on stone. In fact, the tablets themselves speak to us of this in that Moses broke those carved out by Father and Moses made the next set with human hands although the Words are Spirit as written by Father's own fingers. For Joshua this "death" meant a changing of the guard so to speak. For us it is so written by the Apostle Paul, "Wherefore my brethren, ye also are become dead to the law by the body of Christ..." (Romans 7:4). It is as if Father God were declaring again to us through Paul, Moses is dead. In the very first few words of Joshua we see a revelation of change by relationship as

Father called Moses His servant and He addressed Joshua as the son of Nun, the sprout of repropagation, the shoot.

It was Jesus who came to deliver us from the bondage of the law into life by the Spirit, being born of God as sons and daughters. "That He might redeem them that were under the law that we might receive the adoption of sons" (Galatians 4:5) And just as Father lays out our inheritance as sons and daughters in Ephesians, so He described the physical inheritance first to Joshua. Then Father gave instructions to Joshua that we know he could not keep as we also cannot keep, "Only be thou strong and very courageous, that thou mayest observe to do according to all the law, which Moses my servant commanded thee…" (Joshua 1:7) No one has ever kept all of the law, no one except One, and His name is Jesus. Was not this an identification of another who was to come? Was not this a descriptive prophecy of the real Son, the real shoot, of the real root of Jesse? Is not this speaking of the real rest, Jesus? For only One has ever fulfilled the perfect law of God, He is Jesus!

Father then told Joshua to "go over this Jordan."(Joshua 1:2). Four hundred and thirty years after God had promised Abraham this deliverance of His people from the bondage of sin or Egypt He came down and delivered them out. After the last of the prophets had been written there was a four hundred plus year drought of hearing from God, before Jesus came forth from the silence in heaven, just as Israel waited for their deliverer four hundred years. It was a time of waiting for all things to be made ready. The people had to be prepared to see the deliverance and the place had to be prepared as well. That which was promised was already there but a separation existed or blocked them from attaining to it. It was a place of crossing over. A river blocked them from the promised land just as sin once blocked us all from the promises of God. This was a river of separation keeping those promised from the Promises. It is through Jesus that we can see the promise of the Holy Spirit in us being fulfilled. "I will never leave nor forsake you. I will be in you and you will know it"(John 14:17-20) is evidence of a new life from the inside out, not by the letter of the law but by the leading of the Spirit from within. The promises cannot be accessed without struggles and battles and with patience we posses our souls. With great tribulation we enter into the kingdom of God. Faith is proven in trials and struggles, so it was then for those crossing the Jordan- so it is today. Two crossings- one a sea of baptism into Moses- a second across a raging flooded river being led by the ark of God, His presence. The fear that had held out those promised to enter and possess the land had died off in the wilderness of disobedience and a new generation willingly entered into the promises of God. I believe there is another generation coming who will walk worthy and stand fast in the promises of God knowing of their eternal security of being seated in the heavenlies "in Christ Jesus." They will have a knowledge of "as Jesus is so are we in this world." Not a seeking to attain but to reveal that which was always inside, being the sons and daughters of God, showing forth His glory through their lives, secured in His grace, a promise of never failing or falling, no self focus on themselves or on sins long ago paid for by the risen One. But still, we must first see death!

And so it is for us brethren. We must see Moses dead! The law must be dead to us who are born of the Spirit of God, born again of true righteousness and holiness by the incorruptible seed of God, for only then can we live before our Father who promised to never leave nor forsake us just as He did Joshua and just as He so promised Jesus. But before any inheritance can be taken we must see this death to any right standing before God by the law for if we see this as a part, any part, of our relationship with Father God, we are still servants and not yet sons. Today in many churches across this land and around this world, the laws are being held up as a way to keep in relationship with Father God when there is no other way but One, Jesus and Him crucified for our sin.

Satan is still seeking to use Moses to condemn those who are free from all condemnation and set free from the law of sin and death; those who are alive and live by the law of life by the Spirit are free from all laws of sin and death, the laws of Moses. It was Father God who hid Moses' body, and it is never to be seen again! Same as with the law! It is as it is written in Revelation 12:10, "And I heard a loud voice in heaven saying, 'Now is come salvation, and strength, and the kingdom of our God, and the power of His Christ; for the accuser of our brethren is cast down, which accused them before our God night and day.'" This "now is come" is the power of salvation through the completed works of Jesus on the cross on our behalf, for us who believe and receive this truth. Verse 11 follows this scene with this truth, "and they overcame him by the blood of the Lamb and by the word of their testimony, and they loved not their lives unto death." You see Jesus sprinkled the heavens with His own blood and forever has cleansed the heavens of Satan's right to appear before the Throne of Grace because His blood has washed and continually washes us clean leaving no more right by the law to accuse us of sin before God who cannot see anything because of the blood.

This is freedom brethren, a yoke removing truth given to set us free, all accomplished by our Joshua, our Oshea, our Sprout of the root of Jesse, our Savior and God, Jesus the Christ. Only at the throne of judgment can we be condemned and we know Father is not there for us but sits on the throne of grace awaiting us but to come to Him in the light of His love for us. This is explained even better in the New Testament version of Joshua

> And to make all men see what is the fellowship of the mystery, which from the beginning of the world hath been hid in God, who created all things by Jesus Christ. To the intent that now unto the principalities and powers in heavenly places might be known by the church the manifold wisdom of God. According to the eternal purpose which He prepared in Christ Jesus our Lord; in

whom we have boldness and access with confidence by the faith of Him.

Ephesians 3:9-12

Can all men see this is us? Can they identify God's working in and through the church? Or do they still see rules and regulations and regulators sitting in judgment? It is in the holding up of the cross that the death of Christ Jesus is seen, not sin and judgment! It is His death that speaks of a change of covenant beloved, not rules and regulations and traditions. It must be seen by the world and openly displayed through the church that Satan has been cast down by the eternal blood of Jesus. His blood was sprinkled in heaven and the heavens are eternal, and so then is His blood. Our lives should be open books of wonder before the world, displaying the mighty works of God…His multiplied and many venues of power.

You see there can be no change of covenant unless a death has occurred. This is why every covenant Father made was done in blood sacrifice as a living testimony of its existence. Look with me in Hebrews 7:11-12,

> If therefore perfection were by the Levitical priesthood, (for under it the people received the law,) what further need was there that another priest should rise after the order of Melchisedec, and not be called after the order of Aaron? For the priesthood being changed, there is made of necessity a change also of the law.

This question is one of a need being raised up and being met and fulfilled by a new priest to carry it out. As each old covenant priest died another had to be raised up which also affected the law and therefore changes. Even the old priesthood allowed at the death of that priest a freeing of those held in the cities of refuge. They were allowed to go back home. Then the new priest would set in his laws as well. If you do not think this is so of humans just look at how each new congress establishes itself with more and more laws. But look at little farther into this "death" and change with me

> For there is verily a disannulling of the commandment going before for the weakness and unprofitabileness therefof. For the law made nothing perfect, but the bringing in of a better hope did; by the which we draw unto God. And inasmuch as not without an oath he was made priest; (for those priests were made without an oath; but this with an oath by Him that said unto Him, "The Lord sware and will not repent, Thou art a priest forever, after the order of Melchisedec:) by so much was Jesus made a surety of a better testament. And they truly were many priests, because they were not suffered to continue by reason of death. But this man, because he continueth ever, hath an unchangeable priesthood. Wherefore he is able also to save them to the uttermost that come to God by Him, seeing He ever liveth to make intercession for them.
>
> Hebrews 7:18-25

This is a lot of Scripture but of a key to see this truth is that for the first to be disannulled, another had to replace it; this both the priest and the weakness of the law "he" enforced. No one was ever made perfect before God through or by the law and therefore it was replaced once for all by a better covenant and testament of this covenant in the blood of Jesus, who is our high priest forever. For God Himself so swore, and there is none higher.

If then there was a death, and there was on a cross, then this speaks of a new priest and therefore a new covenant which replaced the weaker covenant. This was not a patching up of the old, this was not a call to a renewal of Levitcal laws, this was not a blending of the two into one new covenant. For if these things were so, then we too would need Levitical priests over us. No, no, no! This is a testament of a changing of covenants and therefore priests as well. In order for Jesus to be our high priest forever, unchangeable, immoveable, never ending, strong and without challenge, innocent blood had to be spent above the innocent blood of any animal which only covered the sin. It had to be the perfect blood of God in Christ Jesus spent for us that He might be made our high priest. His death not only brought us life but it ushered in the new covenant and totally replaced the old, no mixing in of two as one, no old wineskins repaired with new cloth nor new wine put into old bottles, it spoke of a newness of life under a new order—grace! Jesus brought us into this grace at His own expense for no one else could do this. His death brought us into life eternal! If Jesus were dead and not alive then another covenant would be given but He lives forever and Father so swore. This is our assurance and our testimony. Death brings life. A seed must die and fall to the ground before new life can come forth. Can you see this? What death have you been facing that you are resisting? Let Jesus walk you through this valley and into the life abundant He has engineered for you. There is no permanent death for those in Christ Jesus, just a passing from death into life both now in this world as well as into eternity, of which you already are a part.

I saw this in my life as the death "clothing" of this world was being removed and replaced by spiritual clothing, true righteousness and holiness. The new man was being put on as the old was being put off and out. You see for new life to come there must be a pruning away of the old and the dead and the death that once held us in fear. This is often painful to us for we cannot see what Father is doing through Christ Jesus by His Spirit in us. It often hurts, and we are confused and afraid, but I say to you: lay back into His hands and trust Him who loves you beyond all imagination, beyond all you could ever ask or know. He is worthy of all trust. He gave up His life for you and for me. We must love not our lives unto death but willingly give them to Him to do with as He so wills for us for He loves us and sees everything from an eternal perspective, and not worldly as we all do. Even in the loss of our son new life has come forth that has eternal ramifications growing out of that seed. It has brought forth newness of life in many areas of my life, to our lives and through our lives for others to see and share in. We lost no son, we gained eternal vision and everything has and is being restored double. You will never receive from Father in a spirit of fear, but in boldness in faith knowing what Jesus has done for us. I began this by sharing that love is the key to believing. It believeth all things, but we must know we are forgiven of all things, and know that we have rights to inherit all things. "He that overcometh shall inherit all things; and I will be his God and he shall be my son" (Revelation 21:7). Only a son can inherit, never a servant or a slave! In the knowledge of inheritance, what is ours through the cross of Jesus, already done for us, can we. As sons and daughters of Father God through Jesus Christ we have access to His great and precious promises- but they can never be attained when we are servants- only the Son abideth forever, John 8:35 '…and He shall divide the spoil with the strong…' Remember the Words Father so spoke to Joshua…only be strong and very courageous…for I will never leave nor forsake you…" (Isaiah 53:12) and (Joshua 1:5-6).

I will write to you of this Joshua, this Deliverer, this Savior, this Restorer of all things, this Eternal Priest, this Jesus and of what He has done for us all. I pray that in seeing these truths many yokes that have been placed upon you for many years by those who still are yoked to the law are removed! I pray that the angels of our churches today will see and hear and believe! For it is as Paul declared many years ago and still today to those who have an ear,

> Be it known unto you therefore men and brethren, that through this man is preached unto you the forgiveness of sins; and by him all that believe are justified from all things, from which ye could not be justified by the law of

Moses. Beware therefore, lest that come upon you, which is spoken of in the prophets; "behold, ye despisers, and wonder and perish; for I work a work in your days, a work which ye shall in no wise believe, though a man declare it to you.

Acts 13:38-41

Are you justified from all things? If not, then you are still under the law! What you were warned of has surely fallen upon you! Just as Job declared, "that which I have feared the most has surely fallen on me" (Job 3:25) is being declared by many who need never have to face any judgment from Father for any violation of the law through the full payment of God's grace, His gift to us, Jesus, His only Son. This is the Gospel of Grace, the nearly too good to believe good news. Come home. Moses is dead! But is he dead to you?

A Great Dam of Sin

So many believers are stuck on the wrong side of the Jordan River, seeing themselves through their natural eyes and having their minds formed with natural words, never fully entering into the Promises of God. It was Joshua (Jesus or Jeshsua or Oshea) whom God called to lead Israel into the Promised Land. The river Jordan was at full flood stage and stood between the promises and them and it had to be crossed over before they could enter in or into what Father God had spoken to them, a land flowing with milk and honey. It is the same today brethren; there is nothing new under the sun. It is why the church looks so similar to the world. We still see ourselves in it as natural or carnal people. Look with me at how Father sees this "crossing over Jordan" and you will be more free to enter into His great and precious promises. They are ours.

"And the priests that bare the ark of the covenant of the Lord stood firm on dry ground in the midst of Jordan, and all the Israelites passed over on dry ground, until all the people were passed clean over Jordan" (Joshua 3:17). This verse has in it the ability to help us see what Jesus has already done for us on this journey if we will but allow the Spirit to speak to our hearts. The firm ground is the sure work of Jesus, the midst of Jordan is the place where Jesus was baptized for "our" sins and not His, and through what Jesus did, we pass over "clean" into Father's precious promises.

Joshua 4:10 says this: "For the priests which bare the ark stood in the midst of Jordan, until everything was finished that the

Lord commanded Joshua to speak unto the people, according to all that Moses commanded Joshua: and the people hasted and passed over." If Jesus had not finished His works here on the earth and from the cross, if Jesus had not come and taught us what Father had planned for us who would follow after Jesus, no one could cross over the Jordan. Father had brought Israel *through* the Red Sea but *to* the river Jordan. Moses led Israel through but only Jesus (Joshua) can take us into the Promised Land. It was a time of flooding in the valley where Jordan overflowed its banks making it impossible to cross over on "dry ground" or sure works, sure footings, solid rocks. Father led them and us to this place for only here can we see the miraculous work of the cross clearly.

> That the waters which came down from above stood and rose up upon an heap very far from the city Adam, that is beside Zaretan: and those that came down toward the sea of the plain, even the salt sea, failed and were cut off: and the people passed over right against Jericho.
>
> Joshua 3:16

This could be John 3:16 if we look through His eyes. Father had led them (and us if you will) to the Jordan in a time that they could not pass over because of the flood. So Father cut off the flow from above, by His power, and all who were there passed over clean on dry ground. The city of Adam speaks of the sins of mankind from Adam until Jesus came, the last Adam, who stepped into the river Jordan "for" us who would but believe upon His sure work on the cross. Only through the cross can we go over or cross over Jordan seeing all of our sins, past, present and future sins, cut off for us through Jesus. This flowing of sins from Adam (natural man and his efforts) flowed into a sea of salt that allowed no water to flow through it. It was a sea of dead works, but because of Jesus, His righteousness became ours, a fresh and new and living way had caused that which was dead to become alive.

I like how Joshua 4:23 says this, "For the Lord your God dried up the waters of Jordan from before you, until ye were passed over, as the Lord your God did to the Red Sea, which He dried up until we were gone over." The word for *gone over* here is the Hebrew word *abar* which means just that. The breach was opened by faith in what Father said until they were gone over. It is a passing over a boundary one time until we are gone over, completed and on the other side. It is never "gone over" until we see what has just happened to us and in us as a finished or completed work. Father has ended the reign of sin and death that entered in through Adam by cutting off the root of the tree, literally the tree of life that was cut off to mankind through Adam's disobedience. Jesus has then from that root, Him being the root of Jesse, the Seed, has for us acquired a new source of life once more, the spiritual life, the eternal realm, the unseen realm, and only by faith can we enter in.

Can you see this yet? We all cross over at the "cross" and through the "cross" all the flow of sin was cut off by Jesus's sure works, a foundation on dry ground, and solid ground, into the promises of God, but to Gilgal, and at Jericho. Salvation gets us in, but reproach must be removed before the battles begin, and there will be many who oppose us.

Look at how we are to cross over: Joshua 4:12-13, "And the children of Reuben, and the children of Gad, and half the tribe of Manasseh, passed over armed before the children of Israel… about forty thousand prepared for war passed over before the Lord unto battle, to the plains of Jericho." You will never be ready to fight for the Promises of God unless you can see the sure work of Jesus, cutting off the flow of sin from Adam to now through the cross. You will be on unsure ground if you try to fight "for" victory and not "from" victory. Rueben means "behold a man," Gad means "a troop of good fortune," and Manasseh means "one who causes to forget." Can you put these into a sentence? It might look like this: I know a man who has led a troop into good fortune, into a place where he causes us to forget all of our pasts. Can you name this "man"? I know you know Him. His name is Jesus. He has cut off the sin that has flowed since the fall in the garden. He has removed the law that was against us (the law being the power of sin, "the strength of sin is the law" (1 Corinthians 15:56), nailing it to the cross, a place of assurance, fulfilling the righteous requiem of the law in His own flesh) not based upon our works, shifting sands, but upon His work on the cross. Only here can the flow of sin be cut off and seen as it is—behind us and powerless to control us ever again—to His glory! But we must transform our minds, not our brains, but our inner thoughts and conform them to another image, Jesus. In Jesus we became a new creation with new and living thoughts, seeing the unseen, operating by faith and no longer by physical or carnal ways, seeing the futures He has already promised. And it must be acquired by faith. This is a place of pain we all must pass through and cross over until we are gone over, never looking back again. Be patient with even yourselves. This is a journey, not a sprint.

The Stone Is Rolled Away

Love keeps no record of wrong…

1 Corinthians 13

After the children of Israel had crossed over the river Jordan and after they had seen that God was truly with Joshua (Jesus) Joshua had an encounter with the Lord Jesus seen as commander of the armies of heaven. He received instructions, and then he was to lead the people Israel to a place called Gilgal, the place of rolling away. This is no coincidence on the Lord's part as He brought forth the nation to a place where they were to begin to conquer the land promised to them many years before.

It was at Gigal that the Lord God said that He would "begin to remove the reproach" (Joshua 5:9) of His people. Reproach is another word for shame, and we all know that shame first fell upon mankind in the garden when Adam and Eve first violated the Word of God and sin and death entered into the earth realm at their hands. They had been standing naked and unashamed before God and in only a few verses, after consuming the knowledge of good and evil, they discovered that they were naked and ashamed. Sin brought forth an awareness of something Father never wanted them to experience, yet He watched as His creation moved from total God consciousness into an ever increasing self-focus, a form of death. Once delivered from the bondage of Egypt the nation of Israel was led out by the strong arm of the Lord to a place where they proclaimed that they were more than able to do whatever the Lord asked them to do. It was at Mount Sinai that the laws of God were given replacing or adding to the covenant that Abraham had lived under—grace. The law was not given to keep the people from sinning but just the opposite, it was given to draw out the sin that was hiding just under the surface. Its purpose was to further expose the weakness of human flesh and a need for a Savior, a God to help them. The shame of the people came forth as they began to better understand the laws of God leaving them at a distance from the One true God, afraid to approach Him, ashamed and filled with reproach.

The parallel story of this is of course written in the New Covenant teachings of Paul where he helps us to see that our shame has indeed been rolled away. It is explained in many ways for us to see that when Jesus died he took our shame, our reproach upon Himself and became the very payment for our sins. When His death came upon the cross it came with Jesus fully carrying the burden of the sin of the whole world upon His own shoulders. Into the grave He took it and there it remained. His resurrection then became the announcing to all who would but believe that their sins had been forgiven. "And if Christ be not raised, your faith is in vain, ye are yet in your sins" (1 Corinthians 15:17). When the stone was rolled away from His tomb it was not to let Jesus out but to let us see in that not only had He risen from the dead but that the body in which He had born our sins was resurrected as well. Only sin and its very nature were left in the grave. Jesus is alive. The two angels that sat upon the place of His burial were as the cherubim over the Ark of the Covenant that once held the rebellion of mankind under the mercy seat of God. They were there as if to declare to us all, Jesus has overcome the sin of the whole world and they will never be seen again. It is written in the book of the Psalms concerning this "reproach" or shame. "For the zeal of thine house hath eaten me up, and the reproaches of them that reproached thee are fallen upon me…" (Psalm 69:9) and "Reproach hath broken my heart, and I am full of heaviness; and I looked for some to take pity, but there was none; and for comforters but I found none" (Psalm 69:20). If we were to read this Psalm it would reveal to us that this is indeed a Messianic Psalm or a foretelling of the life of Jesus.

But this showing forth of Jesus wasn't just done to teach us a lesson; it was the very will of Father God to remove our shame and guilt and be freed from sin to come once again in the cool of the day to visit with Him. Sadly, this seems to have happened all over again, and no one is immune to the legalism that is imbedded in religion today. But know this for sure, the stone was rolled away from the tomb where Jesus's body laid long ago, to free us from the law of sin and death to be made alive in Him, to have life to the abundance of God our Father's grace. He came that we might have life to the full, overflowing abundance. Do you know this?

Rolling Away the Stone

How many are there who are alive by the resurrection but live as though still dead, bound in the clothes of death—the law. No joy, no peace, no life! When Jesus comes into our lives, into our hearts, we should become new creations- different than before. It should be seen and recognizable. When Lazarus was resurrected he caused the religious of his day to want him dead and gone just as they wanted Jesus dead and gone. How do they see you and me today? Someone dead brought to life, or someone alive but still dead? If we are still yoked to the law, the stone is too heavy for us to carry, but if it is grace, Jesus said that His yoke was light and easy for He rolled the stone that bound us in death away. Which side of the stone are we going to see from? For from *here* we will show forth new life to the abundant or we will be alive but still wearing the clothes of death.

"Take ye away the stone." (John 11:39). What a declaration of faith! Jesus spoke these words before a group of people who had just come to the grave of a man named Lazarus, and he had been dead for four days. This boldness of speech surely set each and every person in attendance on edge even prompting Lazarus's sister Martha to declare, "He stinketh by now!" (John 11:39). But despite all physical and natural knowledge Jesus called a man once dead back to life to the glory of God and Jesus and to the amazement of all those who stood by and watched the event unfold. There were even those there who saw what happened and knew of the entire event and yet they ran back to the Pharisees and reported the event as one to be afraid of. One would think that this event alone would have changed the hearts of those who saw this and those who also heard the report, for they knew it was truth. Look at this truth from John 11:46-51:

> But some of them went their ways to the Pharisees, and told them what things Jesus had done. Then gathered the chief priests and the Pharisees a counsel, and said, "What do we? For this man doeth many miracles. If we let him thus alone, all men will believe on him; and the Romans shall come and take away both our place and our nation." And one of them, named Caiaphas, being high priest that same year, said unto them, "Ye know nothing at all, nor consider that it is expedient for us, that one man should die for the people, and that the whole nation perish not."

Do not over complicate what is being spoken here by Caiaphas for if we fail to see this, we miss a large truth for us all. Caiaphas spoke or prophesied that Jesus was to die for the people and for the nation that none of them should perish. This he did from the Scriptures that had forecasted or foretold of the coming Messiah. He "knew" this was according to Scripture, and still he acted out his part. They did not need to see any mighty miracles for they knew and believed in what was reported to them, yet they did not see Jesus as he truly was and is and always will be, God! They acted out of envy and out of fear declaring that if Jesus continued to do what He was doing Rome would take away their places and finally their nation. This too came to pass, just as Caiaphas prophesied, albeit seventy years later. In seeing the physical they missed the spiritual event that took place! What a truth for us today as well as we look at the rolling away of the stone from the grave where Jesus once was laid.

I have written in other places of how that in Scripture Father God tells by the prophets and by Moses of this event but often in parables or comparables; Jesus is hidden in the Old Covenant for us to see as well as the New. Jesus even identified or revealed

Himself to the men on the road to Emmaus in these Old Testament stories until they said "Did not our hearts burn as he opened up the Scriptures to us?" (Luke 24:32). Jesus was also showing us the way to see Him just as they did, in the Scriptures, both Old and New Covenants.

But of interest to this journey and its teaching is this truth once again brought forth, once the children of Israel had crossed over the Jordan, they were led to a place called Gilgal. It was named Gilgal or "the place of rolling away." It was at this place that God spoke to Joshua and said that "here" will I begin to remove the reproach or shame from Israel. And so it is with us today. It is when we see the stone rolled away that we also should begin to have the shame and reproach removed from our hearts. Yet often in the telling of what Jesus did many still feel shame and reproach even feeling the need to bear guilt that Jesus already has done for us. It is why He came! But I do not want to wander away from what the Lord has spoken to my heart today. It is from your heart that the stone must be taken away! After we are born again of God we have become a new creation or creature in Christ Jesus. This implies a death of the old; before the new can become a reality the old must be dead. Before a new tree can become a tree a fruit must be yielded that has seed in it and when it dies and falls to the ground and is accepted, it becomes a new life with the capacity to reproduce of itself, and that of a different species than when it died. What was buried was corruptible, what was raised was incorruptible. This is symbolized by the baptism in water or being "old" at the submersion but being "new" at the raising out of the water. But I want to take us just a little deeper into the baptismal waters and see if there is not something else Father wants us to see by His Spirit today.

Look with me at what the Lord has so spoken in Ezekiel 36:25-30:

> Then will I sprinkle clean water upon you, and ye shall be
> clean from all your filthiness, and from all your idols, will

I cleanse you. A new heart also will I give you, and a new spirit will I put within you; and I will take away the stony heart out of your flesh, and I will give you an heart of flesh. And I will put my spirit within you, and cause you to walk in my statutes, and ye shall keep my judgments and do them. And ye shall dwell in the land that I gave your fathers and ye shall be my people; and I shall be your God. I will also save you from all your uncleannesses; and I will call for the corn, and will increase it, and lay no famine upon you. And I will multiply the fruit of the tree, and the increase of the field, that ye shall receive no more reproach of famine among the heathen.

Surely the sprinkling speaks of baptism and its significance in our lives and to Father God but look at the removal of the old heart, the stony or stone heart, hardened by sin and by life itself. It is followed by a removal of reproach or shame as Father God blesses us among all the heathen nations of the earth, a visible blessing, prosperity, wellness, joy, peace, fruitfulness or replication. And do not miss the Lord's Supper, communing with Jesus and Father and the Holy Spirit, as spoken by Father in Ezekiel. The corn is the bread, the increase of the field is the grape and wine, and the fruit of the tree is the olive oil or the anointing.

There is great power in this truth for us to see and chew upon. But for now, it is to the hearts of those who are hurting that I share this today. A hardened heart is a heart of stone, hardened by the circumstances of life, often even at Father God. Often we do not understand what is happening in our lives as we pass through this life. We have lost someone or something in our lives we feel we cannot live apart from or without. I too once cried out to God for understanding as we lost a son to death when he was just beginning his new life with Father God. Yet it is not what we are saying or crying out that I want to address, but the results of this—hardness of heart.

I know a man who has written a book on the hardness of the heart and it so helped me to see some of the truths I now see I would be remiss if I did not acknowledge *Hardness of Heart* by Andy Wommack. It has much truth in it for the believer as it pertains to not only hearing but receiving what Jesus is speaking to us. But to summarize the entire book in a few words, it is simply opening up our hearts to see Jesus as He really is. He is God! What Jesus was showing all those gathered around Mary and Martha, and us as well is more than His ability to raise the dead back to life, and right now, not some time in the future. He is a present help in our time of need. He is our life. He was openly declaring Himself God in the flesh come down to the earth. Look at His own words from the telling of the event in John 11:25-26, "I am the resurrection, and the life; he that believth in me, though were he dead, yet shall he live. And whosoever liveth and believeth in me shall never die. Believest thou this?"

You see, Jesus was breaching or trying to break through hardened hearts, hurting hearts, damaged hearts, hearts that God created to see Him as He is and to be loved by Him; hearts crushed in the garden of Eden and filled with shame and reproach ever since by sin and its ultimate conclusion, death itself. Shame came instantly to Adam and Eve in the garden but it took hundreds of years for sin to create death in mankind who was created by God to live forever. The Bible tells us that even when God did not impute men's trespasses or sins against them death still reigned, until Jesus came into the world to save us from sin and free us from death! It is at this place, the cross, that our old natures are forever destroyed by what Jesus accomplished for us. He being made sin, and for sin, not His but ours, entered into death, and passed through it because it did not have enough power to hold Him. And He came out with the keys to death and Hades, triumphing over the powers that once controlled us with fear.

The stink of death will always remain on those who will not receive the truth of His Word just as Martha said of her brothers' death. Do not be as those who do not acknowledge His very presence. He is God you know! And if you have asked Him into your hearts, He indwells you. Your sins are gone. The stone is rolled away, but do you still feel the weight? If you do you must read on…

A New and Living Way

It is right here, at this place, at our Gilgal, at the place of rolling away, that life is to begin. A new and living way speaks of an old and dead way passing away. This is "life" by the Spirit, which is of faith, not life under the laws of Moses. There can be no spiritual life under the law for the law is not of faith. 2 Peter 1:3 says this, "According as his divine power hath given unto us all things that pertain unto life and godliness, through the knowledge of him that called us to glory and virtue…" This did not say that he gave unto us all things according to our ability to keep the commandments of Moses nor our own personal goodness, no matter what measure of it we have. And he gave these "all things" that pertain unto life, not the ministration of death as written upon stones. And all of these things come not by what we do but by who we know, or rather by who knows us, Jesus Christ in us, the hope of glory.

Jesus came to give us life, not a better way, but a new and living way, life by the Spirit, His. Being forgiven of all our sins was accomplished on the cross in order to be made alive to God, for we were all born into death, spiritually. When Adam fell, he died to God spiritually, unable to relate to God's image any longer. Adam had been created in God's image but after the fall all of his children, starting at Seth, were born of his own likeness, his image, natural man only. "And Adam lived an hundred and thirty years and begat a son in his own likeness, after his image, and called his name Seth" (Genesis 5:3) The name Seth means a "substitute." God replaced by a substitute—man's image for

God's. Romans 5:10 says this truth to us, "For if, when we were enemies, we were reconciled to God by the death of his Son, much more, being reconciled, we shall be saved by his life." This simply means that if when we were without God and on our own, as natural men and women, enemies, God atoned or sacrificed Jesus for us, reconciled or atoned for us back to God through His death on the cross. Now, being made right with God through what Jesus did, shall we be saved by His life.

You see, true Christianity is not about doing what is right or wrong through external controls, it is about a new and living way by the Spirit of Jesus in us, His life in us, Colossians 1:27. Just as the water baptism is unto a remembrance of his death and resurrection and the forgiveness of sin, the Spirit baptism is unto the life of the Holy Ghost in us, Jesus. It is a submission to the life of Christ Jesus in us, and this by the leading to truths that free us by the Holy Spirit, whom Jesus sent. Jesus said this to John in Revelation 1:18 , "I am he that liveth, and behold, I am alive forevermore…Amen…and have the keys of hell and death."

I am not sure what you see in this truth, but for me this says that what Adam gave away, life by the spirit to God (Being alive to God), Jesus took back for us through His own death, and He then could give us His life, not a continuation of our own. This is a life alive to God, and Jesus holds the keys in His hands. Jesus did not come to make us good enough to speak with God, He came to make us alive, reborn of God by His Spirit. Only someone born of God's Spirit could do this. This is why Jesus was born not of an earthly man, but by the Holy Spirit. This is the life Jesus came to give to us. For this is the life alive to God our Father. Sadly, many believers see Jesus as a get out of hell card, a means of escaping God's judgments on sins, lessening the truth of life and life abundantly as Jesus promised in John 10:10.

We are "living," if that is what we call it, way below or beneath what Jesus has already purchased for us. It is a life with the knowledge of a Father who so loves us, a Savior who so loves us, a Holy Spirit in us that loves us and is sent to teach us and lead us to this truth. "For God so loved the world that he gave his only begotten Son, that whosoever believeth in him should not perish, but have everlasting life" (John 3:16). This is a very well exposed and known verse but few really read it in light of what we are now seeing. If we believe in Jesus, 1) we are not going to perish in judgment and 2) we are given everlasting and eternal life. The question is this one: Is this at physical death or at spiritual birth? Eternal life is "eternal," meaning without end. Just as Jesus is, so are we in this world (1 John 4:17). We are eternal beings, without end, now! It is life Jesus came to give, and it must be lived in order to be life. There are so many believers who have accepted Jesus as the good teacher and prophet and healer of long ago, one who will help us to keep the rituals and requirements of God and step in for us when we fail to keep God from smacking us around a little. But this is the spirit of error as is all teaching that does not teach life by the Spirit, from within and no longer from without. This spirit to overcome death and sin is in us. It is Christ Jesus in us, the hope of glory. Be careful who you listen to. "We are of God: he that knoweth God heareth us; he that is not of God heareth not us. Hereby know we the spirit of truth and the spirit of error" (1 John 4:6). If you are born of God, this truth you will accept!

Runnin' Wild Grace

I read once in a book about a man who was called to teach grace to a group of church leaders. When he came he began to instruct them on grace and as he went on he looked up and could see that they were not receiving grace very well. He asked the preacher who had invited him to come how they were receiving the teaching they were listening to. The preacher replied, "not very well…but teach on." His reply was met by an angry old man who asked this question (paraphrased): "What you are saying to us is that these young people today won't have to jump through the same hoops that we did?" To that question he answered, "Yes, of course." They had no idea of what grace actually is, and yet they claim not only to be Christians but leadership of the church. Is it then anything too far out of line to say that this is more normal than rare? I think not!

I was once told by a pastor that a little guilt goes a long way in *controlling* others, keeping them conscious of the dangers of sin. If this were truth, and it is not, then why did Father send Jesus to the cross? Why not just do the law? This running wild or out of control is often called lasciviousness. It means without any boundaries or controls, and it is in fact a word that accurately describes how many believers spend their lives. But when fear is used to control the children of God, they become fearful of ever approaching the only One who can help them. Fear may hold you for a short period but when you finally fail, and you will, the fall will be great.

This kind of teaching causes exactly the opposite of what Father has intended to happen. Instead of drawing His children to Him they are driven away. It also causes the family of God to look inward instead of upward, toward self dependence instead of God dependent. It causes many to write books describing a seven or eleven step methodology to a better life. It creates a need to hold onto that which has already is past, and I mean the law as a way to seek or follow Father God. It creates a hold onto attitude, which leaves all of us in a form of bondage never receiving the kingdom we are created to occupy. It causes us to refocus on that which is done away with, and I mean the carnal man in any way coming to God, who is the answer. It is a self dependency in the flesh.

I relate it a little like this: I recently brought my mother home to stay with us after she had a bout with pneumonia. She became so weak during her hospital stay that she needed to use a walker to keep herself upright. As we came to enter into our home she got to the two steps in our garage on which we access the entry into our kitchen and as she tried to step up on them she became a little too wobbly to enter. I told her to place her arm around my neck and I would carry her up the two steps and on into the house to a chair that awaited her. She did not let go of her walker as I slid my head under her arm and picked her up to carry her. As her entire weight was now in my arms she still held onto the walker as if it was the device that would move her from one place to the other. Despite my repeated requests for her to let go of the walker she held it fast. We were unable to enter into the kitchen through the door as the walker together with her in my arms would not pass through or cross over the threshold. Finally after what seemed to be two or three minutes she let go of the walker and it became hung on her jacket and was being literally drug behind us as we tried again to enter into the house. I finally gave it a good kick and it became unattached and I carried her safely to her chair.

This is what many believers are instructed to do when well meaning preachers and teachers tell them that they must still follow the law, the rules, the order, the denominational traditions and so forth. Life by the Spirit will not begin as long as you hold fast to the law which governs the flesh life only, and it is supposed to be dead! Her fears of falling or failing were not truth as I held her safely in my arms, but nonetheless it took quite a bit of convincing to get her to finally let go. The promises of God are yes and amen "in" Christ Jesus not Moses. In fact, the "works of the law" void faith and leave those chosen to walk by faith under the curse of the law.

It is clearly written in Galatians of this truth, "For as many as are of the works of the law are under the curse for it is written, 'Cursed is every one that continueth not in all things which are written in the book of the law to do them...'" (Galatians 3:10). This is not being written to Jews but to believers who had resorted back to the law after having received Jesus by faith. These were not under the law but under the works of the law, trying to access Father by what they did like fasting or even praying. It sounds something like this: "Father, I have been fasting and praying for two weeks now and still You have not answered my prayers." This is the works of the law: trying to access Father via self efforts and not through faith which is simply what Jesus has already done for us.

The following verse tells us that no one is justified by the law for "the just shall live by faith." (Galatians 3:11). Faith then is a way of life, not efforts. So many then fail to hear from Father because their consciences are filled with thoughts of sins unconfessed and they are accused by their own conscience drowning out the voice of the Holy Spirit that indwells them. They not only feel cursed but they have in fact placed themselves without knowledge back under a system of penalty for failure and rewards based on self achievement. If we believe we will be blessed if we tithe then it is through our giving we are blessed and not through Jesus on the cross. I indeed tithe but not according to any law. I give from the heart and because I know when I give I give declaring Jesus is alive, (Hebrews 7:8). My tithe then declares faith in Jesus in whom I am already blessed. I have every spiritual blessing in "Christ Jesus." The line is a fine line, but it must be clearly seen less we find ourselves under the works of the law "trying" to receive at our own effort that which Jesus alone has freely provided at His own cost, His life. I can never receive anything He did not freely give up for me because He loved me first. "He became poor, that I might become rich." (2 Corinthians 8:9). That is grace! We do not forgive to be forgiven but because we already are forgiven we then forgive. It must come from faith in what Jesus has already done on our behalf, and never from what we are doing. Those are works of the law.

In Paul's writings in Romans 6 it sounds something like these two questions, which are never asked in most churches across this land, just as we looked at just before this, "What shall we say then? Shall we continue in sin that grace may abound…What then? Shall we sin, because we are not under the law, but under grace?" (Romans 6:1 and 15). Paul was surely teaching grace in a way that aroused questions that I have never heard asked in a church. The easiest way to keep from having these unanswerable questions asked then is to just assign the congregation to a little law and grace mix which Paul calls spiritual adultery. Jesus said that He would spit the lukewarm out of His mouth, and this is exactly where many are today.

Look with me at a few verses from the Old Testament which direct us back into grace and grace alone- for this throne of grace is where Father dispenses everything we need….in fact it is where He calls us to come boldly in time of need. He did not say come explaining or working in order for Me to do for you. He called us to the throne of grace where everything we need is already finished via the cross of Christ Jesus. Faith then can access what is already finished and prepared in advance for us to do as it says

     LARRY HERNDON

in Ephesians. Father has already prepared the good works we are to do- He did not say we had good works to do in order to receive from Him what we need. The law and the works of the law are not of faith and therefore no promises are ours- for they are attained solely through grace which is simply saying, something we are gifted or given. He can carry us to the promises or we can stay at the door and hold fast to our walkers and security blankets. Using fear to control simply will not work- it will ultimately drive those away who are seeking the face of God but have been taught that this is not possible except by works.

"If thou, Lord, shouldest mark iniquities, O Lord, who shall stand? But there is forgiveness with Thee, that Thou mayest be feared" (Psalm 130:3-4). This is a great contradiction if in fact what is being taught is correct for in this verse forgiveness of sin draws us closer to God and reverence is increased as we draw nearer to Him. A man is never more secure than when he has an audience with his heavenly Father. I recently asked a small group of people this question, and I will now pass it along to you. How could Moses, the giver of the law, stand before God, face to face, speaking right to Him with the knowledge of murder in his heart (for he killed an Egyptian man in a failed attempt to begin his ministry in his own power and time)? How could this man Moses stand before Father God on Mount Sinai as he was given the Ten Commandments, specifically, "Thou shalt not kill"? In fact, look at what Moses said to the people immediately after they had heard the voice of God speaking from the fire and smoke and darkness on Mount Sinai.

> And all the people saw the thunderings and the lightnings, and the noise of the trumpet, and the mountain smoking; and when the people saw it, they removed, and stood afar off. And they said unto Moses, "Speak thou with us, and we will hear, but let not God speak with us, lest we die. And Moses said unto the people, "Fear not; for God is come to prove you, and that His fear may be before your

faces, that ye sin not." And the people stood afar off, and Moses drew near unto the thick darkness where God was.

Exodus 20:18-21

Moses knew Father God's forgiveness was greater than his fear of being rejected. Moses had already faced death and he knew now his life was not his own. None of these wanted to listen to the voice of God, by His Spirit, for they were afraid (a fear of death) and stood afar off. They believed if they spoke with God they would die, they knew what they had done, they had just received the laws of God and they knew. But Moses saw this event as an opportunity to draw nearer to Father God, not run away; and certainly not to have others tell him what Father was speaking. Moses said God had come to prove them that His fear might be before them always and sin not. This word *prove* literally means to show how this will work, to prove this to them. This is what we just read in Psalm 130. If God wanted to hold us accountable for sins, He could, but He is a forgiver of sins, in fact, He not only forgave them, He removed them forever from His sight by the blood of Jesus. It is in facing our fears that death is overcome and life, new life becomes a reality. It requires a letting go of the old and an embracing of the new. For Moses it was a wooden staff turned into poisonous snake: and God spoke to Moses to pick it up by the tail. If you tried to pick up a Cobra by the tail you would be bitten and quickly. You would be dead. But when Moses picked up the serpent by the tail it became once again *a* staff, but not Moses' staff, but the staff of God, Jesus. Moses faced sure death and received life even though he knew he had been a murderer. Sin will never disqualify a person from service for in fact if this were true no one could ever serve Father. Yes, the Ten Commandments had not yet come but the Bible teaches us this: the laws of God are written on our hearts, from the inside, according to Romans 2:15. Our consciences both accuse us and excuse us as we base our judgments on how others act or on what they do, but a guilty conscience can only condemn us, and we are left unable to hear the still small voice of Father.

Every man that actually sees God (in his heart) has this reverence that restrains sin because we can see His overwhelming love for us in the total forgiveness of sin in our lives. Each and every man who saw or heard God believed that they would surely die but in fact this death brought forth life anew kindled in a relationship of faith. Seeing and hearing Father's voice is the answer to all of our struggles and the end of all fears. Once He has spoken and we have heard Him, is there anything to fear? Is He not able to fulfill His promises? It is in believing what others say or tell us about Him that causes fear and doubt. It is what Job declared when he said, (paraphrased by me), "I had heard of You by what others said of You but now I see You clearly and I repent in sackcloth and ashes." Jacob was attacked and wrestled with by the Lord (some say Jacob wrestled with God, but this is not Scriptural for no one can go up to Him. He clearly came down and accosted Jacob) until he also declared, "I have seen God and lived." Samson's parents saw the Lord and lived and from this came new life.

It was in the acceptance of the sacrifice that this freedom came and an understanding of life given through the sacrifice for no one can see God and live, yet we live. As He has so interacted with each of us we too have found life in the shadow of the death we once lived in. Jesus said that "knowing God and Jesus Christ, whom He sent" was eternal life. Everything else, every lesser position, is a form of death and bondage. Jesus did not come to make us good but to give us life with the knowledge of access to Father, who is eternal life. The proof of our acceptance is seen in the fact that just as Father accepted the offerings set before Him and He consumed them up in fire, so Jesus was consumed in His fiery judgment and received into heaven forever. If we have been called and elected as His children, and we have, if we are in fact the brethren or brothers and sisters of Jesus, and we are, then relationship is what should become the paramount of our focus, not the knowledge of good and evil. In this there is no life, but knowledge of death and shortcomings. I would that you look once more at this truth, "awake to righteousness and sin not." (1 Corinthians 15:34). This verse is not telling us that by not sinning we will become righteous but by acknowledging Father has given us His righteousness, Jesus, we will move away from sin altogether. When we know that we have been made righteous before God and this by His own hand, when we awake to this truth, sin has been defeated. It has lost its power in us who believe. Only a man who knows this truth would ever dare to approach God, and He is beckoning His children, come.

The next piece of this need to be controlled is for all who control or are controlled by their pasts. We are saved but live like we are still in bondage, free in Spirit but dead and without any life. To you I offer up this truth, for I too have walked this road. It was an encounter with the risen Jesus where He healed my heart, covered with scars from battles in this life. It may be emotional scars or physical scars from abuse or rape or molestation. It may be financial scars having lived in some form of mental poverty. It may be from a death or a loved one being bound in death clothes, or from a divorce or other betrayal. In fact, it can come from almost anywhere and at any time, disabling us, forcing us to be controlled and seek freedom to control ourselves and then others who have likewise controlled us. It is a form of death that holds many in the body of Christ, freed but living in the knowledge of boundaries being in place we cannot cross over—fears!

I can speak of even preachers who having been controlled by others who then seek out pastorates with a heart to help but when given the opportunity to help simply control others as they were controlled when they feel a fear of loss of control. I can speak of those who were molested or raped or abused by family or friends and never "allow" themselves to be hurt again by controlling or attempting to control their lives by "not allowing" others in. I can speak of much bondage including the ultimate need of being accepted by any and all, of being always right. All of these are bondages that Jesus came and freed us from, yet we still have them over us because we will not let go of them nor them of us. They are familiar spirits, depression, anxiety, fear, hate, anger, doubt all thriving in our minds while being manifested in our lives. They are all in fact, death clothes.

It is a fear of being found out and hurt again-so instead we control ourselves, or think that we do, and all the time we are still being deceived. The only true control then is no controls at all. It is why Jesus came, to set the captives free. The church is full of those hurt but teaching, controlled and preaching, hiding but leading. It is the opposite of lasciviousness, but it is just as hurtful, even more dangerous than allowing others to hurt us is the fear of failure. I hid here for many years myself and if I am not careful I will run to this place when anything past my control comes up. It is a place where we admit we are saved, but still being saved, until we learn we can trust the One who died for us, and just let go. "I know whom I have believed, and am persuaded that He is able, to keep that which I've committed unto Him against that day...."(2 Timothy 1:12). It is a beautiful Scripture and a beautiful lyric for a song but do we truly know this One? And if we are fully persuaded that He is able- then why do we still try to protect ourselves and control our circumstances and fear anything we are not controlled by or control. This is not freedom....it is a more sinister form of bondage...it is the spirit of fear from which anger comes- doubts arise- sin is manifested here- it is in fact- a form of death, trying to resurrect the dead life of flesh. Even the Apostle Paul sought to control his circumstances trying to enter into places to preach in human wills but the Spirit stopped him. He tried to get Father God to remove the thorn in his flesh, sent by Satan himself, Jewish men who hunted him everywhere he went trying to stop him- but Jesus's reply is still the same. "My grace is sufficient for thee..."(2 Corinthians 12:9). Paul concluded this truth, "for when I am weak then I am strong- for in my weaknesses Your strengths are made perfect or complete."

(2 Corinthians 12:10). It is trusting past sight- seeing the grace of Jesus as coming or already there- a provision made not because we have earned it or have any controls, but because He has loved us and already died for us- now what else won't He do for us being in us? It is not trusting in self- but trusting in Him- and even Paul himself said he had not yet mastered this but had at least moved away from the dock.

To those of you still in this bondage I pray for you a revelation of His love for you- an understanding of His greatness, of His compassion for you- even greater than yours for you- Someone you can trust and depend upon-always in all things- in His sufficiency, and not in your own. This then is not manifested in our strength to keep ourselves from being hurt- in our controlling either our own selves or others- letting go of the fear of loss of controls- and simply seeing Jesus as He is-worthy of our trust. This is a process and it will take time but at each battle see Jesus seated next to Father God, at rest, and see yourself seated with Him, in Him….as it is in heaven…for this is how we show forth the love of God to a hurting world….even in the hurt…we trust and embrace all that He sends to us as our provision…we let go- and when we do, His strength is seen in Him holding us fast and steady- let go and simply believe. It is already defeated…. Jesus has already healed your broken hearts- won't you receive this truth even now- it is the anointing of Jesus- to free us- to break every yoke- all of them- but we must let Him have access to our hearts- I know this- for He touched mine- and He has made me whole again. This is why I can never go back to the law…for perfect love casts out fear…for fear has to do with punishment. And this is the flesh…..but you are Spirit, born of God, and in Him is no fear…including fear of failure…fear of losing controls…fear of anything is not of faith…and faith works by love. We fear because we do not trust in His perfect love! Ask Him to reveal His love, this love, to your hearts- it is for freedom He came, to set us free…and only those set free are free indeed.

The Iron Entered His Soul

I am most concerned for the church today as it is for the position it has assumed is a lesser position than Jesus wants His bride to be. It is often seen as an angry bride, one that is always looking about and focusing on anything that takes away from its own beauty or position- but the bride has simply lost focus of her husband- the One who died for her. She must return her eyes to Jesus. I have tried to share what the Spirit of God has so taught me concerning this but especially now, in these last days, I pray that these truths will bring light into a darkened corner we were never intended to stand in.

"He sent a man before them, even Joseph, who was sold for a servant; whose feet they hurt with fetters; he was laid in iron; until the time that His Word came; the word of the Lord tried him" (Psalm 105:17-19). I would like to have emboldened the part of this verse I wish us to look at closely, "He was laid in iron." The actual Hebrew translation of this part of the verse is, "His soul came into iron." From this verse I want us to see that Joseph was in leg irons so long that his soul actually entered into the iron, they became a part of him. Joseph had done no wrong to be in this position yet here he was in a prison wearing leg irons. I believe many believers occupy this position today despite having the knowledge of total forgiveness of all sin, all of them. I have and will continually spell this truth out to you from the Scriptures, for in this truth you will be set free. There are so many believers who have, for whatever reasons, accepted a lesser or fallen state. They have accepted "their sickness or disease" because they have had it or them so long their minds have accepted the condition they are in as a permanent one.

We are called to not see physically here but spiritually by seeing Jesus and everything in this earth realm as temporal or able to be changed. Only the unseen, the spiritual realm, is unaffected by the physical- and this is accessed by faith alone, and faith works by love: that in the knowledge of the completed works, it is finished, in Jesus. Don't look at what you are doing wrong as you wait for the answer to come forth but look rather at Jesus, at what He has already done for us. It is nothing more than a ploy of the enemy to self examination which will always leave us feeling just a little short of what we need to do to receive whatever we need. It in fact is a very self righteous act to set ourselves in the center of the room and beat our selves senseless with our own failures.

It takes no faith to self examine- it does however take faith to believe what the Word says of the new creation in Christ Jesus, "As he is, so are we in this world." (1 John 4:17). The "he" is Jesus and it is through what He did that we receive by grace through faith, being heirs through the promise. Any return to self is a departure from faith which came with Jesus, in Him. It is all about Jesus and nothing about us, we are crucified with Jesus and we now live by His faith. Any examination of the new creation must be one of examining Jesus who now sits at the right hand of Father. 2 Corinthians 13:5 tells us to examine ourselves to see if we are in faith, and so we should…do we believe what Jesus has already done for us? Do we truly believe He removed all of our sin? Do not try to raise Judas from the dead. Look instead at the One Father sent to correct what had been destroyed by sin and death- He was and is and always will be the answer.

There is a teaching in Numbers 19 about a red heifer being sacrificed and burnt up and her ashes mixed with water called the "water of separation." This water was to be applied anytime someone touched death as death had no part in the encampment of Israel. This application of water was given to each person and they were unclean until the evening. The ashes speak of a finished work, a completed burning and purification where no more could be done with the heifer. Look with me at Numbers 19:2, "This is the ordinance of the law which the Lord hath commanded, saying, 'Speak unto the children of Israel, that they bring thee a red heifer without spot, wherein is no blemish, and upon which never came a yoke.'" This is a sacrifice which is a type or shadow of the real sacrifice, Jesus. It speaks of what He has already done for His bride, the church. These ashes of sacrifice mixed with water cleansed the death from those alive.

Look now at Ephesians 5:26-27, "That He might sanctify and cleanse it with the washing of water by the Word. That He might present it to Himself a glorious church, not having spot, or wrinkle, or any such thing; but that it should be holy and without blemish." Now right here is where many will struggle but take this into your hearts first and let truth be discovered: Jesus's finished works on the cross (the ashes speak of finality) when taught correctly declare to the church that He, Jesus, has already sanctified it. And it need but only be washed with the Word, encouraged, edified, comforted, in its struggles in this world. Just as Jesus so washed the feet of Peter to remove the dust of this earthly walk, and not his whole head and body, (for Jesus said, "You are already clean because of the Word that is in you…"so now should we follow after the example of the Master and wash one another in the finished works of Jesus by the Word.

Just as Moses declared in Exodus 33:16, "For wherein shall it be known here that I and Thy people have found grace in Thy sight? Is it not in that Thou goest with us? So shall we be separated I and Thy people from all the people that are upon the face of the earth." The separation of the church from the rest of the world is not that we do not sin any more but that all of our sins are forgiven and when we get a little dust on us from our walking in this life we are to wash one another with the water of the word. The finished works of Jesus are the waters of our separation for He has declared that He will never leave us nor forsake us, never! We are not to condemn one another but to wash one another's feet in the love of Jesus with the Word. Just as the Jordan separated Israel from its promised Land- sin once separated us from God. But the water was parted for them to cross over into His promises. It is the blood of Jesus. Can you see it now?

Josephs' soul had accepted the state of his being until the word of the Lord came and tried him. This sounds a lot like 1 Peter 1:5-7, speaking of God's family,

> Who are kept by the power of God through faith unto salvation ready to be revealed in the last time. Wherein ye greatly rejoice, though now for a season, if need be, ye are in heaviness through manifold temptations; that the trial of your faith, being more precious than of gold that perisheth, though it be tried with fire, might be found unto praise and honour and glory at the appearing of Jesus Christ.

Nothing new under the sun is there? Often in our trials and tests we too accept the iron into our souls seeing our places and conditions as terminal or never ending, we are all alone or so we feel (once again this is an acceptance in the mind or heart) but just as the Word came and tried and delivered Joseph....so He has and will deliver you and I. The children of Israel were about to cross over the Jordan and enter into the Promised Land in Numbers but before they could the red heifer was brought forth. So it is for all of God's children who are waiting for His promises, and they are great and precious promises.

We too must see the work of the cross of Jesus as the finished works that they are, "it is finished." (John 19:30). No promises of God can come forth except through His finished works. Faith then draws from what is already done, it does not move God to do; for His works are all finished as well. I recently heard a man teach this verse and I believe that this is exactly where it should be placed. "So Christ once offered to bear the sins of many, and unto them that look for Him shall He appear the second time without sin unto salvation" (Hebrews 9:28). I too, as this young man so taught, always believed this meant Jesus was coming for His people, His church, His bride, as soon as we could be found without sin. It would be a long wait if this is truth for in fact we will never quit sinning in this flesh house, never. So look at this in another translation which better explains this verse, the Amplified Version, same verse, "Even so it is that Christ, having been offered to take upon Himself and bear as a burden the sins of many once and once for all, will appear a second time, not to carry any burden of sin, nor to deal with sin, but to bring to full salvation those who are eagerly, constantly, and patiently waiting for and expecting Him."

Can you see this now? Does not this truth set your hearts free? We all have been yoked in this life to something or someone but Jesus never bore any yoke, except the cross of our sin- He is the red heifer for us, to wash us clean with His Word, having been forever cleansed by His blood on the tree where He was cursed for us. "And it shall come to pass in that day, that his burden shall be taken away from off thy shoulder, and his yoke from off thy neck, and the yoke shall be destroyed because of the anointing" (Isaiah 10:27). This is what God has called us, the church, His bride to be and to do for one another, we have an anointing to break these bonds from off of the body- it is our calling and our purpose to free those God has set free in Jesus Christ. Shame on those who still place burdens upon those set free by the Lamb. I have been called forth to teach others that indeed their shame has been removed, the yoke and burden removed by Jesus, and that we may have shackles on our feet for a season, it may even enter into our souls, but once His Word comes forth, once we have been tested and tried (or the rather, we have sufficiently tested and proved Him and His Word. We can trust in what He says), we will shine forth as a sun brighter and brighter as the day approaches. Don't accept any condemnation for in Jesus we have been set free. Those whom the Son sets free are free indeed! To His honor and glory forever and ever, amen!

Sin is not controlled but exposed by law. The greatest freedom that exists is in the knowledge of having all of our sins already paid for while remaining in the very Presence of our Father. The forgiveness of sin then does not allow me to run wild but to draw nearer and nearer to the One who would do such a thing for us all. It is almost too good to be truth, but it is indeed the Gospel of Grace. It is the New Covenant in Jesus's blood wherein we draw near to Father in full assurance of total forgiveness. How else can a man approach God? If you even believe there is a little bitty sin left you would surely die! No wonder they all ran from Mount Sinai at the hearing of the law and asked Moses to speak for them and to speak to them. But David sought out an audience with God in seeing Jesus's coming afar off so to speak. He dared to approach the throne of grace, to bring the very Presence of Almighty God into Jerusalem, to place His Presence in a tent, a tabernacle so to speak, giving access to all- a Father who willing forgives when asked, knowing He is a merciful God, a loving God- how else dare anyone approach Him? Surely "this" is the tabernacle of David that is being rebuilt according to the Scriptures. It is a place where all can come to the throne of God's grace and mercy through His Son Jesus Christ.

This is what James agreed with when Paul came and confronted the church in Jerusalem. The law was given to drive us back to Father, not show Him how good we can be and therein earn an appearance before Him! Grace is the freedom from sin, not the right to sin as often as we wish. It is found in not being condemned because of Jesus's finished works that we approach the throne of all grace- and never because we tithe, or fasted, or went a day without cussing. There is absolutely no continuing assurance in fleshly efforts, none! The answer to the sin issue is grace, not the law. Where sin abounds, grace super abounds. It is not until we see this amazing grace that we dare to approach Father in boldness.

The question is this: Is grace truly sufficient for me? Is God's promise greater than my sin? All of them? What about the ones I just committed? Those I will commit tomorrow? How can I depend upon grace? We will look at these all the way through this book but let me assure you of this: God already has forgiven you all trespasses in Jesus through the obedience He showed all at the cross. The question is not how can God declare us righteous even as we sin but how could He declare Jesus a sinner when He never sinned? Our safety is not in our goodness but in His righteous judgment against all sin as seen displayed upon Jesus on the cross for us all! God can't declare me righteous unless His divine wrath against unrighteousness has been satisfied. Let's look a little at what happened on Calvary. Let's take a look at what cup Jesus drank for us all.

THE CUP NO ONE ELSE COULD DRINK

I often hear people say that people who speak and teach grace are sin minimalizers. To them I would say that sin-focus minimalizes what Jesus has done for us on the cross. To those who believe they can keep the law of God and attain to Him by self-effort or by sinning less, I pray a revelation from Papa for you now. For of a truth if any of us could pay for our own sin we would have had to first been perfect and without the very sin we are seeking to pay for. Only a perfect lamb was acceptable before God as inspected by the high priest.

If you really believe that you can drink of this cup, and you cannot, you will find yourself hanging on a cross for the sins of the whole world. It is written of in the gospels that Jesus asked the Father three times to remove this cup from Him. However, Jesus submitted to the will of His Father for us and He who knew no sin, who had never felt separated from His Father, endured something so terrible that few ever want to even think of it. Jesus consumed the sin of the world and therefore he alone bore the weight of the sin upon his shoulders and took all wrath for sin into himself. The Bible says that "he who knew no sin *became* sin…" (2 Corinthains 5:21). Jesus, the perfect sinless lamb of God, became sin itself and then also for sin and in the likeness of sinful flesh; it would be like taking our precious children or grandchildren and throwing them into a prison filled with pedophiles and then standing and watching them defile them. It was here that all sin (a noun and not a verb) was punished and the sinners set free from the bondage of sin itself.

Here God's fury against all sin was exhausted on Jesus for us….forever. Jesus faced the fury of God's wrath on sin for us, that we might never have to face it, ever! Look at Isaiah 51:22, "Thus saith thy Lord the Lord, and thy God, that pleadeth the cause of His people, 'Behold, I have taken out of thy hand the cup of trembling, even the dregs of the cup of My fury, thou shalt no more drink it again….'" This then becomes our promise from God our Father to us because of His wrath against all sin as taken out on His Son Jesus for us. "For this is as the waters of Noah unto Me; for as I have sworn that the waters of Noah should no more go over the earth, so have I sworn that I would not be wroth with thee nor rebuke thee" (Isaiah 54:9). And because the payment was in fact paid in full and more than that, overpaid, God is justified in declaring the sinner righteous by faith knowing fully in Himself and by His own will and wisdom that the payment for sin has been satisfied fully.

What Jesus drank for us was a cup of wrath no one else could drink- but He did for us in obedience to our Father who loved us so much that He sent His only son, a perfect Son and beloved of God, to die for us all. We are left with the dilemma of all dilemmas. Dare we believe this gospel?

I am not a man who condones sin or lawlessness but the rather, I am a man who sees what Jesus has already done and has declared as His finished works greater than all of our sins combined together- grace greater than all of our sin. Where sin abounds, grace super abounds. But first, sin had to be identified and removed. "Moreover the law entered that the offense might abound. But where sin abounded, grace did much more abound" (Romans 5:20). The law could identify sin, but it could not restore or bring life, it cannot remove sin, only the knowledge of sin. And once sin could be clearly seen, God's amazing grace as seen in Jesus Christ on the cross for all sin, it, sin was destroyed by Jesus and faith and life in Him by the Spirit came forth for all who would but receive right standing before God, not of their own good, but through the torn flesh of Jesus for them, forever. I do not condone sin; I hate it, but I see grace as it is—the only answer to man's depravity. A cross on a lonely hill, the perfect sinless Son of God naked before all who passed Him by for us and innocent blood running down for us all, to whosoever will, and all by God's own plan. Amazing grace, is it not?

In truth, grace has set me free from sin by seeing all of my sins upon a righteous and holy Savior, because Father God so loved me. It is all about me, about us and His love for us. It helps me to forget about me and I pray it will so help you to lose your own self focus and fix your eyes upon Jesus, who is both the author and finisher of our faith. If we will but believe who He has made us to be! He will forever free you from the bondage of the law and it entanglements. Won't you let Him? It is the only place of assurance you will ever know and have and it is the only way you will ever be able to stand in front of Father God and receive His amazing graces which are endless. Remember that Jesus became sin, but He became sin that we might become the righteousness of God in Him. This being said that you might now see yourself and your prayers as He sees them. "The prayers of a righteous man availeth much." (James 5:16).My prayer is for you to see and believe, but if you do not- I am in good company for Isaiah also asked the Lord, 'who will believe our report? To whom has the arm of the Lord been revealed?' To me Lord, be it unto me!

From Under the Altar

I write this for those who were like me, stuck and unable to move forward even though I have always wanted to. When I was eight years old I was "saved" at a revival at our church when an evangelist called us into a fear I remained in until I was forty-nine years old. He said, "If you die tonight without Jesus in your heart you will spend an eternity in hell because of your sins." This is true but it is not by the law that a man is saved or regenerated. We will never approach someone we fear! In fact, we will hide behind a bush or a leaf from the very One we desperately need. As he called out for those who did not want this to happen to them I hurried down the aisle to the safety of "not going to hell." Fear motivated many into the angry arms of a vengeance seeking Father….sadly no one ever told me the truth of the gospel. Fear is not of God for God is love. In fact, they are opposites…for perfect love casts out fear….let Him cast this fear from your hearts forever….His name is Jesus, the Savior of the world.

It is from this place the Lord Jesus has helped me to escape. I stood as though in darkness, never coming to the truth that the light of God, Jesus, was in me even as I walked in the filth of this world. Bent down with fear, I could see judgment and justice. From here the shadow of death, the lord of the flies, using the law, blinded me to the light of Jesus's finished works, seeing my sacrifice, my bloodshed, never seeing the precious flow of Christ that had washed away every sin. Aren't you one who is there? Did I not see you there and hear your voice as well? Weren't you under this altar with me?

> And when He had opened the fifth seal, I saw under the
> altar the souls of them that were slain for the word of God,
> and for the testimony which they held: and they cried with
> a loud voice, saying, "How long, O Lord, holy and true,
> dost Thou not judge and avenge our blood on them that
> dwell on the earth?"

Revelation 6:9-10

This revelation of Jesus to us is intended to help us better understand what Jesus has done when He opened up the fifth seal and released this truth for us: and to see all of this- not from our perspective but from a heavenly perspective, from the throne of God, the throne of grace.

Several years ago the Lord led me into this place seeking to understand what God is doing and about to do from Revelation 10 when He showed me many men marching into the darkness and away from the light of God's truth. In this chapter we see a strong angel, Jesus, His church which is His body, standing with a rainbow upon His head, clothed in a cloud, with a face like the sun, and His feet like pillars of fire, proclaiming that "time shall be no more." This is Revelation 10:6. Following this announcement came this information from verse 7: "but in the days of the voice of the seventh angel, when he shall begin to sound, the mystery of God should be finished, as He hath declared to His servants the prophets." This mystery is unveiled in verse 15 of Revelation 10 where we see that the kingdoms of this world become the kingdoms of our Lord and of His Christ and in them He shall reign forever more.

As I read this tenth chapter of Revelation I began to weep as I thought of these young people marching out into the darkness that beckoned them. I cannot remember ever weeping any harder in my life except to express the loss of our own child and the acknowledgement of my own sin. I began to acknowledge that this was the very thoughts and heart of Jesus in me weeping for those who would not make it. I began to pray for more time, more chances to talk with them, to tell them about Jesus, about salvation and of all of God's promises to us who believe in Jesus. For the past eight plus years I have been in training learning exactly what I believe the Lord wants us to see and what He is asking us to do at this time. I have also come to see that there are many children of Father God who for whatever reasons have failed to remain in the New Covenant but have became harlots or spiritual adulterers seeking to remain under the New Covenant of God's grace through the blood of Jesus His only begotten Son and return to the law and legalism at the same time. This cannot be and it must be addressed with all diligence and honesty and in truth.

First, to clarify a few things I have set before you, this strong angel upon whose head a rainbow sits I have declared as Jesus. In Revelation 4:1-3 it is revealed to John to "come up hither, and I will show thee things which must be hereafter." The Word declares John was in the Spirit and he saw a throne set in heaven and He that sat on the throne looked like a jasper and a sardine stone and the throne was surrounded by a rainbow that looked like a brilliant emerald. This is in no doubt the Lord Himself. But what about the rainbow? I take you back to the days of Noah where in God made an agreement that He would never again destroy the earth with water and His signature was a bow in the clouds, a bow in the rain, a rainbow. "I do set My bow in the cloud, and it shall be for a token of a covenant between Me and the earth" (Genesis 9:13). The Lord God went on to declare that when He caused a cloud to come upon the earth the bow would also be there as a remembrance of His everlasting covenant between Himself and every living thing upon the earth. It was a promise from God to never again judge the earth and every living thing with water and that every time He sees this rainbow He will remember this covenant.

In the fifty-fourth chapter of Isaiah, God again records more for us concerning this rainbow as He speaks of His Son Jesus and what He will do upon the earth when He comes, all according to the prophet Isaiah. In Isaiah 54:8 we see God speak that He was angry for a few moments, not with Jesus, but at sin itself, (Father could not stand to see sin upon His sinless Son) for our sin and not for His own, and that He hid His face from Jesus as Jesus bore the sin of the whole world upon His sinless shoulders, only to treat Him with everlasting kindness and mercy forever more. But look at His promise because of what Jesus did for us:

> For this is as the waters of Noah unto Me; for as I have sworn that the waters of Noah should no more go over the earth; so have I sworn that I would not be wroth with thee, nor rebuke thee. For the mountains shall depart, and the hills be removed; but My kindness shall not depart thee, neither shall the covenant of My peace be removed, saith the Lord that hath mercy upon thee.
>
> Isaiah 54:9-10

This should be enough for us to see that the rainbow is a sign of a greater promise than no more flooding; it is a promise and a covenant between God and all who stand under the rainbow, under Jesus. This promise is one of no wrath ever on His behalf toward those who are "in" Christ Jesus by faith and an agreement forever of His peace toward us. So many believers still see themselves under the law of Moses where they stand awaiting punishment for sins Jesus paid for and even worse, they stand awaiting God to punish those who have harmed them, even asking God for retribution. I have heard many people openly demand judgment and justice for wrongs done to them in this life and I understand their feelings in this but this is not a release to extract a pound of flesh for a pound of flesh or an eye for an eye.

These are old covenant sayings, for those under the Mosaic covenant of the law—do good, get good, do bad? But for those standing under the rainbow, there remains a covenant of peace and no wrath, a promise from God. If we know that God is not angry at us, if we know that His intentions toward us is peace, why do so many still see God as an angry judgmental God awaiting to destroy those who get cross ways with Him? God openly declared His plans to us, that through His long suffering He intends to redeem every one who will but let Him, intending that none should perish. From this truth according to His Word we must add the truth that God has already dealt with all sin one time in His Son on a cross two thousand plus years ago as Jesus paid not for His sin, but for ours, as well as the sins of the whole world. It was John the Baptist who declared "Behold the lamb of God who takes away the sins of the whole world" (John 1:29). This only happens when we behold Him upon the cross for our sins and we give them to Him forever, one time. For a greater purpose than just the removal of sin Jesus came into this world as He established a new covenant signed in His own blood, the blood of His Father who conceived Him in Mary by the Holy Ghost. Jesus came to give us life, His. Jesus was all man, but He was not born of man, but of God via the power of the Holy Ghost. It is the same for us today. We are forgiven through the blood of Jesus by faith, but it was Jesus who gave to us the power to become the sons of God-and this is life eternal.

This is the conception of the Holy Ghost to whom we receive just as Mary did. "Be it unto me according to Thy Word." "If you being evil know how to give good gifts to your children how much more will the Father give the Holy Ghost to them that ask?" (Luke 1:38 and Luke 11:13). This is very simple and straight forward. This endowment of power from on High is spoken of by Jesus before He left His disciples. It is the power wherewith we, the sons and daughters of God, are to reign in life by the One, Jesus Christ having received, "abundance of grace and of the gift of righteousness." (Romans 5:17). A person who does not know they are forgiven can never reign in this life. A person who does not see and know they are the recipients of the abundance of grace God has extended toward them can never reign in life by

Jesus Christ. These too are gifts that must be received by faith. Believing we are God's righteousness is much different than just saying it in church. It means that even when we fail to live up to the standards we are still viewed by God as holy and righteous, even when we fall short of that which is right.

This is not received by being holy and good on our own, but receiving it by grace, an unmerited gift from God, it can never be earned, never! If we earn this gift, if we are worthy of it, Jesus died for us in vain. The abundance of grace is only toward those who know and acknowledge their need of it. I pray this is laid out clearly before your eyes for without this truth being settled into your hearts, you might as well stop now and throw out this writing. 2 Corinthians 3:18 says this, "But we all, with unveiled faces beholding as in a glass the glory of the Lord, are changed into the same image from glory to glory, as by the Spirit of the Lord." This simply says that once the law has been removed that veils us from seeing Jesus clearly; we can begin to be changed into His image from glory to glory, and by the Spirit. This is not from without or external but from the inside out, by the Spirit, as He reveals truth to us.

As the glory of God is revealed to us and through us we too are being changed ever more like Jesus each time. This is better stated in 2 Corinthians 3:15 this way, "but even unto this day, when Moses is read, the veil is upon their heart." It is with the heart that we believe unto righteousness, and a heart that is blinded by the law and not bathed in the abundance of grace, cannot see the truth of the gospel, nor the revelation of Jesus. The truth of the Word is revealed by grace and not the law. God's glory is revealed when we become more and more like His Son, doing what Jesus did as He walked this earth. And because of what Jesus has done in fulfilling the perfect plan of our Father (in His death on the cross Jesus fulfilled the holy and righteous requirements of God's Law) we remain in a covenant of peace, in grace forever. Some of you will say that this is only when we do what is right but if you do what is right, why does God declare a covenant of peace? If we do nothing wrong, which is not possible for us, why then declare there is no condemnation? If we have done no wrong we cannot be condemned! Are we not in peace with Him if we see ourselves as doing nothing wrong? God can't be wrathful toward us if we do not sin, right? Of course this covenant of peace and grace never applies more than when we do fail and slip up. Don't be too quick to abandon the mercies of God as revealed through His grace and covenant of peace we have in what Jesus did for us. Wrath was declared on all sin once two thousand years ago and Jesus who knew no sin became sin *for* us and declared us righteous by faith through this grace and covenant of peace; remember, this is His plan, not yours or mine. His mercy toward us who believe cost Him everything!

For the next few pages of writings I want to begin with this; if this does not minister to you through the eyes of grace, it will not. That being spoken and explained, let me share what the Lord has shown to me. First, in the fifth chapter of the Revelation of Jesus Christ we see that it is Jesus alone who is empowered to open the seven sealed book by His own worthiness, established on the cross. In verse 8 we see the elders fall down before the Lamb, Jesus, with instruments and with vials containing the prayers of the saints. Why are they in bottles? Did they not go straight to God? The answer might be a bit confusing but it is no! Why you ask? Because many of these prayers were offered from a place prayers cannot be heard. You see, many believers still see God sitting on a throne of judgment but the Bible says we are to boldly go to the throne of grace where we can receive in our times of need. So many of us have cast up prayers to an empty throne seeking judgment and justice, often even seeing ourselves guilty before God. James says a man who asks God doubting shall not receive what he asked for he is double minded and unstable in all of his ways.

The prayer of a righteous man availed much according to James who spoke of an old covenant man named Elijah. Elijah had like passions as we do but his righteousness is declared by the Word of God, not by what he did, but by what Elijah showed in faith believing God. Righteousness is never established by right or wrong but by faith, what and Who we believe in and what He says that we believe. James say that Elijah was a man subject to human passions just as we are and so it isn't that Elijah was more holy, but he believed God. Romans 1:16-17 says righteousness is revealed faith to faith and so it is. Righteousness is not revealed through works but through faith alone. God hears the prayers of the righteous but that righteousness must be of faith and not self attained righteousness. I hear many people pray declaring the righteousness of those they pray for or even in themselves. It sounds something like this, "Lord God, help old Steve, he is a good man and he goes to church and loves his family and he tithes and he is working hard for You." If these are the reasons God answers prayers what will happen when we forget to do them one day?

So many are taught that God won't answer our prayers if we sin that many prayers are cast up in doubt and in fact, often when we ask God, we begin to disqualify ourselves judging ourselves without any encouragement from the unseen enemy. God will never answer the prayers of a person who is worthy of their own account, He will only answer prayers of men and women made righteous in the blood of His only Son by faith. Know this: God always answers the blood! In fact, if you wish to see this in Scripture go to Luke 7:1-10 and read of "great faith" in a Centurion, a Roman who asked Jesus to help his servant. In this we see this sinner, born in sin, having heard of Jesus ask those in the Jewish synagogue to send for Jesus.

He did not go himself for he knew he was not "worthy" to ask but the Jews that went to Jesus declared this in verse 4, "And when they came to Jesus, they besought Him instantly, saying,

'That he was worthy for who He should do this; for he loved our nation, and he hath built us a synagogue.'" Certainly these good deeds should qualify this man according to the law and to the Jews but look what this man said when Jesus went to seek him out, verses 6-7.

> Then Jesus went with them. And when He was now not far from the house, the centurion sent friends to Him, saying unto Him, "Lord, trouble not thyself; for I am not worthy that thou shouldest enter under my roof; wherefore neither thought I myself worthy to come unto Thee, but say a Word, and my servant shall be healed."

Jesus declared "this faith" a great faith such as He had not seen in all of Israel. The Jews tried to qualify the healing by works to Jesus but the centurion qualified Jesus to do the works. He did not see it necessary to establish himself worthy but to correctly see Jesus as He is, Lord. In Jesus, all prayers are yes and amen. In fact Jesus declares Himself the Amen in His Revelations. Condemnation is not a spiritual gift, it is a lie from the pit of hell and yet it is held widely in the church today to use this guilt and shame and condemnation to manipulate the body of Christ. Failure is almost certain. If fact, this teaching drives us away from God when it is prayer that we need most, just talking to Papa. If we see Him as a judgmental and angry God, why would we go there except for just a quick passing request for forgiveness which is already given anyways? Do we need to manipulate Father with our attempts at being good enough to sway Him into doing for us? This is a sad truth in the churches across the land today, and I know this saddens the heart of the Father who loved us so much that He sent His own Son to die in a physical body for our sins that we might believe and return back to Him without fear of judgment or punishment.

Quit trying to qualify yourself before God with what you have done for Him and quit disqualifying yourself through what you have done wrong: "Only believe" are the Words Jesus instructed us with, and so it is. If we see Him as able, if we see Jesus as worthy, if we see Him as willing, then it is Amen. Remember: there is no more remission of sins where "this" blood is. (Hebrews 10:18). It is His blood!

It gets a little more slippery here but bear with me as I do my best to share what the Lord has so spoke to me. Revelation 7:9-17,

> After this, I beheld and, lo, a great multitude, which no man could number, of all nations, and kindreds, and people, and tongues, stood before the throne, and before the Lamb, clothed with white robes, and palms in their hands; and cried with a loud voice, saying, "Salvation to our God which sitteth upon the throne, and unto the Lamb." And all the angels stood round about the throne, and about the elders and the four beasts, and fell before the throne on their faces, and worshipped God, saying, "Amen: blessing, and glory, and wisdom, and thanksgiving, and honor, and power, and might, be unto our God forever and ever, Amen." And one of the elders answered, saying unto me, "What are these which are arrayed in white robes? And whence came they?" And I said unto him, "Sir, thou knowest." And he said unto me, "These are they which came out of the great tribulation, and have washed their robes, and made them white in the blood of the Lamb. Therefore, they are before the throne of God, and serve Him day and night(remember day and night) in His temple: and He that sitteth on the throne shall dwell among them. They shall hunger no more, neither thirst anymore; neither shall the sun light on them, nor any heat. For the Lamb which is in the midst of the throne shall feed them, and shall lead them unto fountains of living waters; and God shall wipe away all tears from their eyes.

> Psalm 105:17-19

This is a lot of Scripture to go over but I want to present this to you in this manner, where is this taking place? It cannot be in heaven for in heaven there is no night and day. Remember the covenant of the rainbow to Noah? "While the earth remaineth, seedtime and harvest, and cold and heat, and summer and winter, and day and night shall not cease" (Genesis 8:22). We must see with the eyes of Jesus to see truth of the hidden manna He promises to us. It is when we pass through the great tribulation (we enter the kingdom with great tribulation) for the message of the abundance of grace and the gift of righteousness that our prayers are changed.

> And when he had opened the seventh seal, there was silence in heaven about the space of half an hour. And I saw the seven angels which stood before God; and to them were given seven trumpets. And another angel came and stood at the altar having a golden censer; and there was given unto him much incense, that he should offer it with the prayers of all saints upon the golden altar which was before the throne. And the smoke of the incense which came with the prayers of the saints, ascended up before God out of the angels hand. And the angel took the censer, and filled it with fire of the altar, and cast it into the earth; and there were voices, and thunderings and lightnings, and an earthquake.
>
> Revelation 8:1-5

Why were the prayers of those in Revelation 6:9 prayers of revenge, vengeance for *their* blood? Is it not the same cry of the spilled blood of every saint before Jesus came? Is it not the blood of Abel crying out from the ground, vengeance, vengeance! And Father God always answers the cry of the spilled blood as He so spoke to Cain as Abel's blood cried out to Him in Genesis 4:10. It is here that I want to take you into the book of Wisdom: "The Lord is far from the wicked, but He hears the prayer of the consistently righteous, the righteous, in right standing with Him"

(Proverbs 15:29, AMP) Again we must see this as an occurrence not after death but before- what is it that makes our prayers heard, is it our own righteousness, or is it the righteousness of Another? And did He not pay for the sins of the whole world, all of them?

You see, the law is a place wherein a man must approach God in his own ability to be good, or at least in a place where his sin is covered by the blood of a bull or a goat, as it was with Cain and with Abel. The offering up of 'the firstlings of his flock' was a lamb sacrifice of blood, a type and shadow of Jesus while Cain's sacrifice was from the ground which Father had cursed because of the fall of mankind. But this altar was a place of waiting for those who died in faith believing in a future deliverance from sin forever. You see, we must decide where we will cast up our prayers to God, either on Mount Sinai or Mt. Zion. The Law was delivered on Mount Sinai to Moses and it could only point out right and wrong and could bring forth no life. But the heavenly Jerusalem, the city of the living God, is Mount Zion and it is accessed by faith now! At the first Pentecost Father God gave the Law- but the Bible says that when Pentecost had fully come- when all had been accomplished- Father God gave the Spirit. One brought death, the last one brought life by the Spirit to all who believe. Remember that the Law is not of faith! Only prayers of faith are answered!

Hebrews 12 speaks of Mount Sinai as a place where even Moses feared to go and the Words of the Law spoken by God so frightened the people that they would not go up and asked God to not speak them anymore. Anyone who touched that mount was stoned or thrust through with a dart, and a fiery one at that, because the mountain was on fire and full of darkness and blackness and tempest. In fact only the voice of God was there. But a closer look at Scripture says in Hebrews 12:22, "but ye are come…" indicating a present time and in verse 24, "and to Jesus the mediator of the new covenant and to the blood of sprinkling, that speaketh better things than that of Abel." Jesus declared "Father, forgive them they know not what they do." (Luke 23:34). He could have declared vengeance, revenge, but He did not. Abels' blood cries out vengeance until the blood of Jesus was shed.

The two voices are still crying out, friends, one from earth and one from the heavens. "See that ye refuse not Him that speaketh. For if they escaped not who refused him that spake from earth, much more shall not we escape, if we turn away from Him that speaketh from heaven" (Hebrews 12:25). The verses that follow speak to us of a promise God made through the prophets of a shaking like an earthquake once again of everything that can be shaken, both on earth and in heaven, signifying a removal of all things that can be shaken leaving only the things that are not shakeable. The lightning and thunder speak of Jesus's willing sacrifice for us as Father so spoke. "Father glorify thy name. Then came there a voice from heaven saying, I have both glorified it and will glorify it again. The people therefore that stood by and heard it said that it thundered" (John 12:28- 29a). Add to that John 12:31: "Now is the judgment of this world; now shall their prince of this world be cast out." Can you see the thunder and lightning and earthquake spoken of in Revelations 8? All that we might see, "Wherefore we receiving a kingdom which cannot be moved, let us have grace, whereby we may serve God acceptably with reverence and godly fear" (Hebrews 12:28).

You see, even in the heavens, it must be by grace, just as it is now on the earth. Those prayers offered in heaven in Revelation 6:9 were not of grace but of revenge, of the law that demands justice and judgment and a payment. In Revelation 6:11 we see these souls from under the altar receive white robes and told to rest for a while until all was accomplished . But recall that it is Jesus who is opening these seals and He is releasing His people from these seals: number one, false doctrine on a white horse appearing as Jesus: number two, terrorism on a red horse; number three, famine and pestilence on a black horse; number four, death and hell on a pale or dappled horse- these all spirits. Number five is another nasty one, it is judgment and justice and a cry for vengeance by the saints themselves, many deceived by one or more of the first four. You see, we must first receive false doctrine before the enemy can come in. He comes in with a flood of words that are false and are intended to imitate the very voice of God. This is revealed by Jesus to us in Revelation 12:13-17:

> And when the dragon saw that he was cast unto the earth; he persecuted the woman which brought forth the manchild. And to the woman were given two wings of an eagle, that she might fly into the wilderness, into her place, where she is nourished for a time, and times and a half a time, from the face of the serpent. And the serpent cast out of his mouth water as a flood after the woman, that he might cause her to be carried away of the flood. And the earth helped the woman, and the earth opened her mouth, and swallowed up the flood which the dragon cast out of his mouth. And the dragon was wroth with the woman, and went to make war with the remnant of her seed, which keep the commandments of God, and have the testimony of Jesus Christ.

Here we see Jesus revealing to us that the enemy will spew out great floods of water or false doctrine claiming it is the judgment of God. The flood always speaks of God's wrath on sin until we again see the rainbow which declares a covenant of peace and not judgment for those in Christ Jesus. The enemy will always declare judgment upon those who follow after Jesus; and he will use those in the church to do it. This is why we must grow in grace, be solidly established in grace. We will all continue to fall short but remember, we are under grace and not the law. This false doctrine of God's judgment with a flood of false doctrine isn't some future event but a completed event. How many churches are declaring grace and how many are declaring God's judgment on sin with a flood of words? Think about this and pray over these Scriptures before you judge this not correct. In chapter 7 of Revelation we remember those who had come out of the great tribulation and had been washed and had washed their robes in the blood of the lamb. This is what Zechariah 3:1-5 says,

> And he showed me Joshua the high priest standing before the angel of the Lord, and Satan standing at his right hand to resist him. And the Lord said unto Satan, The Lord rebuke thee, O Satan; even the Lord that hath chosen Jerusalem rebuke thee; is not this a brand plucked out of the fire? Now Joshua was clothed with filthy garments, and stood before the angel. And he answered and spake unto those that stood before Him, saying, Take away the filthy garments from him. And unto him He said, Behold, I have caused thine iniquity to pass from thee, and I will clothe thee with change of rainment. And I said, Let them set up a fair mitre upon his head. So they set a fair mitre upon his head, and clothed him with the garments.

He was given a clean white robe, and a new way of thinking, no more condemnation because the Lord has selected the Way of Jerusalem, of peace. Satan, the accuser of the brethren is cast down by Jesus. Remember that Jesus has ascended to Father and has also sprinkled the heavenlies for us who believe. The enemy had stopped the construction of the house of God, now the body of Christ, with condemnation and false accusations and once freed from them Joshua along with Zerrubabel began to rebuild the temple. This is what is still happening today as the church itself preaches and teaches fear and control and condemnation and guilt and shame and returns those set free back into the bondage of the law.

If we look at chapter four of Zechariah we see this angel appearing again to Zechariah and showing him two men standing by a candlestick, one on each side. And when Zechariah asked what these men were doing there he was told, Zechariah

4:6, "Then he answered and spake unto me saying, This is the word of the Lord unto Zerrubabel, saying, Not by might, nor by power, but by My Spirit saith the Lord of hosts." And now see verse 7, "Who art thou, O great mountain? Before Zerrubabel thou shalt become a plain; and he shall bring forth the headstone thereof with shoutings, crying, 'Grace, grace unto it.'" I am sure you can now see the Mount Sinai, the law, being used by Satan to control and even stop the bringing forth of the headstone, Jesus the Christ, until Zerrubabel began to speak *grace, grace* to it. The law will flee in the light of the power of the Spirit of God Grace—the abundance of grace and the gift of righteousness. Jesus is not on Mount Sinai, He is in Mount Zion and in the heavenly Jerusalem. He is in the light and not on the mountain of darkness and blackness where fiery darts are hurled at us by the enemy. It was Jesus who taught us to speak to the mountains. It is grace, grace we speak and by the Spirit.

I would like to share more revelation with you. You see it is the enemy who sends out the flood of false accusations and judgments from God when we know that it was Father God Himself who sent Jesus, His perfect and only begotten Son, to the cross for the sins of all mankind. It is His declaration we must see in and through the Words of Jesus, for all revelation is for us but always through what Jesus did on the cross, our altar. I share with you this as revealed by Jesus Himself in Matthew 23:18-19: "And whosoever shall swear by the altar, it is nothing; but who soever sweareth by the gift that is upon it, he is guilty. Ye fools and blind: for whether is greater, the gift, or the altar that sanctifieth the gift?" Jesus concludes this with this verse from verse 20, "Whoso therefore shall swear by the altar, sweareth by it, and by all things thereon."

Father God chose the altar, the place, the time, and He chose the sacrifice, the gift that was to be placed upon the altar. It is all about Jesus. It is never about what we do or do not do, what we bring to Him or do not bring, but in whom we believe and trust.

It is about His Son and our faith in what He has already done for us, for of a truth, what can we add to the greatest sacrifice ever offered? If judgment is being passed onto this world for sin, it means Jesus did not pay enough, and therefore, we too must offer up for any and every shortcoming. Face the truth friends and brethren, Father God does not need our money or our praise or prayers. Of a fact, it is just the opposite, we are in desperate need of Him.

The only thing I can bring is my faith and trust in what Jesus has already done for me. Once we see how much we are loved of Father through sending His only Son for us we will freely give all, tithing becomes an honor we give without any thought, our hearts are changed by love to give as we have been given to. When Father swore to us in His Word that He would no longer be wroth with us, He meant it and He was speaking from a place we cannot understand unless we see this single truth, He loves us. For Father spoke this and swore this upon an altar He Himself prepared, even growing the very tree His Son's blood would run down into a thirsty world, offering up fellowship through His blood to any and all who would but believe. The blood of Jesus still cries out to Father today, and Father always answers the blood. The Bible says in Hebrews 10:18, "There is no more remission of sins where this blood is." "This blood" is speaking of Jesus's blood shed for us.

Father loves the world and all therein. How dare anyone, including me or you, approach Father without a full knowledge of His sacrifice which through a gift of faith we now approach His throne seeking grace and mercy based on the finished works and full payment of another. Do you now see this? I will not remain under the altar, the legalism and law demanding justice and judgment when in fact if I do I too must be so judged; no, the rather, I will dance and sing and praise and bring offerings from my heart which is overwhelmed with the love I now see for me by One who needs nothing but freely offers all to those who will see and believe and accept His great and awesome gift of love, and therefore, I love. A person who sees their sin as beyond their own abilities to render a payment for them comes humbly seeking forgiveness and receives it by faith.

Jesus said, "He who has been forgiven much, loves much, but he who has been forgiven little, loves little." (Luke 7:47). My ability to love then is not established by what I have done right but by my seeing the greatness of my sins and the high cost of removing them and believing in what Jesus has done for me; I love much for I had much debt and I could never have paid it, never! I could never confess my sins away enough or sincerely enough, I could but humbly accept His payment of love for me, there is no other explanation, no not one! I have only me to offer, and I give myself completely expecting nothing in return based upon my right doings, but in full assurance of His promises, for He alone is trustworthy; He has earned my trust with His blood and my trust is always growing as I continue to walk humbly at His side each day, not in declaration of my unworthiness, which is still self focus and prideful, but in His ability to keep me and to save me now and forever. It can never be based upon what I offer or do, for then all of His promises are based upon my failings which are far more numerous than my 'good' deeds. Don't be moved back into the legal system; if you are in it, get out now, and stay out; for only death can be found at that altar. Our ability to love others reveals just how much we believe we are forgiven.

What I am going to share with you now I received from the Lord by the same grace He has saved me with, for it is always by grace through faith. It is His grace in me that brings forth whatever I share. The altar on which we present our prayers and offerings is an altar human hands are not able to form. In fact, as the Lord has so shown us before in other writings, His altar is not to be defiled by human hands or efforts. Yet if we look more closely at the passages in the Revelation of Jesus to us, to His bride, to His church, we can see an altar in which those who are standing under are not able to get their prayers answered.

We have looked at why a cry for vengeance is not acceptable before the throne that dispenses grace but I want us to see this even more from the Word of God our Father. It is called a brazen or bronze altar and it is made of brass which speaks of judgment. It is declared as a type or foreshadow of Jesus to Moses in Exodus 27:1-2:

> And thou shalt make an altar of shittim wood, five cubits long, five cubits broad; the altar shall be foursquare; and the height thereof shall be three cubits. And thou shalt make the horns of it upon the four corners thereof; his horns shall be of the same; and thou shalt overlay it with brass.

These burnt offerings were sacrificed to God for judgments on sin and for guilt by the priest. It is written of in the days of David and Solomon of men grasping the horns of this altar where they knew they would be receiving judgment. Brass always speaks of judgment. There was also another altar to be built, an altar of incense and it is seen in Exodus 30:1-2:

> And thou shalt make an altar to burn incense upon; of shittim wood shalt thou make it. A cubit shall be the length thereof; and a cubit the breadth thereof; foursquare shall it be; and two cubits shall be the height thereof; the horns thereof shall be of the same.

But look at verse 3, "And thou shalt overlay it with pure gold." Its place was to be: "And thou shalt put it before the veil that is by the ark of the testimony, before the mercy seat that is over the testimony, where I will meet with thee" (Exodus 30:6). Gold always speaks of righteousness and so we see the altar of incense, covered in gold in the inner sanctuary or Holy of Holies where Father would speak or meet in His mercy; and this altar was smaller than the brazen altar which was to set in the outer court area. The bronze altar was bigger but only because more sacrifices were made on it.

Only priests could enter into this Holy of Holies. But we now know that the veil, the flesh of Christ Jesus, was torn to give us access through faith into the Holy of Holies in fact declaring us as His house or tabernacle. This is more Scripture to show us that if we are to enter into the Holy of Holies, to the mercy seat, to the Throne of Grace, it is an altar for incense, for prayers, not for sins or judgments on sins or wrong doings committed against us. For if we are still offering up declarations for judgments and for sins, we are not dead but still alive in the flesh or carnal realm.

Mercy is above judgment! Mercy on an altar of gold is being near to Father God's heart through what Jesus did for us. There He hears our prayers. The bronze altar is abandoned because of what Jesus did. There can be no more judgment on it. This is a place where only New Covenant believers can enter in and that through the blood of Jesus who has sprinkled the heavens for us to enter in. In Hebrews 10:16-18 we see this truth concerning what we bring to the altar,

> This is the covenant that I will make with them after those days, saith the Lord, I will put My laws into their hearts, and in their minds will I write them; and their sins and iniquities will I remember no more. Now where remission of these is, is no more offering for sin.

Jesus cleansed the altar of incense for us and has made it possible for us to no longer come before Father at the brazen altar but to enter right inside to His mercy seat where our prayers are offered on an altar only believers under grace alone can enter into, Hebrews 13:9-10,

> Be not carried about with divers and strange doctrines. For it is a good thing that the heart be established with grace; not with meats, which have not profited them that have

been occupied therein. We have an altar, whereof they have no right to eat which serve the tabernacle.

Fleshly doings will not establish your hearts and in fact the Word declares these as "strange doctrines." I pray you will go and to read the next teaching on Strange Fires for in that is more revelation for us who seek the mercy seat at the Throne of Grace. We are to be established in grace and not in a blended gospel of law and grace. Go with me now to Deuteronomy 28 where we see curses proclaimed on all who fail to do all that the law commands, a large portion of this chapter for a large altar of sacrifice; and also the chapter in which the blessings for obedience to keep all of the law is also written, a small altar for no one has actually ever kept all of the laws save Jesus, the perfect Son of God. There are 14 verses (1-14) to proclaim the blessings and 53 verses (15-68) to proclaim the curses for failures.

But I want you to see that right in the middle of these curses, right in the middle of the brazen altar, "And thy heaven that is over thy head shall be brass, and the earth that is under thee iron" (verse 23). Remember the revelation Jesus is showing to the church, His body and bride,

> And when He had opened the fifth seal, I saw under the altar the souls of them that were slain for the word of God, and for the testimony which they held; and they cried with a loud voice, saying, "How long, O Lord, holy and true, dost Thou not judge and avenge our blood on them that dwell on the earth?"
>
> Revelation 6:9-10

Can you see it now? Their testimony was judgments for their blood and not for grace in the blood of the Lamb. The altar of brass, of judgment sat over their heads and the earth became as iron to them. And upon all who they judged and cried for vengeance upon, just as the blood of Abel cried out over Cain, a mark was upon Cain. Only under the blood of Jesus can all judgments be removed, all of them. It is Revelation 13:9-10 that tells us this, "If any man have an ear, let him hear. He that leadeth into captivity shall go into captivity; he that killeth with the sword must be killed with the sword. Here is the patience and the faith of the saints." We cannot hold others captive in our judgments or kill people with our condemnations but free them to Jesus with forgiveness just as we have also been forgiven much. It is my prayer that in this you can see Jesus, a better revelation of what He has done, is doing, and will do soon.

I present to you this as an offering to show that it is by God's Spirit this will be done and not by man's abilities and it will come when the church begins to stand in grace and grace alone. It must be declared and only those who come in that grace that is given in abundance can plead to God who sits upon the throne of grace waiting for His children to come to Him boldly. The answers to these prayers under the altar will be voices, and thunderings and lightnings, and an earthquake. But those in grace will be fed by Jesus, they will receive life giving water and their prayers will be before the throne of grace night and day. Will we continue to send up our requests to an empty throne in judgment and justice and crying for vengeance and for God to avenge our blood or will we stand before the great throne of grace and plead for those who need grace, grace, abundance of grace- will we plead for time to get this message out before the great church under the rainbow declares time shall be no more? Will we offer up our prayers to God never having them heard from under the altar of condemnation and fear or will we step out boldly in grace and declare the gospel of grace before the little season of rest comes to an end?

You see, the sixth seal releases the great earthquake spoken of in chapter 8:5 of Revelation but before this occurs all of heaven, having been shaken just as the earth is being shaken, is silent awaiting our decision. "And when he had opened the seventh seal, there was silence in heaven about the space of half an hour" (Revelation 8:1). It is now that the silence begins, as all wait on our decisions. Father God has fulfilled in Himself every requirement He would require. It is when we see this and understand this that we finally come to the throne of all grace expecting good and no longer judgment, even expecting it. It is here that the silence is waiting to see what each of us will decide, to trust in His grace and mercy or to try to approach an angry God in our own goodness? Will we come performing before Him or as we are, in need of His amazing grace? Will we remain in fear under the altar expecting judgment? Will we run with a knowledge of His love for us, even in our weaknesses and failures, before His throne of grace to dance and sing? Only the latter one will lead us into the fullness and richness of God's favor, for His favor or grace toward each of us was not established by our doings but by the completed works of another. Do you remember His Name? Jesus! Can we afford to cry out any longer from under the altar to an empty throne? Won't you join me in grace and see your prayers answered as they are poured out before God on the altar before the throne of all grace. And if you come and join me, come boldly; for you are a son of God!

Strange Fire

It is a very hard thing to see and understand but if you will but look through Another's eyes for a few moments I will offer up something to you that I believe will forever free you and bring a greater awareness of God's amazing grace, shown in the giving of His only Son Jesus for our sin and new life. This is a teaching that has been brewing in me for a long time and even now I am still trying to listen closely to the Spirit as He speaks of what Jesus has done for us on the cross a long time ago. In the sharing of this I am sharing a huge part of what the Lord has called me to do and to be because it was in this that I came to see and better grasp the grace of God, Jesus. Grace was too important for a man born of the flesh to carry out; God required His own flesh and blood to bring it forth with truth that sets free. The Word tells us in John that "the law was given by Moses but grace and truth came by Jesus Christ."(John 1:17). This sounds strange to us but of a truth, truth is found in grace, not the law.

It is of importance to be reminded that the Holy Spirit was given to "lead us into all truth" and that He was not needed for the interpretation of the law. The flesh can easily see the laws and understand them, but the Holy Spirit is vital to grace and its understanding. Jesus taught us that He is the truth and that in knowing the truth, we are set free. He did not say in having the truth we are set free but in knowing, in having knowledge, freedom comes. It is better defined as eternal life, "This is eternal life, that they may know You, the only true God, and Jesus Christ whom You have sent" (John 17:3). It is in the knowledge of the eternal that the temporal lets go, in seeing the spiritual that we let go of the physical.

Paul said to look upon what is unseen and not to look upon what is seen for what is seen is temporal and what is unseen is eternal. This requires faith, and that pleases God. "It is impossible to please God without faith." (Hebrews 11:6). And God gives us the faith we need according to His Word in Romans 12:3. We know that faith comes only by hearing and hearing by the Word of Christ and that faith works by love according to Galatians 5:6 so we see a process being laid out wherein many are led to begin at the wrong end of the rope in an attempt to stay or keep away God's wrath through efforts and offerings He will not accept. Their journey, as was mine, was in the wrong direction. In fact, it is just the other way around, God has already shown us how much He loves us, and He is seated with Jesus awaiting us to join them in rest from all human or fleshly or carnal efforts.

This all works when we come to see and believe the love that God has for us. "This is love, not that we loved God, but that He loved us; and sent His Son as an atoning sacrifice for our sins" (1 John 4:10). It is from this place we must see with His eyes, from God's perspective, from our Father's heart, not what He did to Jesus, but what love He had for us in sending the Son He loved for us. How great is that kind of love? We have only a small glimpse through human suffering at the loss God felt in His Son's death; and in so doing opening a door to the very throne of all grace and mercy by a cross on a hill on a tree He Himself grew knowing this- one day it would be the tree that would have His own blood run down its trunk and pour into a dry earth. This love was given in order that we, who acknowledge we have sinned much and great, will return His love with our own. Jesus said this, "he who is forgiven much, loves much; but he who is forgiven little, loves little."(Luke 7:47). Do you know how much you are forgiven? In grace you and I are forgiven all! Everything in grace works together! Grace brings forth life.

It was one of the prophets who asked several questions of Father God concerning sins? He finally came to the highest of all human sacrifices, their own flesh and blood. He asked, "Shall I offer up my own children for my sin?" (Micah 6:7). Of course the offer is ridiculous for all flesh is tainted with sin through Adam. It also shows us how badly we know we need to be forgiven as well as how poorly we recognize Father God. Sin is cleansed for us and not for Him. If a sacrifice of human flesh could have removed sin then Jesus had no need to be the perfect plan of God for us. Only perfect sacrifices are acceptable to Father God; that is Jesus. But while all other man made so called deities require sacrifices, often children and virgins and flesh and blood, God showed from His own heart a love we can only see in the cross where He graced us His only Son whom He loved. Is there any greater love than this? It is from here that Father began to bring me from under the old altar and to see the sacrifice He required as more than anyone could offer, no matter how hard I tried and wanted to pay. It may sound good and even feel good to our flesh, but of a truth it is like spitting on what God freely gave declaring Jesus not enough. It is this freedom of grace He has so given to me to offer to you now.

I want to start this with a teaching I believe so many of us have accepted that we dare to even question its requirement; for it is long held that by confession we are forgiven. There is a truth in this but the question the Lord has posed to me is exactly what is it that God desires from you and from me in regards to sin? The Bible clearly tells us that without the remission of blood there is no forgiveness of sin and so we see that every time sin was confessed blood had to be offered and a body burned with fire. There were two different altars on which the sacrifices were made- one for sin outside the gates; a second one on the altar of incense before the Holy of Holies.

On this altar of incense the offerings were burnt and arose a sweet smelling savor before God while sin offerings were with dung (self righteousness) outside the city gate. Jesus has fulfilled both of these sacrifices for us and His sacrifice was acceptable to God, a sweet savor to God. And He was sent outside the gates to be burned with the righteous judgment of God's wrath on all sin. Many teach that Father could not look upon Jesus as He died but the Word declares to us that Father was "in" Christ Jesus reconciling the world unto Himself. Clearly His life given was the plan of God our Father. These altar sacrifices were a practice under the Mosaic covenant of the law for many years until Jesus came; they were a type and a shadow of the true to come. His teachings on forgiveness are often viewed out of time by the readers of the gospels as Jesus was born under the law and He ministered to the Jews. Once they had rejected Him, as prophesied, Gentiles began to come to Him signifying the end of His life on earth. Jesus then was taken by the very ones He came to free along with the Romans to a cross where He was crucified. But He was not crucified for any sin He committed just as He was not baptized by John for the remission of any sins He had committed.

Jesus did all of this that all righteousness might be fulfilled, and the law is righteous. Jesus did not live here on the earth and do all that He did because He did it through His own power or ability; in other words Jesus did not cast out demons, raise the dead, heal the sick, and stop the winds of nature because He was God's Son. No, He emptied Himself of all of His own power and came as a man and was identified with man in calling Himself the Son of man. Jesus did all of these things because He lived a sinless life in the time of the law, for the law required a sinless sacrifice. It was through the power of a sinless life that these things were accomplished and it is "this" life that He gave to us, His righteousness. Even Pilate said he found no fault in Jesus. He fulfilled the laws of God perfectly showing forth the righteousness of God's law.

God's righteousness was revealed in a greater manifestation than if we all had to be killed by His judgments on sin as He sent in His own Son to bear the sins of many, all who would but believe that He was dying for their sins, in their place. In doing so, Jesus forever satisfied all payments for sin, consuming all righteous wraths against sin, for all who will but accept this amazing act of love and mercy and grace. I will lose many of you here for this is still the thrust of the religious today; we still are told we must confess our sins in order for them to be forgiven.

If this is true, which it is not, how will these sins get under the blood shed so many years ago? Will Jesus once again have to come down and pay? Faith does not speak in this way Paul teaches us in Romans 10, for Jesus has already done everything He had to do for us. Faith is then believing what He has already done. Or do we really have the audacity to approach our Father who loved us so much that He sent His Son in our place, to come to Him with strange fire, sacrifices, He does not require or accept? And do we do this in order to appease our need to "feel" better, to make some sort of payment, to receive some kind of praise for our appearance before Him?

It is quite like the man who buried the talent Jesus gave him and when Jesus came to receive it back the man dug it up claiming what he thought he knew of Jesus: "you are a hard man that reaps where he doesn't sow and gathers where he has not laid straw." When we see God our Father in such light we will always hold back in fear, always have an accusing heart before Him denying what He has already done for us in order to find some place for self preservation. If in our confession, we see this confessing as a payment, we have then earned some form of forgiveness and it is no longer by grace. Let me say this very clearly for you once and for all: if you can do anything, if you believe you can do something to be forgiven, you have fallen from grace. Jesus plus anything equals nothing.

The Word clearly defines this for us in Ephesians 1:7, "in whom we have redemption through His blood, the forgiveness of sins, according to the riches of His grace." Do not try to make this say something different, for in truth, forgiveness of sin must be according to the riches of God's grace lest it be by our confessions. So many of us wish to live at the cross or even at the tomb of Jesus but He is risen in the hearts of those who can see this truth. The resurrection confirms the forgiveness of sin. "For if Christ be not raised, your faith is vain; you remain in your sins" (1 Corinthians 15:17). The resurrection life of Christ in us is our confirmation of total forgiveness, not just in the earth realm, but also in heaven forever. Do not forget that Jesus entered into heaven with His blood where He sprinkled away the sin before God and the very place where Satan once could stand and bring accusations against us until Jesus cleansed the heavens. The Bible tells us in Revelation 12 that he is cast down from heaven by the blood of the Lamb and the word of our testimony. Jesus said that He saw Satan fall like lightning and this I believe to be how this occurred. Through man's sin, we gave him access to God's throne, a legal right, because we gave him the authority we had been given. But Jesus took back what was ours and has returned this to us through His grace and sacrifice, and by His sacrifice alone. Any righteousness that is not a gift or a grace to us then is self righteousness based not on what Jesus did but upon what we have done.

In so stating these truths I do not magnify sin but the payment for sin instead. The righteousness of God was glorified in what Jesus did, not in any human confession. When Jesus knew the time had come He declared to His Father, "Glorify your name." The response was this one, "I have glorified it and I will glorify it again." By placing His only Son Jesus, the fulfiller of God's righteousness, perfect and holy and without blemish, upon the altar of sacrifice, the cross, the righteousness of God's Law was magnified evermore than if we all had to pay individually for in us is no perfection. Jesus did not remove the law but He instead perfectly and completely filled its righteous requiem and glorified His Father's righteous judgments against all unrighteousness before all mankind and before the heavens and all who dwell in them. Any sacrifice by man would glorify the man and rob God.

The proof of this truth is in the acceptance of the sacrifice one time for all as stated in Hebrews chapter 9. A sacrifice can be made that is not accepted as we will soon see in the sons of Aaron. But an acceptable sacrifice is one that is consumed completely- and they all speak of a future sacrifice in the Old covenant and of Jesus alone in the New covenant. Go back and study out the acceptable sacrifices in the Old and see that they are but types and shadows of the real sacrifice they only saw in a distant image, Jesus. Father God accepted the sacrifices with 'fire' in the Old as Gideon sacrificed before Him in Judges 6:21, Moses and Aaron in Leviticus 9:24, and others. (See Solomon's sacrifice and Samson's parents' sacrifice and Able's sacrifice accepted while Cain's was not and Elijah's sacrifice in 1 Kings 18:38.) Only those taken in fire by the Lord were accepted and received.

What I am saying is that in what Jesus did for us on the cross, in His sacrifice for all sin one time for all forever, in that Father's full wrath on sin was satisfied and displayed for all to see, Jesus not only magnified Father God and glorified His righteousness. He fulfilled ours as pertaining to the law, actually becoming a great overpayment for our sin both individually and collectively. The very fact that Jesus ascended first into the heavens to cleanse the heavens themselves for us, and He was accepted and allowed to do this. In so stating His works finished, they are then finished and accepted by God. His sacrifice was greater than the debt and He speaks eternally to Father, and according to His own will, on our behalf. That is why Ephesians declares our acceptance before God is "in Christ Jesus." Our part then is revealing Jesus's righteousness and Fathers' righteousness in faith alone (Romans 1:16-18, righteousness is revealed only in faith). All other sacrifices remain "on the altar" of self sacrifices and the prayers of those under this altar blocked.

In Hebrews 10 we are taught that the law is only a "shadow" of the good things that are to be and that they, the law and its requirements, are not the realities of God. They are not eternal but temporal, they are seen and not unseen. But hidden from all was the reality of Jesus until He came and laid down His own life willingly, and not of force, for no man or spirit could have forced Him, for us and our trespasses. It goes on to say that this sacrificial system, which was based on the Mosaic Laws, only shadowed the truth of grace through Jesus Christ. And even though carried out all day and night, shedding more blood than we can imagine, could not make those who desired to draw near to God the Father in worship perfect; and that a perfect conscience concerning sin toward God. There is and there was no earthly payment that could do what needed to be done on our behalf.

The Word tells us that if these sacrifices could have made the offerers perfect would they not have then ceased? And if perfected, this ceasing of sacrifices would have permanently removed all of their guilt and consciousness of sin! But much the rather the very sacrifices that they believed covered their sins actually became a reminder of their sinfulness, because all of this blood could not remove their guilt or take away sin. In Hebrews 10:5-17 we then see Jesus begin to declare a truth to us who can see and hear, "Sacrifice and offering You did not desire, but a body You prepared for Me; with burnt offerings and sin offerings You were not pleased. Then said I, Here I am, it is written of Me in the scroll. I have come to do Thy will O God." So we are then told that in setting aside all sacrifices for sin God then became willing of His own will to send and accept only that which Jesus was going to do.

The Word tells this truth then to us, "and by that will we have been made holy through the sacrifice of the body of Jesus once for all" (Hebrews 10:10). I am not sure any magnification is needed here but if you need to see this just see the "once for all."

There then can be no other sacrifices, none, not even one. In the kjv of Hebrews 10:8 it declares God was not pleased and took no pleasure in animal sacrifices "offered by the law." This is a heart condition friend, a way or means of approaching Father God, not a methodology or theology. If we approach God thinking we can do anything more than His Son has already done, we are bringing forth strange fire, unacceptable sacrifices moved by fear and the human need to be in control through self righteousness. Grace declares this to us, I, Jesus, have finished all of the work, will you receive it? Law declares this to us, you must do something, some kind of payment must be made, and you must do it!

We are not made holy by what we confess, but by Who we confess by what Jesus did for us. We are called to reign in life by the gift of righteousness and the abundance of grace. These are both His work, not ours! Here is a great fault in our confessions which must be in faith. I do not declare my sins but my Savior's payment for my sins, for His sacrifice is the only one Father will accept. If Jesus has been seated next to the Father as the Word declares then His work must be finished, but the priest by the law never finishes his work of sacrificing animals and shedding blood, it never ends. It is in Hebrews 10:13 we read of this position Jesus is in, seated, "from henceforth expecting till His enemies be made His footstool." Paul declares these enemies as "enemies of the cross" in Philippians 3:18 where he urges us to follow His example by laying down all of our self righteousness and begin to walk in the righteousness we have been given by Jesus's sacrifice on the cross.

Paul declared he had not mastered this yet but that he had began a journey in a righteousness he could not attain to by any effort, which included the killing of those who believed in Jesus. Paul declared his heritage, his birth rights, his church position, his education, and anything else he could boast about in his own self as "dung" compared to the gift of right standing he now could see in what Jesus had done for all who believe. (Remember the altar for sins was outside the city gates and it was to be burned and consumed with fire- and it still contained the dung!)

The writer of Hebrews, although debated by scholars I think it is Paul, wrote this in Hebrews 10:14, "for by one offering, he hath perfected forever them that are sanctified." There is no more offering for sin friends; Jesus has paid the debt in full to the satisfaction of God's righteous wrath according to Isaiah 54:9-10 where God declared He would never be angry with us again on account of what Jesus did for us who will but accept and believe. The next few verses in Hebrews 10:15-17 speak of the purpose of the Holy Ghost to us who believe, He comes to remind us that our sins and iniquities Father God will remember no more. The payment has been made, I cannot remember any sin that Jesus has paid for. The question is not is this the truth, but do you believe it? Hebrews 10:18, "Now where remission of these is, there is no more offering for sin."

Wow! No payment can be made- nothing more and this according to His Word. How can we confess a sin that God has declared He will never impute to us? (This is Romans 4:8- 'blessed is the man to whom the Lord will not impute sin.') We have all been taught in church that the Holy Spirit will remind us of sins and convict us of them but that is just not the truth, it is religion. It will benefit us to look at John 16:7-12 once more to see the false teaching by many of the purpose or ministry of the Holy Ghost.

> Nevertheless I tell you the truth; it is expedient for you that I go away; for if I go not away, the Comforter will not come unto you; but if I depart, I will send Him unto you. And when He is come, He will reprove the world of sin, and of righteousness, and of judgment.

I pause here that we might see a few things before we finish looking at the ministry of the Holy Ghost: first, Jesus is telling His disciples and us that we are better off with the Holy Ghost than we would be with Jesus Himself being present. This is a lot to take in but simply put, Jesus was confined to an earth suit and He could not be everywhere at once, but the Holy Ghost can. He also said that as long as He remained, the Holy Ghost could not come. Until sin was dealt with, until Jesus was glorified, the Holy Ghost could not come. But once Jesus was resurrected and he had ascended, the payment accepted in heaven, the Holy Ghost was sent into the world at Pentecost. His mission, to reprove or convince the world of sin, not the believers. It is the convicting power of the Holy Spirit that calls a person to salvation and grace. This is what we have faith in, what Jesus did on the cross!

This is seen in the next few statements Jesus says in John, "of sin, because they believe not on Me." This is the sin He convicts the world of, not believing on Jesus. "Of righteousness, because I go to My Father, and ye see Me no more." The Holy Ghost speaks of Jesus's righteousness and that His place at the right hand of His Father declares what He did settled the righteousness issue forever. He declares Jesus's righteousness to us who believe that we are righteous and to the world that Jesus's righteousness is something they lack. "Of judgment because the prince of this world is judged." Satan and his followers have received their judgment which awaits them because of what Jesus did for us and all guilt is back where it began. But look at verse 12, "I have yet many things to say unto you, but ye cannot bear them now."

Many things that Jesus said the disciples could not understand until the Holy Ghost came and brought them back into remembrance of what Jesus had said. At Pentecost Peter declared to all who would hear,

> This Jesus hath God raised up, whereof we are all witnesses. Therefore being by the right hand of God exalted, and having received of the Father the promise of the Holy Ghost, He hath shed forth this, which ye now see and hear.
>
> Acts 2:32-33

This is that baptism of fire and the Holy Ghost that Jesus spoke to them before and it manifested in seeing and in hearing through the Spiritual gifts and miracles that occurred on Pentecost. Today we simply do not believe in this because we have long been taught it is no longer "for" us. They could not bear to hear this then, they could not understand, but once Jesus sat down and sent the Holy Ghost, the promise for us who believe, Jesus sent Him down and there was evidence of His arrival. There was prophesying and tongue talking and three thousand were saved the first day.

I heard it once said that what Jesus did not accomplish in Peter in three years the Holy Ghost did in one day. Peter declared this to the Jews who resisted the truth of grace to the Gentiles in the retelling of Cornelius's conversion in Acts 11:15-17,

> And as I began to speak, the Holy Ghost fell on them, as on us at the beginning. Then remembered I the Word of the Lord, how that He said, "John indeed baptized with water; but ye shall be baptized with the Holy Ghost." Forasmuch then as God gave them the like gift as He did unto us, who believed on the Lord Jesus Christ; what was I, that I could withstand God?

I doubt many see their denial of this as "withstanding God" but when this is not taught the people wander or perish. Don't settle for less than all that God has for you my brethren, do not let wise men rob you through vain words and traditions of men.

But see the ministry of the Holy Ghost is not to convict the church of sin, but the world. He reminds the world of Jesus righteousness and us of this truth, God our Father will not remember our sins and iniquities any more for we are declared righteous by faith alone! Having said this I feel it important to sow some more truth into your hearts. Look at Exodus 20:22-26, remembering that these things of the law are types and shadows of the reality of Jesus.

And the Lord said unto Moses, Thus thou shalt say unto the children of Israel, Ye have seen that I have talked with you from heaven. Ye shall not make with Me gods of silver, neither shall ye make unto you gods of gold. An altar of earth thou shalt make unto Me, and shalt sacrifice thereon thy burnt offerings, and thy peace offerings, thy sheep, and thine oxen; in all places where I record My Name I will come unto thee, and I will bless thee. And if thou wilt make Me an altar of stone, thou shalt not build it of hewn stone; for if thou lift up thy tool upon it, thou hast polluted it. Neither shalt thou go up by steps unto mine altar, that thy nakedness be not discovered thereon.

(Mark and remember "in all places where I will record My Name I will come unto thee and bless thee.")(Exodus 20:24). The Lord gave this to me several years ago and it has always been a Scripture that did not quite seen to fit until the Lord began to speak to me not only of what we bring to Him but of where we try to come to Him. It was in the telling of the Law being given that we are to see clearly that the first stone tablets were hewn of God's own hands and the second ones of Moses. In Exodus 31:18 we read this, "And He gave to Moses, when He had made an end of communing with him upon Mount Sinai, two tablets of testimonies, tables of stone, written with the finger of God."

This is almost too beautiful to pass by so let me share with you these truths. Father gave the laws to Moses in one moment of time, as seen in Exodus 20 but it took Father almost over ten chapters to commune with Moses about His Son Jesus Christ. Yes, the forty days and nights were not defining law all flesh can understand in one second, but Father drew pictures for Moses of the sacrifices and the instruments used in the Temple and of the dimensions and purposes of the Temple and it services and helpers, all of which would help us to see Jesus more clearly. Father's focus was not upon laws He knew none of us could ever keep but upon the fashioning of those things which were shadows and types of Jesus who was to come.

I love it that the Holy Spirit called this time communing with God. This is what those on the road to Emmaus did with Jesus as Jesus opened up the Scriptures to them and revealed all about Himself from Moses and the prophets. I love this that this is called communion- eating with Jesus, seeing our Savior revealed in every Bible story. It is then a truth for the Lord's Supper or Holy Communion that it is not a ritual but a remembrance of Jesus for us in every way He can be seen in us through the Word. What do you remember when you take communion? Is it your sins or His victory over them for us at the cross? Father wants us to see His Son and not our sin. The law could only point out those which Jesus would soon die for and remove forever.

So many come to God as if He were sitting on a throne of judgment but He has declared to us to come boldly to the throne of grace. Grace is a place where we come with nothing of our own good or abilities, having no control of self or of others, not controlled or controlling, free and freed, simply trusting in what Jesus has already done for us. I like to say that if He did not pay for it and finish it already, it won't be acquired or done. If forgiveness is not already taken care of, how will I be forgiven? If healing is not already furnished through Jesus's broken body, how will I acquire healing? If He did not become poor for me, how will I ever become rich through my life walking in His completed works? Yet looking back at the shadows we can see Jesus more clearly in these verses.

God does not want us to make any gods for Him or for ourselves. But in even the hearing of God's voice and His commandments sin broke out in Israel and they made a golden calf as God Himself cut the Words of the Law into stones. But blessings of God do not come from the judgment seat but the mercy seat of grace, the cross of Jesus. For this cross is the altar God chose for Jesus to pay for all sin and through that sacrifice to bring many sons to God the Father of us all. It is at the cross we will be blessed, never through the things we do. Let me add this to what is being shared- in the passages from Exodus were written these words, "In all the places where I record My Name I will come and bless thee there…" I asked you to mark and remember this. This truth then is seen in the revelation of Pentecost, when it is fully come as was written in Acts 2:1, "When Pentecost was fully come." Pentecost then had not ever fully come until Jesus had finished all of the work Father sent Him to do and had ascended in the heavens and cleansed even them with His own blood. Then the Holy Ghost fell with power from on high.

In the book of Leviticus 23:15-17 we read this, speaking of Pentecost

> And ye shall count unto you from the morrow after the Sabbath, from the day that ye brought the sheaf of wave offering; seven Sabbaths shall be complete; even unto the morrow after the seventh Sabbath shall ye number fifty days; and ye shall make a new meat offering unto the Lord. Ye shall bring out of your habitations two wave loaves of twp tenth deals; they shall be of fine flour; they shall be baken with leaven; they are the firstfruits unto the Lord.

At the end of the Passover, at the fullness of Pentecost all were to bring a new offering of bread baked with leaven symbolic of what Jesus did for us- sin no longer separating us from God. All other offerings of bread were baked without leaven…but this one, when Pentecost had fully come was a new and living way- and He is the bread of life-and the place where this was to be was a place of blessing, a place only God's Name was to be honored- a place where nothing human, no efforts of flesh were to be- it was a cross. Look at this verse from Deuteronomy 16:2, speaking of this place of blessing, "Thou shalt therefore sacrifice the Passover unto the Lord thy God, of the flock and the herd, in the name which the Lord shall choose to place His Name there."

Oh, can you see this truth beloved? It is through the Passover sacrifice, Jesus, the Lamb of God, we are blessed, and He is the sacrifice that brings the blessing, not human obedience, but His alone! When we pray in Jesus's name we are asking for Him and through what He has done for us and God has so promised to bless us. But if we come declaring what we are doing or what we have done, controlling or being controlled, we will find ourselves before the judgment seat, and it is empty, for now. But take special note of how this altar, a shadow of what Jesus was coming to do, was polluted. God said that we are to take no tool to shape it or hew it reminding us of the futility of human efforts trying to earn or attain to what God has determined was the place and cost of sacrifices.

Look now at the second set of tablets: "And the Lord said unto Moses, Hew thee two tablets of stone like unto the first; and I will write upon these tables the words that were in the first tables, which thou breakest" (Exodus 34:1). Oh there is food here beloved for those with eyes to see. Father said in Hebrews that He would write upon our mind and hearts His laws in Hebrews 8:10, "For this is the covenant that I will make with the house of Israel after those days saith the Lord, I will put my laws into their mind and write them in their hearts..." But look at Hebrews 10:16, after Jesus, "This is the covenant that I will make with them after those days, saith the Lord, I will put my laws into their hearts, and in their minds will I write them." It was in Proverbs 3:3 that we were taught that our hearts are tables on which God's mercy and truth are written. A heart of stone was removed from us and we were given a new heart made of flesh when Jesus died for us and we saw this, our old heart died and was replaced. The stone rolled away for a new and living way.

Only on a new heart, a fleshy heart, one that knows of His mercy can the laws of God be understood and received into the mind. The stone tablets show us the hearts of God's family under the first covenant and they never understood the truth of God's mercy and love and truth. One written on the minds in the old; the new covenant written from within on the new heart God gives us. Law given by man produces death as we make our own tablets of stone with our own self-focused efforts. The first tablets were carved from another Rock and by the loving hands of His Father, one of faith. His name was Jesus- He Is the rock of all salvation. (We will either fall upon the rock, Jesus, and find life, or be crushed by the rock of law, self efforts and fall and die.)

It was anger or wrath that motivated Moses to throw the two tables of stone down and break them and it was anger that provoked Moses to strike the stone after Father had told Moses to speak to the stone. James tells us that the wrath of man works not the righteousness of God and so it is. It is a strange phenomenon that those under the law could not see their Savior but He was easily seen and sought after by the blind Gentiles. The law is not the way to see Father God, He has chosen grace. It is only in Jesus's heart filled with love that Father's laws can be kept or ever would be. Surely as Moses hurled the tablets at the sinful Jews Father's heart was broken seeing His Son rejected and broken for them all. There is no altar of human effort that can bridge man and God save Jesus on the cross. There is no second Jesus coming through human effort, but the same Jesus is coming a second time- and now for those, as it is declared in Hebrews 9:28, (Amplified),

> Even so it is that Christ, having been offered to take upon Himself and bear as a burden the sins of many once for all, will appear a second time, not to carry any burden of sin nor to deal with sin, but to bring to full salvation those who are eagerly, constantly and patiently waiting for and expecting Him.

All of this to bring us to clearly see His Son Jesus and Him crucified for our sins. Jesus is the only altar whereon any man dare to come to Father God, for only in Jesus can we know that our sins are forever removed, freeing us to come in such boldness. Remember, it was God's will to reject animal sacrifices and require a body, and that was the body of His own Son for us who will accept this. This is Galatians 5:3-4, "For I testify again to every man that is circumcised, that he is a debtor to do the whole law; Christ is become of none effect unto you, whomsoever of you are justified by the law, ye are fallen from grace." Trying to come before God without the imputed righteousness of Jesus, a free gift given by faith alone, we will be discovered and our nakedness found out as was Ananias and Sapphira in the book of Acts. They tried to make unacceptable sacrifices to God by linking theirs (although done in deceit) with those who gave from their hearts to God through the name of Jesus.

I do not believe these two were even believers but they sought out a relationship with God through what they offered. You cannot mix light with dark- any mixture brings death- loss- tearing- and confusion. Just as the offerings of those who do so in deceit brought death to them when they tried to mix them with the true church so does any attempt to mix law and grace. Yes, even our tithes and offerings are made acceptable to Father through the cross of Jesus and according to Hebrews 7:8, "And here men that die receive tithes; but there He receiveth them, of whom it is witnesses that He liveth." Just as His resurrection speaks of our forgiveness, so our tithes speak of our faith in that truth, testifying of it in the heavenly realms. Everything we have is polluted by the world until we give back to the Father a first fruit or tithe in which, *'if the first fruit is holy the lump is also holy.'* By giving to God whatever is unholy, through the cross of Jesus, it is made holy and everything that remains is then holy. When we sacrifice to God we must sacrifice that which He requires, and He has declared praise of His Son, and of His love in the sacrifice for us, as acceptable offerings on His altar. All other sacrifices are strange fires.

In the book of Leviticus we see in the ninth chapter Aaron making those sacrifices that were shadows of Jesus before God on the altar He had declared but in the tenth chapter we see two of his sons, Nadab and Abihu, bringing forth what God records as *strange fire.* It is not that the fire was strange for it came from off of the altar nor was the incense probably strange although the Bible is not clear on this completely. But in Leviticus 10:1 we read this, "And Nadab and Abihu, the sons of Aaron, took either of them his censer, and put fire therein, and put incense thereon, and offered strange fire before the Lord, which He commanded them not." The Word tells us that God sent down fire and devoured them both. The name Nadab means liberal, to present or to volunteer and Abihu means the father of him. It would seem to declare that we cannot bring offerings to God the Father that He does not require for in so doing we defile the place of offering and the required offering by declaring another, actually diminishing the cost of the original and required sacrifice.

In chapter 9, we see the high priest Aaron, a type of Jesus, making the required sacrifices in the prescribed way and we see that God consumed those offerings and when Aaron stepped away from the altar, the glory of God appeared after the blessing was spoken over the people. God's plan was carried out in detail and His shakina glory showed up. When we worship God we are called to worship in Spirit and in Truth. We are not called to offer up strange fire, other things mixed in with the precious blood of His Son, the Lamb of God who has taken away the sin of the whole world. The blessing of the high priest then is not tied to some command but to seeing Jesus as our acceptable sacrifice for all who believe and are blessed with every blessing Father has. Every offering was to be offered in fire to God the Father in a shadow of the consuming fire of God upon His Son for our sin and iniquities. The full wrath of God's righteous and holy judgment on sin was put upon Jesus and just as the offering of the animals under the law was taken up to heaven when offered as prescribed, so it was when Jesus was taken up into heaven to sit next to His Father having satisfied forever all wrath on sin for those who are believers. It is in this that God brings forth His sons and daughters by His choice, His own predetermination, His election as He knows all who will believe. We are not born of God by our wills or efforts, but by His choice and calling. (And His calling goes out to all!) In this truth we see this love that must be in place for us to receive all that He has for His children.

The sacrifice on the altar was consumed with fire, the sacrifice less than the requirement: but when Jesus crawled up and onto the cross, the fire and wrath of God's Holy Judgment was met by a greater sacrifice that consumed the fire. His love consumed all judgment and punishment forever. This is the baptism of fire and the Holy Ghost, an all encompassing love that consumes everything that prevents that love from coming forth in fullness. When love met sin and God's righteous judgment against it, love overcame and won the victory for us. Only here at this altar is Father's righteous wrath against all unrighteousness exhausted forever. It is here that we are proclaimed righteous and Father's righteousness against all sin has been satisfied and completed. Can you see it yet?

There is not a question of 'sin or not' in this for us but of what do we say God has done for us concerning sin? If we continue to see through our own eyes we will return to the law wherein there is no more sacrifice accepted according to the law. The law requires confession of sin and transference of these to another while grace requires only faith believing that this has already happened for us when we believe. For it is by the law that sin is revealed but we are not under the law but under grace. But here you must know that you are dead to sin.

> For when we were in the flesh, the motions of sins, which were by the law, did work in our members to bring forth fruit unto death. But now we are delivered from the law, that being dead wherein we were held; that we should

serve in the newness of spirit, and not in the oldness of the letter.

Romans 7:5-6

We then born of the spirit of grace turn toward our Father and away from our self efforts and begin to walk in trust and not in fear. It sounds something like this, Thank You Father for loving me so much that I struggle at times to see it as I should. But today, I come to You in the knowledge of what Jesus has done for me before I was born. What I could not do He has done! I am accepted not based on what I do, but on what He has already done and I am seen in Him. He who knew no sin became sin and gave me His righteousness and confirmed your righteousness in so doing. Your Word declares that I am forgiven and seen according to Ephesians 1:4 "holy and blameless in Your sight." Help me not to look backwards through my human eyes of understanding but through the eyes of the Spirit. Help me to see Ephesians 1:7 through what Jesus has done, "In Him we have the redemption through His blood, the forgiveness of sins, in accordance with the riches of God's grace that He lavished on us with all wisdom and understanding." You see, Father, we sometimes think we are forgiven when we confess our sin but Your Word tells us that we are forgiven in accordance to the riches of Your grace, not our confessions. I declare to You that I believe that Jesus has satisfied all payments required and if I could have paid, it still would not have been enough. I know I still sin and do wrong but I declare to You Jesus, He died for my sin, for me, and His payment was greater than all of my sin. It should have been mine to pay, but Jesus came instead. There is no more I can do than to declare what You say of me, I am the righteousness of God in Jesus, not by any effort on my part, but because He came to do Your will, and pay for all sin that we who believe might begin to walk in the love You have shed into our hearts by the Holy Ghost declaring to us we are forgiven and all in forgotten. I am leaving the walk of self efforts and the bargaining for forgiveness based on what I say or how sorry I act and I am moving away as did Paul from human effort into acceptance of a greater reality than the law, the reality of Jesus on the cross for me. I thank You and praise You for who You are and for Your plan for me and I pray to better understand grace and share it with the world that they too might receive the forgiveness of sin and the gift of righteousness through the abundance of Your grace. In His Name, Amen.

I want to begin to draw this to an ending but I must share this little piece of truth with you. In Hebrews 13:9-15 we see all that I have shared capsulated in these verses.

> Be not carried about with divers, and strange doctrines. For it is a good thing that the heart be established with grace; not with meats, which have not profited them that have occupied therein. We have an altar, whereof they have no right to eat which serve the tabernacle. For the bodies of those beasts, whose blood is brought into the sanctuary by the high priest for sin, are burned without the camp. Whereof Jesus also, that He might sanctify the people with His own blood, suffered without the gate. Let us go forth therefore unto Him without the camp, bearing His reproach. For here we have no continuing city, but we seek one to come. By Him therefore let us offer the sacrifice of praise to God continually, that is the fruit of our lips giving thanks unto His name.

This is so beautiful to see in the heart if we can just remove our traditions and personal beliefs for a moment. Anything but grace is a strange doctrine, a strange fire offered upon an altar only those who believe can partake from. It is not through any law or rituals that we are profited but through Jesus we have been invited to the supper, the feasting on His body given for us. Just as Jesus was crucified outside the city in our shame we too must bear His reproach for the grace He has offered to us, and you will be if you stand in grace alone. But in so doing we are going to Him having ended our own efforts and attempts to settle forever the crisis of sin. Our sacrifice to God our Father through Jesus's blood, is not confessions of sins long put away but praise for His Son, and our Lord who bore our shame and guilt freely and according to the will of the Father. It is not what we do but Who we confess that is an acceptable sacrifice to Father, and He is looking at us in Jesus's finished works, for He is seated next to the Father's right hand having ascended. Those under the law or under the works of the law cannot partake at this altar, only praise for the completed works of Jesus, His finished works, "It is finished…" (John 19:30) is accepted.

Now I wish to finish this off with a teaching I have often shared with others as it was so shared with me from the story of Joseph, a type and shadow of Jesus, from Genesis 50:15-18. In this story we see Joseph's brothers coming to him after their father, Jacob or Israel, had died. Joseph had been placed into Egypt by his brothers who sold him into slavery but ultimately by God to make a provision for them during a seven year famine. They lived under his care for those years and even more and through Joseph they were cared for and provided for.

In the forty-fifth chapter of Genesis we see Joseph embracing his brothers and loving them and insuring their care but look at verses 14-15, "And he fell upon his brother Benjamin's neck, and wept, and Benjamin wept upon his neck. And he fell upon his brethren, and wept upon them, and after that his brethren talked with him." Benjamin was Joseph's brother by the same mother, Rachel, but the other ten were brothers by other women. They did not return the love of Joseph although Joseph gave the love to them. It reminds me of the parable Jesus taught concerning the forgiveness of sin and how a person who had knowledge of the many sins they had forgiven loved Jesus more than those who saw their sins as but little sins and therefore little forgiveness and little love. Let's look now at those verses in Genesis 50:15-18,

> And when Joseph's brethren saw that their father was dead, they said, Joseph will peradventure hate us, and

will certainly requite us all the evil which we did unto him. And they sent a messenger unto Joseph, saying, Thy father did command before he died, saying, So shall ye say unto Joseph, Forgive, I pray thee now, the trespass of thy brethren, and their sin; for they did unto thee evil; and now, we pray thee, forgive the trespass of the servants of the God of thy father. And Joseph wept when they spake unto him. And his brethren also went and fell down before his face; and they said, Behold, we be thy servants.

This broke the heart of Joseph, a foreshadow of Jesus, in that although he had already forgiven them, they still sought out forgiveness. It made Joseph weep, it makes Jesus weep as well when we do not see that Jesus has brought us into His care and see that although He did die for our sins, it was a plan of God and Jesus and the Holy Ghost before the world ever began. Look at Genesis 50:20, "But as for you, ye thought evil against me; but God meant it for good, to bring to pass, as it is this day, to save much people alive." Although sin was in our lives it was God who in His infinite wisdom planned the way out before it ever came to be; and He removed our sin by the provision of His plan of salvation, Jesus, His only Son, whom He loved, for those who would but accept His gracious gift. I cannot even fathom how God feels when this occurs today.

Before our youngest son died several years ago his life was changed, he became a believer just a few months before he died. There was a young man killed on the highway that I found that moved me to call our son and this began his journey back home and finally into eternity. We went to meet the parents of the boy who had died on the highway to tell them how much the loss of their sons life had changed our sons life, including our own lives. We did not have words to express this properly but in our hearts I will always be thankful to them for what their loss meant for our sons good. There was no need for an apology, giving a cause, there was no need to mention what had happened afterwards, but a simple heart felt thanks and appreciation for their sons life and the fulfillment of his wish, to help just one person in his life.

This is exactly what God did when He sent Jesus into this world to pay and provide a means of escape from the famine of this world. Jesus did what He did because He loved us, and confessing sins long paid for and settled are not what God wishes from us, but much more, praise for His Son. This is what Joseph sent his brothers back to Canaan with when he revealed himself to them, "And ye shall tell my father of all my glory in Egypt, and of all that you have seen; and ye shall haste and bring down my father hither" (Genesis 45:13). Do you want to know how to get the Father down here quickly, brag on His Son, on what He has done? Joseph's brothers never confessed to their father what they had done to Joseph for fear of what he might have done to them. But Joseph knew, and he always knew, and he forgave them all, providing all that they needed from his own heart of love. But love not received leaves us in a mode of defense, under the law, servants and not sons together because of what Another did that we might become sons. I pray this has served your heart's desire to better see this from God's perspective and not from our weak humanness and frailties. It is my prayer that you will walk boldly into the throne room of grace and stand before the Father who so loved you that He sent His Son Jesus to make the Way for you, declaring not your sins, but the glorious gospel of Grace we receive by faith. Jesus is worthy of all of our praise! Amen.

THE END OF RIGHTEOUSNESS

This is a statement if left unfinished would insult any follower of God. For God is righteous and above all imperfection. He is perfect, He is holy, He is God. But in Romans 10:4 we have this written word for us today as it was then revealed to the Apostle to the Gentiles, Paul. "For Christ is the end of the law for righteousness to everyone that believeth." The previous verse tells us that in trying to attain to their own righteousness, the written rules, the Jews failed to submit to God's righteousness which is of faith. This is what I have been trying to lay out for those believers who still feel the need for the controls of the law over them. Jesus is the end of the law, its performance, to be righteous before God. In the pursuit of trying to become righteous they, and often we do also today, fail to accept His righteousness, which is of faith alone. It cannot be mixed.

The Sum of All Fears

I suppose in an attempt to summarize this journey we have yet to see the overall purpose of this writing. "Perfect love cast out fear." (1 John 4:18). This is not a human revelation but a Spiritual one by the Word of God to us who will but receive it. Remember that Paul taught that a return to the law was a return to the bondage of fear. "For ye have not received the spirit of bondage again to fear, but ye have received the Spirit of sonship whereby we cry Abba, Father" (Romans 8:15). A relationship as sons and daughters is not founded upon performance but relationship…therefore we cry, Abba or Daddy Daddy. For the end of all fear is love which both fosters and yields trust. If you trust God you know He loves you and you then love Him. From these truths come all obedience from the hearts of men. (And all true obedience is from the heart!)

You will never obey anyone you do not trust. You might obey out of a fear of loss or punishment but it will be a short lived event. This is what the entire Bible is trying to show us and this from Father's perspective and not our own. You see, we fell a long time ago and none of us knew how to fix the breach between us and a Holy and Righteous God- so we just stay at a distance in which we feel safe. I call it religion. The most fear filled persons Jesus dealt with while on the earth were the very most religious, self righteous, and condemning- the scribes, the Pharisees, the Saducees, the Herodians, the lawyers or law givers- the religious. Their fear was one of losing control or power over others, an exposing of their failures and weaknesses, and all of this while claiming to be the righteous ones. They were even afraid of failures, and the fear held them in bondage unable to move.

It is the same today. Even fear of failure is fear, contrary to what we are taught, fear is not a spiritual gifting. Father did not give us the spirit of fear. The Bible says that sin is deceitful- it also says that law exposes sin hidden in man's flesh- but is it not amazing that the religious could not see their own sins but only those of others. Shouldn't the law have also exposed their sins? You see, religious folk are never wrong even when the Lord of all came down and told them that they were. It makes us wonder what He would say to us today, you know, in your church or mine? Filled with fear they spent themselves trying to stop Jesus from exposing them as nothing more than religious men trying to control- to keep the status quo.

On this journey through life we are all supposed to be continually growing and moving forward toward a higher calling and goal, running in a race to win it, the prize, not just finish the race. So many of us are content to just ride the crest of the flow we are in that we dare not to even imagine we, even us, even our denomination, our group, our church, our families are headed in the wrong direction. I know this, for it was Another who stopped me on my journey and turned me about- and I truly thought I was on the road He would be proud for me to be on. After all, I was reading my Bible every day, I was teaching a Bible study group, I was witnessing to everything and everyone that would but stand still for a few minutes. I was busy at church. I was tithing. I was helping. I, I, I.

My journey became a new and living way when I met Him face to face, so to speak; for I did not encounter Jesus in the flesh for He is Spirit. But I saw Him, and He saw me. It was a love thing that has taken me to places I did not even know existed in my heart. It was sometimes dark and scary and I was afraid- but over the course of ten years I see things in a different way than I did once before. I see everything through eyes of love, His eyes. I have been learning to live my life as one loved and known by God Himself, chosen by Him. I was saved by His grace, called by His Spirit, saved by His Son, baptized into His Spirit, taught by His Spirit, led by His Spirit, held by His love, kept by His power, I live by His faith, and grown by His teaching living on His bread. And so it is. The question is this one: why? Why would a God angry at sin, seeking a payment for it choose to pay for mine and yours with His only Son? Was it to satisfy His wrath only? Was this all done so that we could see how much our sinfulness makes Him sick, even angry?

"Perfect love casteth out fear, for fear has to do with punishment…" (1 John 4:18). I always feared being found out in my deeds of darkness until one day it came to my brilliant mind that God can easily see everything and everyone at the same time. But it was fear of being caught and punished that caused me to hide in shame, cower in fear, lie and cheat, run from the truth. So if God wished to punish us, why is this verse even in the Bible? It has been well documented in this teaching that the law was given to expose that which is hidden in all flesh, a sin filled nature. But the law could never change anyone or anything. But isn't it a strange thing to use the punishment for sin, hell and judgment in the fiery pit, as a means to draw mankind back to God? What does that say about our Father? The very reason He sent in Jesus was to remove sin so that we might come to Him as family, in knowledge of this truth. He loves me! I have been a witness for years to those who get saved and then go on about life. When I say "saved" I mean they answer the call of punishment and race down the aisle of some church or building and receive the fire insurance saying they are sorry for their sins and get the stay cool card which gets them out of the punishment for at least a week or two. Then, hearing the Word of God afresh they see once more just how far away they are from God and race back down the aisle again full of tears and regrets over their most recent actions. Saying they are sorry, they receive what they feel is forgiveness and go on about life as usual. This goes on and on until one day they grow tired of this repetitive course of "living" and they just quit coming to church because they feel convicted of any and every sin each week. I know, I tried this for some time in my own life. So what can be done?

I think it is a sad thing to make what Jesus has done for us, what Father sacrificed for us, all about sin and punishment for sin. Sin has never separated God from man but man from God. God came down and spoke with man did He not? Did He ever find a man without sin to speak to? No! There are none, no not one! You see, in order for us to be given a glimpse of God's true nature, He sent in His Son Jesus. All Jesus did was to draw sinners to Himself, to heal the sick, feed the hungry, free the oppressed, and to forgive all who came to Him. What drew them? Jesus did, and He was simply revealing the Father who loved them all and us as well. If men had known Jesus was indeed God in the flesh they would have cowered in fear, face down in the dust. But Jesus was revealing God the Father to us all, that we might run toward Him knowing He has made a way where no way existed for us to become family—His will but our choice and decision. It is all about having a free choice. If there had been no choice, it would have become by force. Love cannot exist where there is no freedom to decide for ourselves.

Adam and Eve fell because they wanted to be like God, did they not? Is that a wrong doctrine? Is that an evil practice? Isn't that what the Bible tells us we should do? How is that wrong? It is when we try to be like Him without His help- it is religion, our way. You see, trust must be learned, love must be seen and understood…In order to have a family, friends, once a wrong has been done, shame and guilt build a wall, a separation- and the plan seems to have been stopped. We have all been taught that "if we do something nice or say we are sorry" all will be forgiven and all can continue on. We have then earned favor or forgiveness in our doing. But Father set all of this aside and gave to us His grace, Jesus, in order that we who have failed might still have relationship with Him. But seeing our efforts as appeasements toward God leave us torn between "doing" for Him to make things alright or "hiding" from Him until we do. Here we are torn into pieces by life itself, never fully assured of His love. In this there can be no permanent relationship and this is a small way for us to view the Creator of the whole universe. Sin is in its very lowest form, taking what we want, not trusting in Father to provide. It is not obedience He is seeking! It is a calling to see His love for us, trusting in Him. In Wayne Jacobsen's book, *He Loves Me*, he says this,

> One can obey God and yet not trust Him, and in so doing miss out on a relationship with Him. One cannot, however, trust God and be disobedient to Him. For we shall see that all disobedience flows out of mistrust in God's nature and of His intentions toward us.

(Author note: Buy that book and be blessed.)

How can we make any of this about us- about our obedience? God's righteousness against all sin isn't focused upon mankind but upon sin "because" He so loves us and so hates the sin that destroys us. God's wrath on sin was fulfilled in the body of His only Son, and through His obedience, not ours- and all of the Godhead suffered in this, not just Jesus. The sum of all fears was taken by Jesus for us, all of them into His body, our justified punishment. In taking the wrath for our sin, our cup, Jesus was saying to all of us, Father loves you so much that He sent Me to fulfill His righteousness in the law, the perfect law, and glorify Him in so doing- and thereby bring forth a new and living way, a New Covenant in My blood, a cup you can drink, grace! God, our Father, has defeated sin, overcame death and sent out a calling by His Spirit to all through the cross. Come! But not through 'our' obedience, but Jesus's obedience! Just read it for yourself: "For as by one man's disobedience many were made sinners- so by the obedience of one shall many be made righteous" (Romans 5:19). It is the last hour and this is the last calling. Come! If you have a Bible, open it to the last page of the last book and see His will, His hope, His purposes, His plans, His salvation, His eternity, and His love for us all. Isn't it just a simple invitation to whosoever will but come! He loves you, come, please come! Let go and come.

THE END OF FAITH

"If need be" is where we once were and it is where we can remain in that old place as long as is necessary- it is our choice for this is why Jesus came is it not? To set the captives free from "all things." It is written of in 1 Peter 1:1-9 that we are to go through various trials and tests "if need be" until something so wonderful is seen that it passes human or carnal knowledge..... it is called the end of our faith. 1 Peter 1:9, "Receiving the end of your faith, the salvation of your souls." Wow! Not our spirits but our souls- our minds and wills and emotions, all of them. And how is this done? By coming through or out of the places of our trials and tests; simply placing our hope and trust in Jesus, in God's Word, Jesus is the Word made flesh for us, and having a single eye or focus, relying upon His goodness and love toward us. But as we have seen it is not or never has been God testing us but the rather it is us really trying Him and testing Him to see of what He says is truth. Now look at this revelation that ties this all together from Hebrews 6:17-20 one more time, *Wherein God, willing more abundantly to show unto the heirs of promise the immutability of his counsel, confirmed it with an oath; that by two immutable things, in which it is impossible for God to lie, we might have a strong consolation, who have fled for refuge to lay hold upon the hope set before us; which hope we have as an anchor of the soul, both sure and steadfast, and which entereth into that within the veil. Whither the forerunner is for us entered, even Jesus, made an high priest for ever after the order of Melchisedec.'* What is our anchor in the storms of this world? Is it not hope in Him, in what He has declared, in His Word, in Jesus? Is not this in His bountiful *grace* toward those who have no right of their own ability but receive meekly and humbly from that which Jesus has provided? Is this not the place Father invited us to come boldly to the throne of all grace? 1 Peter 1:10, *'Of which salvation the prophets have enquired and searched diligently, who prophesied of the grace that should come unto you...'* The end of faith is that *grace* of Father toward us who believe and trust in Him-even in our trials. The great and precious promises of God, written out for us in His Word, are ours, in this present evil age, for we are the heirs He speaks of here! And it is only sure to us because of *grace*! Romans 4:16, one more time, *'therefore it is of faith, that it might be by grace, to the end the promise might be sure to all the seed...'* Can you see it now? Can you hear it now? The "end" or purpose of the promises of Father is not for Him to give them but for us to receive them- the salvation of our souls, the end of our faith, the completion of faith is not simply in saying we believe but actually receiving the promise itself....but only the bold dare to approach a throne of grace- it takes faith that works by acknowledging His love for us, it takes time, it is trusting in Father's love for Jesus and therefore His love also for us. We have also seen and looked at how God poured out His love into our hearts by the Holy Ghost, (Romans 5:5) and that faith works by love. So what is the end of this trial or testing of God our Father in us? Is it not accepting the truth that we are loved and that we can trust in Him to love us and therefore deliver us in, not from, every trial and everything and in every need? Don't the crises of this present evil age send us running back into His arms? Not for things- but for Him?

Look with me now at 1 John 4:10-19 and let the Holy Spirit rub this into your hearts, receive this as a seed of hope into the darkness you are in currently- and move forward and away from these days of testing God, cross over into faith- because He is worthy of our trust and love and has proven Himself faithful in all things. He has moved us through Gilgal, the place of rolling away-Jesus has taken away our shame and has called us His brethren. Remember, "You will never fail…." He is faithful to fulfill every word we speak- the testimony of Christ is the Spirit of prophecy!

'Herein is love, not that we loved God, but that He loved us, and sent His Son to be the propitiation for our sins. Beloved, if God so loved us, we ought also to love one another. No man hath ever seen God at any time. If we love one another, God dwelleth in us, and His love is perfected in us. Hereby know we that we dwell in Him, and He in us, because He hath given us of His Spirit. And we have seen and do testify that the Father sent the Son to be the Savior of the world. Whosoever shall confess that Jesus is the Son of God, God dwelleth in him, and he in God. And we have known and believed the love that God hath to us. God is love, and he that dwelleth in love dwelleth in God, and God in him. Herein is our love made perfect, that we may have boldness in the day of judgment; because as He is, so are we in this world. There is no fear in love; but perfect love casteth out fear, because fear hath torment. He that feareth is not made perfect in love. We love Him, because He first loved us.' Perfect love is believing that Father is making us into the image of His Son- we will be like Him- even in the trials of this life- He is working "all things" for our good, for us, the believers, His children, His sons and His daughters. Wow! We must see ourselves as Jesus is in heaven, seated right beside our true Father and the One who gave us this eternal life. All fear cowers at Papa's feet! Do you remember 1 Peter 1:1-10? Do you remember "if need be?" Are we past this stage yet? Do we still need to test and prove Father? You see Father sees our faith and trust in Him as "more precious" than any silver or gold- for faith gives honor and glory to His Son- Jesus! It is Jesus we love, and Father for sending Him, for all He has done for us, for the grace and mercy of God come down in His own life given for us all- and we break out into a rejoicing with a joy that has no description- we are filled with His glory- His Presence in us! And in this truth faith is being fulfilled, reached, attained, achieved, its

purpose manifested, culminated- receiving the salvation of our souls- our minds and wills and emotions…..for this is salvation for all who face the evil day! No fear, no trial, no test, no trouble can move you- for you have passed from death to life- from fear into faith- seeing the kingdom of God in heaven brought down to earth to reveal our Fathers plan and to glorify Jesus His Son. And all of this because He has loved me- us- you! All of this was done for us! Because He so loved us! Look with me at 1 Peter 1:10, *'Of which salvation the prophets have enquired and searched diligently, who prophesied of the grace that should come unto you.'* Yes, both the law and the prophets foretold of the coming Messiah, the Anointed One, the Holy One, of Jesus the Christ! And they all searched out the Scriptures to see who it was that this was for. You- me- us- any and all who would but believe-faith! Look at verse 20, *'Who verily was foreordained before the foundation of the world, but was manifest in these last times for you.'* Can you see it now? For you! All of this was done for you, for me, for any and all who would but believe the good news of the gospel….Jesus died for your sins- do you believe this? He was raised from the dead to give us proof of this forgiveness? Do you believe this? He gave up His life that we might have His life in exchange for our lives? Do you see this yet? He did not withhold His only Son did He? This is the grace that was to come and that all the Old Covenant prophets searched the Scriptures to see who would be the recipients of this grace. Do you seek to understand this, for it was appointed unto us?

A Broken Bridge

I am sad to think of this now but this is exactly where this is to be placed in this book. It is a simple and short "bridge" that ties all of this together. It is a quick and very important look at what has happened after the children of Israel entered into the Promised Land. They forgot! It showed up first as disobedience to do what God told them to do by casting away all of those who lived amongst them, and they did not. Judges 2:7, *And the people served the Lord all the days of Joshua, and all the days of the elders that outlived Joshua, who had seen all the great works of the Lord, that He did for Israel.'* But almost immediately, they all began to do whatever they thought was right in their own eyes, no training, no future!

Peter wrote this in 2 Peter 1:16-21, (in my words) We are not following some story about Jesus, we were eyewitnesses to Him and to His majesty, we saw Him transfigured into His full glory- we actually heard the voice of God declare Jesus is My Son and I am well pleased in Him-Hear Him- in other words we saw and heard in physical ways, in this realm….but we have a more sure word of prophecy for you- the Bible, the written Word of God, recorded for you and watched over by the Holy Ghost Himself- and you will need Him to help you understand it. Go and read these verses and let the Word minister this truth into your hearts.

Next, Jesus appeared after His crucifixion and burial and resurrection to many, 500 or more….and then He appeared to two men walking away to Emmaus. He walked alongside them literally hiding himself from them 'in another form.' He did not want them to see Him in the flesh. How then did He reveal Himself to them????? He did this so that we might also be able to see Jesus just as they did, in their hearts. These two walkaways told Jesus all about what had happened in Jerusalem and they even confessed that some of the women "claimed" that they had seen Jesus raised from the dead, just as He had so promised. But they still did not believe. Look at His response, Luke 24:25-26, *'O fools, and slow of heart to believe all that the prophets have spoken. Ought not Christ to have suffered these things, and to enter into His glory?'* This is the same indictment for the church and for us today is it not? But look at what happened next, Jesus began at Moses and all of the prophets, *'He expounded unto them in all the scriptures the things concerning himself.'* Did you see that? Jesus revealed Himself to them in all of the scriptures the things concerning Himself, and so it is today. Jesus is revealed to us by the Spirit of Christ in us and by the Holy Spirit to help us find truth, all things concerning Himself. This is where we gain our faith, how we stand firm. He was revealing Himself not from the New Testament but from the Old for the new was not even written at that time. In verse 32 it says this, *'did not our heart burn within us while He talked with us by the way and while He opened to us the Scriptures?'* No one knows the Scriptures like the One who wrote them, for He is the Word.

It was Jesus who has taught us, *'Search the Scriptures; for in them ye think ye have eternal life: and they are they which testify of me...'* Jesus went on to tell those Jews and Pharisees who sought to kill him, *"For if ye had believed Moses ye would have believed me, for he wrote of me."* And later Jesus also spoke to the believing Jews, *"Your father Abraham rejoiced to see my day: and he saw it, and was glad." Then said the Jews unto him, 'Thou art not yet fifty years old, and hast thou seen Abraham?' Jesus said unto them, "Verily, verily I say unto you, Before Abraham was, I am."* Life is not found in the written words of the Bible but in believing in the One whom is identified in the written words of God- and they all point to the One Jesus Christ. Life is "in" faith in Him.

In 1 Chronicles 28:19 the Lord has showed me more truth about the Word of God and its purpose. Look with me at this verse,*'All this, said David, the Lord made me understand in writing by His hand upon me, even all the works of this pattern.'* This is when David was preparing the things needed to build the Temple of God (David was not to build it but to gather the things needed to build for his son Solomon.) in Jerusalem. The hand of the Lord was upon David to "do" the things He wanted him to do but he understood this from or by the Word of God. In other words, as David heard from Father God He revealed to him what He wanted David to gather or prepare for Solomon- the Temple being a foreshadow of the reality of Jesus Christ. In Ezra 7 we see a pagan king named Artaxerxes write a letter for and to Ezra the scribe saying this "of" Ezra, *'This Ezra went up from Babylon; and he was a ready scribe in the law of Moses, which the Lord God of Israel had given; and the king granted him all his request, according to the hand of the Lord his God upon him.'* This hand of the Lord is not achieved for Ezra's purpose but that God's purposes might be fulfilled. Look at what Ezra 7:9-10 says of this, *'For upon the first day of the month began he to go up from Babylon, and on the first day of the fifth month came he to Jerusalem, according to the good hand of his God upon him. For Ezra had prepared his heart to seek the law of the Lord, and to do it, and to teach in Israel statutes and judgments.'* The hand of the Lord is to say that God is directing someone out of His own power, and according to the Word, the things He wants done. For us it is not in the law but in the epistles of Paul written to the Gentiles the revelation of grace as given to him by Jesus. And so the will of God for us is to be found under His hand which is upon us as we study and search and set our hearts to know Him via His Word. Revelation knowledge comes from both the Old and the New and is drawn out by those who have the hand of the Lord upon them to furnish water for a thirsty man to drink.

If we fail to continue to pursue, to thirst for, to seek after, to enquire about, to ask, to pray for more of Jesus- to see Him in both the Old and in the New clearly, if Jesus does not open up the Scriptures for us, if the Holy Spirit does not lead us into all truth, we too will go the way of Israel- every man doing what is right in his own heart- and we will fall. A disciple is one who continues in the Word, forever. He does not seek in the Word so that he won't fail but because He is still seeking his Savior and Friend everyday, Jesus. I have not seen Jesus in the flesh for He no longer is in the flesh but I see Him each day as I open up the Word, He breaks the bread and blesses it, and I eat the manna of heaven. Do not be as those in the days of Joshua and Moses and even Abraham and forget all that He has done, even if we were not eye witnesses- we have a more sure word of prophecy- are you in it each day? What bridge will you be able to use to cross over the struggles of this life having never used it before? The bridge is faith in what Jesus has done for us. Can you see it now?

Hard To Understand

As I begin to speak of this I want to first pray for those who will read this for this is a crucial step for the believer. Father I pray in the Name of Jesus your Perfect Son for those who will read this next section for I know how much this teaching is maligned in churches today. I pray for open hearts and protection from the evil one who will once more try to rob this truth from them. That they may understand all that Jesus has done for us, I pray the Holy Ghost to help them receive and grasp the importance of His ministry to them. Amen!

It was to His own disciples that Jesus declared, "Receive ye the Holy Ghost." I am not going to debate this issue of Spirit or Ghost but I want us to see a truth in what Jesus was saying to those He was intrusting everything to. They needed to receive Him, the Holy Ghost, when He came. They had to all be of one mind and in one particular place and in prayer and suddenly He came in like a mighty rushing wind. I relate it to a storm blowing a door open and filling a room filled with smoke with fresh air. A vacuum was in the room, a need to be filled to bring a balance or stability to God's perfect plan. Jesus had told them to gather together and wait for Him and that it was better for them that He go away for if He did not the Holy Ghost could not come. Wow!

Which would you rather have and see? If we could call Jesus into the churches today everything would be all right- but Jesus said it would be better if He, the Holy Ghost were sent. He has so been sent. But often He is misunderstood and spoken incorrectly of by us because of what we have been taught by well meaning men and women who claim to "know." The problem is not in the sending forth, for He has come, but in the receiving. You see Jesus was telling His disciples that they must be in the receiving position, a position of expectancy, in order to receive the ministry of the Holy Ghost.

Have you received Him? This is how Mary became pregnant isn't it? The promise in the word became her expectancy, and it was fulfilled. Jesus taught us that when He came He would be in us and we would *know it*. Do you? Is there evidence of His presence in your life? He was sent to 'help' us or come alongside us and to declare to us everything that Jesus said, to bring us into a remembrance of Jesus and of His life, death, burial, resurrection, and ascension, and to help us to understand the Spiritual life of grace. We did not need Him to understand the law—do good, get good, and do bad, get bad. Even the world understands this. Our parents and teachers and policemen all share the knowledge of good and evil. It deals with the flesh or carnal man. If this were not so then why do people hide their crimes and sins? Why not just shoot people or rape and plunder and just like a dog get up and walk away without any fear of penalty. The knowledge of good and evil as controlled from without is what this is, external controls of internal defects.

Then along comes this Jesus fellow and He dies for the sin of the whole world and brings forth through His own sacrifice something we all struggle to understand, grace! Not grace like we are taught, but a radical grace declaring us unable to be condemned- free and loved by a God we once thought was angry at us for each and every infraction seeking to extract some form of penalty upon us. We did not need the Holy Ghost to explain the law but grace. So Jesus chose a man named Saul and changed him into a new creation and named him Paul. He was trained by Jesus via the Holy Ghost for over fourteen years in the wilderness or deserted areas where he actually saw Jesus and received instruction from Him. The thing is this- Jesus had already ascended into heaven and was sitting at the right hand of God. Jesus was revealed to Paul by revelation and not by any man. Paul who had no understanding of grace was taught by revelation through the Holy Ghost everything we now have written about grace. He was born again in grace but he had to grow into understanding by the teaching or revealing of Jesus by the Holy Ghost. Look what Peter declared of this growing in grace.

> Nevertheless we, according to his promise, look for new heavens and a new earth, wherein dwelleth righteousness. Wherefore, beloved, seeing that ye look for such things, be diligent that ye may be found of him in peace, without spot, and blameless. And account that the longsuffering of our Lord is salvation even as our beloved brother Paul also according to the wisdom given unto him hath written unto you. As also, in all of his epistles speaking in them of these things in which are some things hard to be understood, which they that are unlearned and unstable wrest as they do also the other scriptures, unto their own destruction. Ye therefore, beloved, seeing ye know these things before, beware lest ye also, being led away with the error of the wicked, fall from your own steadfastness, but grow in grace, and in the knowledge of our Lord and Savior Jesus Christ. To him be glory both now and forever, amen.

2 Peter 3:13-18

Now this is a lot of scriptures but focus in on these things for now. Peter is writing to the Jewish converts to faith in Jesus Christ who are being tempted to return to the law. This is why I believe Paul wrote the letter to the Hebrews as Peter declares when he said "as was written unto you." The battle in Hebrews and here is an attempt through fear and force to get those who confessed Jesus to recant their confession of faith and return to Judaism. The error of the wicked here is to move these from their faith in Jesus- grace- back into some form of performance based justification- the 'works' of the law. Many were losing their properties which were passed in genealogy or from generation to generation and were being disowned by their families for believing in Jesus Christ. Don't forget that Jesus gave sight to a blind man and the Jews threatened to kick his parents out of the synagogue if they believed in Jesus. The proof of this is in this statement, 'but grow in grace and in the knowledge of our Lord and Savior Jesus Christ...' This was the offense to the Jews and the answer for the believers. But why could the Jews not see? Paul declared it in agreement with Isaiah the prophet.

> And when they agreed not among themselves, they departed after that Paul had spoken one word. "Well spake the Holy Ghost by Esaias the prophet unto our fathers, 'Go unto this people and say, Hearing ye shall hear and shall not understand, and seeing ye shall see, and not perceive; for the heart of this people is waxed gross and their ears are dull of hearing, and their eyes have they closed; lest they should see with their eyes and hear with their ears and understand with their heart, and be converted, and I should heal them.'"

Acts 28:25-27

This is also what brought death to Stephen.

> Ye stiff-necked and uncircumcised in heart and ears, ye do always resist the Holy Ghost; as your fathers did, so do ye. Which of the prophets have not your fathers persecuted? And they have slain them which shewed before of the coming of the Just One, of whom ye have been now the betrayers and murderers; who have received the law by the disposition of angels, and have not kept it.

Acts 7: 51-53

You see in the removal of the law was the removal of control by the church or the Jews over the people. No one ever kept the law but instead they hid behind it claiming to be right in just keeping the external requirements of the law. There is no change in a heart under the law, but there must be a change in grace. There must be a death in order to establish a new covenant- and it is by faith in the spilled blood of another—Jesus our Lord and Savior. Peter warned of falling from this place of security in what Jesus has done for us as revealed to us by the Holy Ghost from within, and returning to the law, which was against us, and according to Scripture. This then aligns itself with this next part of Scripture from 1 Peter 1:8-12,

> Whom having not seen ye love; in whom, though ye see him not, yet believing, ye rejoice with joy unspeakable and full of glory, receiving the end of your faith, even the salvation of your souls. Of which salvation the prophets have enquired and searched diligently, who prophesied of the grace that should come unto you. Searching what, or what manner of time the Spirit of Christ which was in them did signify, when it testified beforehand the sufferings of Christ, and the glory that should follow. Unto them it was revealed that not unto themselves, but unto us they did minister the things, which are now reported unto you by them that have preached the gospel unto you with the Holy Ghost sent down from heaven, which things the angels desire to look into.

Why do we need the Holy Ghost and His ministry? Because it is through His ministry we see Jesus revealed in the Old and New Testaments of the Word. It is through the Holy Ghost conviction of the sin of unbelief is brought forth to those who do not and have not accepted God's gracious gift, Jesus as their own Savior and Lord. The gospel was always in the Old but until the Holy Ghost came down, no one could see or understand- they were being convicted of sins by the law. He is sent to help us understand and to reveal Jesus to us, our need for Him, and confirm all that He has done for us and in us. Everything in the Old spoke of One who was to come who would help us and free us- it is Jesus. He came not to remove the law but to fulfill it and through His death bring us back to Father in a New and Living way, a covenant in His own blood. He did not die in order for us to keep the Ten Commandments and return to the works of the law but to free us from them and to live in the knowledge of grace and no condemnation in the completed works of Jesus Christ as witnessed "to us" by the Holy Ghost from within.

> Whereof the Holy Ghost also is a witness to us, for after that he had said before, This is the covenant that I will make with them after those days, saith the Lord, I will put my laws into their hearts, and in their minds will I write them; and their sins and iniquities will I remember no more. Now where remission of these is, there is no more offering for sin.
>
> Hebrews 10:15-18

Why is the Holy Ghost sent down? To speak to us from within us, Your sins are all forgiven, removed forever, there is no more payment for sin-I was there and I saw it and bear witness to you that in your hearts by faith Jesus lives and He fulfilled the laws and He will renew your minds and write a perfect law of love in your minds! We do not need the Holy Ghost to bear witness of the law but to help us understand grace and forgiveness of sin, of what Jesus did for us on the cross and even now in heaven where He sits beside Father for us, as our high priest. So few ever even ask the questions that Paul wrote in Romans concerning grace or that Isaiah wrote asking Father "Who will believe our report?"

"What shall we say, shall we sin that grace might abound? What then, shall we sin because we are not under the law but under grace?" (Romans 6:1 and15). These are the questions flesh and blood cannot understand and few can accept because without the Holy Ghost sent down, without His witness to us, we will return to the law and to self sufficiency in our own self focused righteousness which is nothing more than comparison to others or blindness to our inabilities to keep God's perfect laws. Paul even scathed the Galatians church who had returned to the law with words that asked this question, both to them and to us. "Received ye the Spirit by the works of the law, or by the hearing of faith?" (Galatians 3:2). You see, the Spirit of God works in faith only- not in or with the law. "For the law was given by Moses but grace and truth came by Jesus Christ" (John 1:17). The law demands but grace supplies- the law brings us to death- grace brings life by the Spirit. If we are good in our own flesh, why do we even need the Holy Ghost? Do you see this now?

"Repent ye therefore, and be converted, that your sins may be blotted out, when the times of refreshing shall come from the presence of the Lord" (Acts 3:19). A time of refreshing, of rest. This sounds good to me. How about you? "For with stammering lips and another tongue will he speak to this people. To whom he said, This is the rest wherewith ye may cause the weary to rest; and this is the refreshing; yet they would not hear" (Isaiah 28:11-12). This is the baptism of the Holy Ghost- Jesus baptizing us into His ministry and bringing us into His rest and into this refreshing by His Presence in us!

This is not a baptism for the remission of sin but of ministry. It is His ministry and we are called or baptized into it. Our efforts to do should be finished now in Jesus- but His works are just beginning in us. They are not our efforts but His- the works He did and greater works- for He has gone to the Father and has sent down the Holy Ghost to be in us and with us and to bring us into all truth- a refreshing, a rest from all of our efforts- they would not receive Him, in fact they openly resisted the Holy Ghost as Stephen said, as Paul declared- will you? But this "refreshing" is a renewal, a revival, a rest according to the Greek word "anapsuxis or anapsucho."

This refreshing is a word used only two times in the entire Bible- this is a significant truth for us. This is the revival of the church, the body of Christ, and it is in each of us. It is not a calling out to God to start a revival but a believing heart willing to submit itself to Father and to the ministry purposes of Jesus in us by the Holy Ghost; revival starts in us- not with Father God. If there were ever a time this was more needed in the history of the church, today would be the day. So many get lost right here that they never progress into the need of this baptism by Jesus while others get all caught up in the "gifts" of the Spirit which are simply tools to do the ministry Jesus has called us into. We should desire these gifts but they should not become our ministry, they are for the benefit of others. Remember the Holy Ghost is sent to lead us into all truth and to remind us of everything Jesus said and did for us. It is a yielded heart Jesus is seeking to work through, not a heart hardened by traditions or fears. This is a call to quit "doing" (self effort) and into "being" (His grace.) Being led by the Spirit is simply yielding our hearts and our minds to His Word. The signs and wonders that follow this are accomplished not by our power but by His. But Jesus said "these signs follow those who believe…"(Mark 16:17). Are you a believer in what Jesus has declared?

I humbly offer my walk to you. "Ask and you shall receive, seek and you shall find, knock and the door shall be opened unto you. If you, being evil, know how to give good gifts to your children how much more will the Father of light give the Holy Ghost to them that ask." (Luke 11:18). Ask Him now and receive Him into your life brethren. We must need Him for Jesus said, "It is better for you if I go away… for if I go I will send the Comforter." (John 16:7). Do you know Him?

Peace in the Land of Rest

This is a place where many of us have failed to enter in because of a lack of understanding. In fact, just as Israel could not enter into this land of promise due to unbelief, few of us do either. Don't be offended. We will not believe that which we do not fully understand- we need a Helper. This place of rest still exists! It is not in a place but now in a person, under a new high priest who lives forever, His name is Jesus. You see rest is in Him, He is our rest, no matter what circumstances we find ourselves in or under. The truth is this- as long as we can- He won't! Our efforts limit His willingness to do for us. It is a place of giving up, surrendering to One greater- One we trust because we know and believe He loves us. All other ways leave us under a burden we cannot remove with human wisdom or effort. We have already seen those under the altar, a place many still are in today. This place of rest is a place where we can see the houses already built for us, where we can see the vineyards bearing fruit we did not plant, where we can see wells and rivers flowing we did into dig nor find- it is a place of completion and finality- it is in Jesus.

It is in His words, "It is finished." (John 19:30). What is finished we ask? Everything! Everything Father sent Jesus to do is finished! Jesus said he had finished everything, all the work Father sent Him to do and so it is. Everything the Promised Land held for Israel was there and yet only two of the original million plus entered into this land of promise because of unbelief. The Word of God declares the promises to us and yet it still requires our faith and no unbelief or doubt to receive all that is finished for us. The Bible teaches us in a story about a rich young man who came to Jesus asking what good thing he needed to do to receive eternal life. Jesus responded to him, "Keep the commandments." The man asked, "Which ones?" Jesus replied and the young man said, "I have kept all of them since I was a child." (Luke 18:18-30).

But the question is this: Why did he still feel the need to do more if he had kept all of the law? The young man shared a truth we all need to see. "The young man saith unto him, All these things have I kept from my youth up; what lacketh I?" (Matthew 19:20). I could write a book from those last three words—what lacketh I? The law will always leave us wondering what else we must do. There is no finished workings for the flesh under the law, it continues on forever. But to a man born of the Spirit, his work has ended as He rests in the finished works of Another. Rest is rest from all works! If this were not true then why do people try to qualify themselves in their prayers? Lord, I tithe and go to church, I work in the nursery, I serve on committees, I don't smoke and have quit drinking. All works that are declaring, "what lacketh I?"

Faith speaks this way: Jesus is worthy. In His Name I ask and for His glory I receive, amen! Faith qualifies Jesus not our selves. There is no rest for the flesh. Most of us can read, and if we would but read the fourth chapter of Hebrews we can see this truth for ourselves. It is written in the eleventh verse, "Let us labor therefore to enter into that rest, lest any man fall after the same example of unbelief..." This warning is followed up with these words, "for the Word of God is quick, and powerful, and sharper than any two edged sword, piercing even to the dividing asunder of soul and spirit, and of the joints and marrow, and is a discerner of the thoughts and intents of the heart."

You see, the Word reveals our unbelief. Even in our heart of hearts, do we believe what He has spoken and if so how do we receive from Father God? It is written in another place in the

Bible that with much tribulation we enter into the kingdom of God and so this is a truth we must also face for this is what stopped Israel, at least that generation, from entering into the Promised Land. It also stops us from entering into the promises of God to which we will address a little now and much more later. You see everything Father wants us to have will come to us "by grace and through faith" that His promises might be sure to all of the seed. We who are born again of God are that seed of promise as was spoke to Abraham through Isaac all the way to our entrance, our gate, Jesus. Isaac was only representative of Jesus, the son offered up for us all, and the real promise was reckoned through Jesus. It is through Him that entrance in and out will come to be. But it is still all by grace—what He has already done for us—and no effort on our parts.

Through faith, a gift given to us to use that works because we know and believe the love God has for us. So many fail here because they see faith as something they must prove they have. They have, as it is said, faith in faith. We do not need to display faith to the One who gave it to us, He knows we have it. We must stand in it, behind it, for it is *more sure* than all that we see or taste or smell or feel or touch in the natural realm. All of these things, in the natural realm, were created by the greater force, the Word of God who is Spirit. Faith pleases God for it is the way He created all things to operate. Our faith then is not in what we show Father God but in what Jesus has already purchased for us in His own blood and body sacrificed on a cross long ago. Our faith is in God, in Jesus, in knowing that they are more than able to do all that is spoken in the Word, each and every promise. Sacrifices and offerings were made according to what God told them to do and He accepted them in the old covenant methods.

It is still so today. We come not seeking Father to do something for us but asking Him to reveal to us what Jesus has already acquired for us through His accepted sacrifice for us. The laboring to enter into that rest is not salvation for we worked not for that which Jesus already has done on the cross for us. No, we must with great trials and tribulations enter in and receive that which is already prepared for us- even facing the giants in the land we are to occupy. For us it is facing the giant lies that have been set into our hearts and minds by the unseen enemy. But rest is just past the first battle- press on- but in faith, not efforts of flesh. We need not pray for faith for healing to be done but to receive that which is already ours in what Jesus did on the cross for us! This is not a way to become rich for we already are rich in Jesus.

This is not a way to become healed for we already are in Jesus. But everything that is stored for us in heaven is only acquired by grace through faith. That it, the promise, might be *sure* to all the seed (Romans 4:16). If it is based upon our own goodness or abilities then the promises can be removed by our failures to be good- this is law. But the Word declares the only way to be sure of the promises of inheritance of this kingdom is by grace through faith. Romans 4:16 is a key for us to see and understand this before it is robbed from your hearts. God had this written just for you. Go there right now and claim this verse as your own as you read it. Amen; so be it.

But is healing a promise? "Bless the Lord O my soul and forget not all his benefits; who forgiveth all thine iniquities; who healeth all thy diseases" (Psalm 103:2-3). Have we simply forgotten how great our Father truly is? Or are we afraid to ask of Him because we know we do not deserve anything from Him? Is it because our faith isn't enough, big enough? Faith worketh by love—His love for us! Our faith to receive is based upon how much we believe we are loved by Father God! His promises are good His word is good, and if you are His, you are good. Receive only! How? He loves you!

It is found in peace, also a gift from God given by Jesus to us before He left this earth. He said "peace I leave you, my peace I give you." (John 14:27). If it is a gift, then it is by grace for grace is a gift. It must be received not earned or purchased. It is a fruit of the spirit and not a root of faith. Faith does not produce peace but it allows peace in. In other words, peace always is because Jesus always is and so faith does not produce peace, it is the method that allows peace into our hearts. Peace is yielded as we keep our eyes and ears and minds "stayed upon the Lord." This is from Isaiah 26:3, and it goes right along with what Jesus declared to us in Mark 6:31 where Jesus sent his disciples to rest, "Come ye yourselves apart into a desert place and rest awhile."

Then it is removed the opposite way. Set your eyes on you, be stayed upon your performance, and you will be robbed. Jesus called His disciples and us to come aside and rest but the rest was with Jesus. Our eyes then are upon Him. So many of us are caught up in ministry and in working for Jesus and even in seeing the miraculous that we forget that rest is being with Jesus alone and apart from everything. Remember, faith is seeing Jesus. Our work and our family and our recreations and our investments and our travels and our friends, all important-but they are not nearly as much fun as when we have just been with Jesus for a little rest.

Look at what Jesus taught us about rest in Matthew 11:27-30: "All things are delivered unto me of my Father; and no man knoweth the Son, but the Father; neither knoweth any man the Father, save the Son, and he to whomsoever the Son will reveal Him." Before we go on to the next verse I wish for us to see that "all things" here means all things, even in the Greek. It is what we who are called to inheritance through Christ Jesus receive according to Revelation 21:7. We will inherit all things. But note that it is through Jesus that these revelations of Father come, for prophecy is the Word of God, and Jesus is the fulfiller of all things prophesied according to Revelation 19:10. Our testimony of what Jesus has already done for us allows others to receive the same- the testimony of Jesus Christ is the Spirit of prophecy.

Can you see this? All things are made by Him and for Him and through Him. How many? All things! He is I AM. Whatsoever you need, Jesus is the Way to the revelation of your needs being met and fulfilled according to the Word of God which brings us into faith knowing we are loved, not the other way around. We believe and then receive-but only according to our faith in what the Word reveals to us about the promises of God and Jesus. Faith comes by hearing and hearing by the word of Christ, a rhema word, the Word made flesh in us, real! Look on with me in Matthew 11:28-30, "Come unto Me, all ye that labor and are heavy laden, and I will give you rest." Again, the law creates burdens, the Spirit gives life, and rest is a gift, a grace from God our Papa to us. The next verse says this, "Take My yoke upon you, and learn of Me; for I am meek and lowly in heart; and ye shall find rest unto your souls, for My yoke is easy, and My burden is light."

It is when and once that our souls receive this rest that we can begin to see the burdens removed, the mountains cast into the sea, but always in His peace. A heart at peace brings a mind at rest. "Beloved, I wish above all things that thou mayest prosper and be in health, even as thy soul prospereth" (3 John 2). This is not a teaching on prosperity, but prosperity is not discarded. It is once the soul at rest is entered into that rest, prosperity comes in health and in finances as well. The key is not his wish but in the soul prospering or being at peace and in rest. It is in the wisdom of Gods Word that a path of peace is laid.

> Happy is the man that findeth wisdom, and the man that getteth understanding. For the merchandise of it is better than the merchandise of silver, and the gain thereof than fine gold. She is more precious than rubies, and all the things that thou canst desire are not to be compared to her. Length of days is in her right hand; and in her left hand is riches and honor. Her ways are the ways of pleasantness, and all her ways are peace.
>
> Proverbs 3:13-17

If we could but see this as it is we would never seek after the temporal things but only after this wisdom from God's Word for in His Word is all we will ever need. Notice again that "all things we desire" are not to be compared to her. Note that Jesus is become *wisdom* unto us. Peace and the pathways of peace are in Jesus and in the wisdom of Him who leads us. Look at His leading in Psalms 23:1-3, "The Lord is my shepherd, I shall not want. He maketh me to lie down in green pastures; he leadeth me besides still waters, he restoreth my soul."

Can you see the quiet waters, the green pastures? It is in them He wants us to rest and lie down, and there He gives *rest* (from restoreth) to my soul. Even as my soul prospers, rest and peace cannot be entered into by doing but by believing and receiving and just being with Jesus. Peace holds fast what grace supplies. If your life is without peace, if your home is without peace, you must receive His at once for in the peaceful place the provision of grace will remain and prosper. Jesus told us to guard our hearts, to let not our hearts be troubled…even as those He instructed watched Him be taken to a cross of suffering and die for their own sin. His exact words were, "let not your hearts be troubled,"(John 14:1). These instructions to guard the heart are where peace reigns. It is His instruction for us. We cannot change the circumstances, what others think about us, even what is occurring right now in our lives, but if we remain in peace, rest will come, things will pass, and our souls will once again prosper. A man at peace, even under fire, is no target of the enemy. It is God's peace in us revealed that works righteousness, not wrath! But we must guard what goes into our hearts.

Move away from the place that seeks to rob or remove your peace, find a place of rest in what Jesus has already provided for us and let Jesus guide you to that place in the desert to hear His voice, for in His Words will be the anchor for your ship in the storm, no matter how large or violent it may seem to be. It was the Word of Jesus so spoken long ago to a raging storm on the Sea of Galilee, "Peace, be still…"(Mark 4:39)…" and know that I am God."(Psalms 46:10).

A Place to *Cross* Over

Well, we have been in a full-out assault of the Law as a means, or a way, to attain right standing with God, and that according to His Word—yet if this was the intended purpose—it would be a simple error on my part. For it was Father "who found fault with the first" (Hebrews 8:7-8) and not me. Father had a better plan, a New Covenant, a better promise, on Another's efforts, more sure ground, and in this He found no fault. It is written in the blood of Father's only begotten Son, Jesus Christ, and in His perfect obedience, not ours. The truth is this; He cannot find fault in this covenant because it is not dealing with the weakness of human flesh or inabilities. So as I finish up killing Moses (the law and works of the law) I open up another area closed to us through our own inability to produce the right standing needed to receive it. The Promises of Father God to us are many but they are "yes and amen" in Christ Jesus, but He must be the single focus—nothing added and nothing taken away; remember, He is our rest. It is not a Christ-plus doctrine or blending of law and grace that will bring forth the promises of God to us—but by grace alone. Galatians 5:4 says, "Christ is become of no effect unto you, whosoever of you are justified by the law; ye are fallen from grace…" What a fearful thought for any believer, that Jesus's death and resurrection—the power of the gospel—are of no effect in our lives. His death is in vain as Paul declares in 1 Corinthians 15:2. This is why I have shared this truth! Nothing in the kingdom of God works without faith and that of what Jesus has done. We must not allow Jesus to be robbed in our lives; there can be no "works of the law" but a simple faith in what Jesus has already done for us. Can you see this now? Faith can only work in grace; the law voids faith! This is why so many believers are failing in this time; they are standing in both the law and in grace, one foot in heaven and one on the earth, one trusting in Jesus and the other their own efforts to be good enough.

I will add in these "great and precious promises" of God in the last section with everything Jesus has shown me in His Word concerning these promises to us, but first another short review—a quick reminder just in case you *fall from grace* or the higher ground above the righteousness of the law. (Because the law demanded our obedience, and we could not!) Look once more with me at Abraham and at what the Word teaches us of these promises. Romans 4:13-16 says,

> For the promise that he should be the heir of the world, was not to Abraham, or to his seed, through the law, but through the righteousness of faith; for if they which are of the law be heirs, faith is made void, and the promise of none effect; because the law worketh wrath; for where no law is, there is no transgression. Therefore it is of faith, that it might be by grace; to the end the promise might be sure to all the seed, not to that only which is of the law; but to that also which is of the faith of Abraham; the father of us all…

These are the verses I told you to claim earlier. Have you? The assurance of Father's great and precious promises to us is not found in what we do *for* Him or removed by what we fail to do but by faith alone in what Another did for us, Jesus. You see, we all were waiting for His coming—that is Jesus—and this according to the Word of God. Moses said that "another prophet like me will be raised up," and in so saying he saw Jesus afar off; in Nehemiah we read of Nehemiah seeing Jesus afar off when he said—speaking of those who had lost their standing in the community of God by genealogies, their rightful inheritance, and positions—in Nehemiah 7:64-65,

> These sought their registry among those that were reckoned by genealogy, but it was not found therefore were they as polluted put from the priesthood. And the Tirshatha said unto them, that they should not eat of the most holy things, till there stood up a priest with Urim and Thummim.

The Tirshatha was a governor, Nehemiah, and he could not allow those who had no proof of belonging to partake of the priesthood and its rightful access to the most holy things until a priest was raised up with Truth and Light. This is, of course, Jesus who is declared both Truth and Light in the Word. In Jesus is our right to these great and precious promises of God. Say you see the Truth!

It was Jesus who declared Himself the "ladder of Jacob" in John 1:51 to Nathanel his disciple. He was the One prophesied to hang between heaven and earth and connect the two. It was not through *our* obedience that this occurs but His obedience on the cross. Many declare the heavens will be "opened to us" when we tithe according to Malachi 3:10, but this is still the old covenant or works of the law. The heavens were not opened to us but to Jesus when He was baptized for our sins and when He received the Holy Ghost, Luke 3:21-22,

> Now when all the people were baptized, it came to pass, that Jesus also being baptized, and praying, the heaven was opened, and the Holy Ghost descended in a bodily shape like a dove upon him, and a voice came from heaven, which said, Thou art My Beloved Son, in thee I am well pleased.

Father God declared this *for us* but *to* His Son Jesus. If heaven is opened to me by what I do, then this must be wrong.

Everything we do and everything that we receive must be seen as done through the cross through Jesus's obedience lest we fall from grace and back into works of the law, which according to Paul in Galatians 3:9-10, "So then, they which be of faith are blessed with faithful Abraham. For as many as are of the works of the law are under the curse- for it is written, Cursed is every one that continueth not in all things which are written in the book of the law to do them."

Of course Jesus was crucified on a *cross* in order to fulfill the Word, which declared anyone hung on a tree to be cursed. The punishment of the days of Jesus was stoning not crucifixion, but in those days the Romans crucified—all of this that we might be even more assured of His identity. Blessings come through faith, and the law voids faith according to what we just read in Romans 4. It is not sin that voids faith but the law and our efforts to attain to God by human efforts or works. Can you see this now? Paul called these works of the law dead works. It is human vanity to try to add to the resume or completed works of Jesus, and as we have already seen it makes His efforts for us of no effect. That is scary, but in fact this is what most of us have been taught for years.

The promises of God as listed throughout the entire Bible are for us who believe and do not *try* to be righteous enough to receive them based on our own efforts but by faith alone, for only in faith is righteousness revealed and that faith to faith. It is through the cross, through Jesus, our High Priest in heaven, for us that we receive the precious promises of Father God and in faith of what He did for us. This is a focus upon Jesus alone, no doublemindedness, no doubting He is enough- we are called to only believe. The road across the sea that swallowed up Egypt was a road of faith; it was through the sea and not around it. It was through the fire the three Jewish boys were delivered from Nebuchadnezzar's fire. It is through the raging river on the dry ground of faith Israel entered into the Promised Land, and so it will be for us today if we are to see these promises work in our lives. For Jesus did not come for us to pray and ask believing in His kingdom to come down from heaven to earth, for it already has come down, but that in so seeing this kingdom life in us others will come to faith in God through Jesus. It is a narrow path of faith we walk on in this life, not the road of self efforts to get Father to do for us but a narrow wooden rail called the tree or the cross.

As we begin to cross over this bridge between law and grace, between the Egypt of our pasts and the Promises of Father in our futures, I wish to share one more piece of truth. 2 Peter 1:1-4 says, verse 1, "Simon Peter, a servant and an apostle of Jesus Christ, to them that have obtained like precious faith with us through the righteousness of God and our Savior Jesus Christ." How did we get this like faith? Where did it come from? Through the righteousness of Father and of Jesus—a gift given, not earned—given because we believed in what They have done for us. Now look at verse 2 of the same chapter. "Grace and peace be multiplied unto you through the knowledge of God, and of Jesus our Lord." How do we get grace and peace? How do we grow in these? Through human efforts? No! But through the knowing of what *They* have done for us. Verses 3-4, "According as His divine power hath given unto us all things that pertain to life and godliness through the knowledge of Him that hath called us to glory and virtue. Whereby are given unto us exceeding great and precious promises, that by these we might be partakers of the divine nature, having escaped the corruption that is in the world through lust." Note that He has given—past tense everything— all things, and we need to live this life; faith does not move God to do something for us but to release what He has already done on our behalf through Jesus. Why must we move away from law and grow in grace, be established in grace, and live in the manifold grace of God? Because only in the knowledge of grace, in what Jesus has already done for us on the cross, will any of Father's promises, great and precious, come to us! By grace through faith!

Grace is simply receiving what God has already done for us; it is not a motivating act of prayer, for all prayers must be in faith. Faith calls forth that which already is, seeing what is not as already finished.

We have all been taught that for us it will be some day yonder, but not for us now. But Jesus came that we might have life in this *present evil age* that we might have life and life to the overflow to the abundance of Father's storehouses. It is yes; I have spoken boldly against the law for the believers in Jesus but not of my own hand or power but according to the scriptures and for your edification and exhortation and encouragement that you might have hope in God, and hope never shames us, never!

I love Father's laws, and in them I have found my way past the laws, which are set to control us from the outside in (the same placenta that keeps us alive until we are born into this world offers no more life after we are born), and I have moved away from Mount Sinai to Mt. Zion, a mountain of faith where we have already come, where Father lives and rules, and where we are invited in and welcomed through the cross. It is a place where an altar now exists. No one of the law can partake, according to Hebrews 13:10, "We have an altar whereof they have no right to eat which serve the tabernacle…" No one! It is only in grace we can be partakers of the divine nature. Let's cross on over now. Let go of the law and embrace grace with both hands; you will not enter into His Precious and Great Promises with one hand on the law.

Effortless Change

There are many who teach and preach steps and methods to change—I have in the past myself done this—but now I see a greater truth. Any real change comes without human efforts; it comes as we go and as we walk in this life. Father does often extend His mighty hands into the realm of the natural to perform the supernatural, but even miracles do not create faith; they left the Israelites always wanting another form of proof. True change comes and is often not even seen until the change is manifested. I will give you some scriptural references to this truth before we begin the next section of this book. I offer to you the tree frog and some sheep.

As we sat on our porch one night with some very close friends I noticed a small tree frog had secured himself to the window directly above our friends, waiting for any small morsel to be attracted to the lights inside the house. As we talked the small frog either let go or released his suction-cup hold on the window and fell upon the head of our friend, startling him. His wife had just asked for the tree frogs to be at her house as we listened to their loud and constant croaking in the night. He thought it was a set up by Debi and me, but in truth it was orchestrated by a higher calling—"your teachers will be hidden no more." Father uses everything to teach us, and in having these little creatures exposed I have been given a gem of truth we all need to see. Yes, she took the little tree frog home and has enjoyed hearing him croak, although now there are many more tree frogs with him, to her dismay. It is not the voice of the frog we are to hear though but to witness his life. You see, we have moved into a new place nearer to our family, and the tree frogs have once again gathered to teach *effortless* change to people who like to work for everything.

I watched as one of the small frogs slowly descended down the metal siding on our barn; he was moving close to the plants that were just beneath him, searching out a good place to eat as the night approached. Our siding color is a very light tan or cobblestone, and I noticed how the frog was almost exactly the same color as was the siding. In a few moments as he neared the green foliage he stopped and just stared at it, almost waiting for something to happen, and it did. He began to turn from the almost light tan into a green color quite similar to the plants he was about to enter into. I then remembered how I had caught others on the oak trees that were almost gray in color—and my lightning quick mind saw it; they did not change by commanding it or by any effort (they did not jump up and down, nor did sweat bead up on their tiny foreheads in self efforts), but simply as they looked at what they were in they changed. If they were on a gray tree, they became gray; if on a green plant they became green; if on the light-tan siding they almost perfectly imaged the siding color, and all without any hoopla or effort. Was this a great teaching or just some metaphysical revelation?

I then remembered Jacob and his father-in-law who often cheated him in business dealings. They made an agreement, as Jacob was so inspired by God to do, to allow Jacob to only receive payments for his labors to come from the lambs born with spots or stripes from those parent sheep that were of a solid color. Do you remember this story? Go read it again in Genesis, for it is rich in spiritual truth. Jesus also received those who are born with spots and deserving of stripes as His treasure and rewards. But an angel told Jacob to strip or stripe the branches of trees and place them by the water trough where the sheep would often come to drink and to mate. Their offspring then became what the parents were looking at—stripes and spots. There is no effort extended by the sheep, but they produced what they looked at. The same is truth for the believers today. Sin focus will lead you into bondage of the law while Jesus's focus will lead you into His grace and by His truth. Sin will lead you into death; Jesus will lead you into life by the Spirit. A man is not changed by denying himself but by carefully and steadfastly observing Jesus—by the Holy Spirit, by His Spirit in us—and not by any self efforts, which are nothing more than the works of the law that place us back under the curses of the law. Remember, faith is voided by the law, not by sin. Romans 4:13-14, go back and read this again and again—go back and read Romans 4:16-17 again and again—and then see 2 Corinthians 3:18 in this light, without any efforts of our flesh, which says, "But we all, with open face beholding as in a glass the glory of the Lord, are changed into the same image from glory to glory, even as by the Spirit of the Lord." Can you see this now? The tree frogs don't jump up and down to change. They don't have a three-step process to observe before change manifests; they simply look at what they desire to be, and they wait until the change comes—without any efforts! Do you want your children to be born into the bondage of the law or into grace? Fix your eyes upon Jesus, and all born of you will be born of Jesus and His grace. Fix your eyes on Moses and the law, and those changed will become law givers and judges. Just as the Holy Spirit told Jacob what to do—for fruit to be born for you—quit looking to the natural but the supernatural—whatever the sheep look at they will produce—why then hold up the law?

How will this truth affect your walk with the Lord, my friends? Will you return to the works of the flesh, to carnal efforts, works of the law? Or will you simply behold the Lord Jesus in all of His glory and splendor, seated at rest next to Father God, and will you not see yourself seated next to Him at rest? Let Him change you from the inside out by the Spirit, for the only thing we can do is wait upon the Lord—everything else is of our own willed efforts—and they will all fail us sooner or later, and great is that fall beloved; I know, for I, too, fell! It was here my journey began back. Where will yours begin?

"All Things"

Perhaps there are no other words spoken that draws our attention more than "I love you." It seems as though every ear is tuned to seek and hear those words. We all have or will at some time hear that phrase in our lives. It may even be a generic type of statement, but it will be heard. The hearts of all mankind were created by Father God, engineered skillfully, to listen and receive love. In that need many things are introduced to us by the physical senses, desiring to fulfill a need that can truly only be met spiritually. Oh, yes, there is a physical love, but it can change and move and even leave us. I believe that is called *falling out of love*. This, of course, then means that we fell into it—love that is—in order to fall out of it again. This is a weak and human term for something, no, for *Someone* greater to reveal to us. It is a love that cannot be contained in human words or thinking for in truth, it has no beginning or ending, and it is alpha and omega. There are no tops or bottoms, no sides, no depths or heights, and no other physical dimensions by which Father's love can be measured. We try to understand it, but in each case, just as we believe we have seen the outer markers of His love, He reveals His love in another way that we cannot see an ending. To hear those words is life to the heart of every man and woman and child, especially when they are so spoken to us from Father God Himself expressed in a way that only He could do—His own personal touch—that identifies this love as more than mere human or physical love. In truth it is life to the heart created to receive love and then administer the same. It was the Apostle Paul who was speaking of this love without end, and only by the Spirit of God who declares to us all in Romans 8:32, "He that spared not his own Son, but delivered him up for us all; how shall He not with Him freely give us all things?" This is a hard-to-believe verse, but if we look at this as Father is speaking it to us it would declare that of everything He created, all things, there is nothing He won't now give to us with Jesus in us, for if He does not do so, He Himself is declaring all things greater than His Son, is He not? But He did not spare His only Son; He gave Him to us who will but believe—He graced Jesus to us—for indeed He is a gift that must be but received through faith. God gave us His life, for He resurrected Jesus from death that all in Him might live eternally with Father God and Jesus and the Holy Ghost. This is why the fear of death was overcome in Jesus for us to release us from its grip and fear and reign of terror.

But of this Father has so spoken through both the prophets and apostles and ultimately through Jesus to us of these things being our choices. Father will not force anything upon us. In Romans 10 we see the apostle Paul, the apostle to the Gentiles, sharing from or drawing from the Old Covenant a truth many of us have missed simply because we do not fully investigate "all things." I must first lay down this foundation; 1 Corinthians 13:7, speaking of love being the more excellent way, says, "Beareth all things, believeth all things, hopeth all things, endureth all things…" Before we can believe *all things* Father speaks to our hearts we must first be assured of His love for us; faith works by love according to Galatians 5:6. In other words in order to believe all things we must know Papa loves us. I have heard many teachings on this, but without the knowledge of His unconditional love for us, faith will never work. All teaching then must come forth from this platform: for God so loved the world…this is love, not that we loved Him but that He loved us first and sent His Son as the payment for all of our sins—all of them! The standard for love is not works, nor even faith, but the truth of the cross—the greatest gift ever given. Love cannot be metered or measured by any other act. First John 4:10 says, "Herein is love…" The words that follow are the only true measurement for love, "…not that we loved God, but that He loved us, and sent His Son to be the propitiation for our sins…"

Having said this we can then move to our part of this love—our response, so to speak. Jesus said, "He who is forgiven much loves much." Our response then to His love is in the knowledge of just how much we are forgiven—if little, then we love little—but if of much, even dare we say of all sin, how great is our love for Him? How can we believe all things or for all things if we cannot see through His act of His love for us, forever removing from us *all sin*? Those set free become free indeed, and then and only then can faith work in us to believe all things. We are often taught these things out of order, leaving many weak and sick and even dying before their time, never fully coming to see the truths of the gospel and the finished works of Jesus Christ, never hearing His voice from the cross, "It is finished," for it is not finished if we still see our sin as separations from His promises and finished works. To this I scold all who so teach this. Let's look a little further into this Romans 10 declaration from our apostle Paul, Romans 10:5-8:

> For Moses describeth the righteousness which is of the law, "That the man which doeth those things shall live by them." But the righteousness which is of faith speaketh on this wise; "say not in thine heart, who shall ascend into heaven (that is to bring Christ down from above) or, Who shall descend into the deep? (that is, to bring up Christ from the dead.) But what saith it? "The Word is nigh thee, even in thy mouth, and in thy heart; that is the Word of faith, which we preach.'

This is simply saying that we do not need to call out to Father in heaven for a Savior, for He has already come and done His works on our behalf. All can see in the next few verses that this speaks of eternal redemption. We use these words for those who will become believers. If we confess with our mouths and believe in our hearts that God raised Jesus from the dead we shall be saved. This is simple truth. With our words we speak salvation, and in our hearts we believe unto His righteousness, being given or imputed to us. But now what about that Romans 8:32 stuff? If He freely gave us His Son, how will He not with Him freely give us all things? Where does the "all things" come from? In other words who will ascend into the heavens for us or come down for us and provide these things? It is the same Jesus, and it is the same cross through which He suffered that He purchased for us eternal life and all of the promises of God; it is a finished work. Faith can only attain that which God has already provided and spoken. The problem is not with God or on His end but on ours—wrong teaching and a lack of knowledge that leads to death—an enemy of God. How can death take hold of us unless we are believing wrong, for Jesus so declared that He holds the keys of death and of Hades.

We must go back and draw off of the Old Covenant, to which Paul so wrote and spoke of in Romans 10 and see this truth from Deuteronomy 30:11-14:

> For the commandment which I command thee this day, it is not hidden from thee, neither is it far off. It is not in heaven, that thou shouldest say, who shall go up for us into heaven, and bring it unto us, that we may hear it and do it? Neither is it beyond the sea, that thou shouldest say, Who shall go over the sea for us and bring it unto us, that we may hear it and do it? But the word is very nigh unto thee, in thy mouth, and in thy heart, that thou mayest do it.

Here we see the word speak of salvation for those under the law; it was in what they spoke and believed in their hearts. It was so then, and it is so now! The answers to our problems and the keys to the promises are not of distance but of a heart condition—

not seeing and knowing just how much we are loved by Father—and not believing in our hearts what the Word has so shown and declared unto us. This is not a faith issue but a *heart* issue! The verses that follow in Deuteronomy are spoken for us to see this truth. Verse 15 says, "See, I have set before thee this day life and good, death and evil…." It is a choice given to believe or not. (Note that death and evil go together.) Look down a few verses to 19. "I call heaven and earth to record this day against you, that I have set before you life and death, blessing and cursing; therefore choose life, that both thee and thy seed may live…" Look at verse 20. "…For He is thy life, and the length of thy days…" Jesus is our life; He is the length of our days. (Do you remember reading from Proverbs about wisdom holding the length of days and riches in her hands and how Jesus is become our wisdom?) He is our health and healing, our wealth and prosperity. He is our all and in all, and to Him everything that is named must bow that His name may be supreme in all. The question then arises; what thing that is named is above His name? What sickness is greater than the name of Jesus? What financial disaster is greater than the name above all names? No, the answer to all of our trials and tests is Jesus in us, the hope of God's glory being shown forth in our lives. It is hidden not from us but in us—in our hearts and then it comes from our mouths—all of the promises of God are yes and amen in Christ Jesus. All things! But this requires us to be finished with *our part*, which of course is to remain in faith knowing how much we are loved of God through Jesus. Our efforts must cease! Our works and efforts to move Father must be seen as they are—useless! Faith doesn't move Father. He gave it to us to access all things. "For the Lord shall judge his people, and repent himself for his servants, when he seeth that their power is gone, and there is none shut up or left…" As long as you can, He won't! Grace is either our sufficiency, Jesus, or He is not! It is in our mouths beloved; you must choose…life or death! But remember, without death, no newness of life can come; the old must pass away for the new to come forth…

FAIL-PROOF LIVING

The journey back began with a revelation of teaching brought forth by the Spirit of God to me. It has been a journey I will always remember for in and on this journey I have came into knowledge of what God and Jesus and the Holy Ghost have done and are doing in my life. I had to lay down all self goodness and human rights and my own abilities in order to receive the grace imparted unto my life. Grace can only be received by faith which works only in love—a place of being loved more and more through understanding all He has already done for us. Law is a place of doing, an arena of earned by effort response…payment for our efforts…a place we deserve to be healed…a place where no one could stand—save One; His name is Jesus! Grace is a place of identity, having lost your self (all of it) and your need to be seen or identified by your efforts or knowledge or positions. It is dying to all natural fears, especially those that seek to preserve us in our old natural states, having lost the desires to return to those things that once bound us—physical or natural things— and identifying yourself as a new creature born again of God, by His will, and for His purposes. It is yielding all to Him, seeing your life hidden in Jesus, a treasure hidden in the earthen vessel, seeing ourselves as He sees us from His Revelations to us, His *rhema,* or Words. And it is learning to trust in a God and Father and Savior and Friend that cannot be seen with the natural eye, seeing His love for us first, and responding there to with love— moving from natural supply to supernatural as He so moves us. It is from here the fall is not able to become a reality; it is a trusting in His ability to keep us and taking up the responsibilities of those things He has given or graced into our lives. There can be no failure here. Do you believe in such a place? It was to this road I called you to join me—a walk for kings—do you remember?

After having studied this truth for several years I began to teach this scriptural truth to my Sunday night Bible study a few years ago. Recently the Lord has impressed upon me that this truth along with a few others are to be incorporated into this book. It is by His leading and by His grace I offer up to you 2 Peter 1:1-11. In this I pray the Lord to reveal Himself to you. Jesus is truth, and truth that will set your heart free in His presence to pursue the kingdom of God as never before, for it has been given to you. I submit to you first verse 11, "For so an entrance shall be ministered unto you abundantly into the everlasting kingdom of our Lord and Savior Jesus Christ." It is through the knowledge revealed in the previous verses that this entrance is ministered with abundance into His kingdom, and His kingdom is in us, to His praise and glory. It is the Promised Land, filled with great and precious promises, and if you are His, these are yours!

> Simon Peter, a servant and an apostle of Jesus Christ, to them that have obtained like precious faith with us through the righteousness of God and our Savior Jesus Christ; grace and peace be multiplied unto you through the knowledge of God, and of Jesus our Lord. According as His divine power hath given unto us all things that pertain unto life and godliness, through the knowledge of Him that hath called us to glory and virtue; whereby are given unto us exceeding great and precious promises; that by these ye might be partakers of the divine nature, having escaped the corruption that is in the world through lust. And beside this, giving all diligence, add to your faith virtue; and to virtue knowledge; and to knowledge temperance; and to temperance patience; and to patience godliness; and to godliness brotherly kindness; and to brotherly kindness charity. For if these things be in you,

and abound, they make you that ye shall neither be barren nor unfruitful in the knowledge of our Lord Jesus Christ. But he that lacketh these things is blind, and cannot see afar off, and hath forgotten that he was purged from his old sins. Wherefore the rather, brethren, give diligence to make your calling and election sure; for if you do these things, ye shall never fall; for so an entrance shall be ministered unto you abundantly into the everlasting kingdom of our Lord and Savior Jesus Christ.

2 Peter 1:1-11

In the seeking of His face, His very presence, the Apostle Peter is instructing the reader of this truth; it is through the knowledge of Him, of our Father God and of Jesus, that His promises are made to us and that by these promises His power *has delivered* (already done) to us everything we need for life and the godly living He *has* called us to, a life of glory and virtue- and thereby escaping the lusts of this life in Him. These promises are accessed by those whose righteousness is not their own but the righteousness of God, a free gift. This is why the journey had to be made first—away from law and into grace alone. These are past tense verbs Peter is using to describe what Father and Jesus have already supplied to us. These truths do not apply to those who are not seeking His face, who are not always moving forward, even in what others might call failures, times of drought or storms, seeing them as stepping stones or steps, a stairway that leads us closer and closer to His beautiful face. You see the pathway out of our circumstances is a road of faith believing in what He has already done and said. I do not believe in healings because I have seen many—and I have seen many—but because He tells me in His Word that He is our healer. Faith then is the access to a finished work, not the source of power to attain the healing. Healing is a part of His gracious character. Romans 4:16 says, therefore, it is of faith that it might be by grace that the promise might be sure to all the inheritance or seed; these promises are ours, all of them, through faith, that it might be by His grace toward us, and here only is our assurance. Grace is not just for salvation or regeneration, but it is a manifold grace, according to 1 Peter 4:10, and is multileveled, going out in every direction to those in faith. In fact Jesus Himself called healing the bread of the children, and we have a better covenant than they did!

It is easy to read over these verses (as I did for about six months straight) and not see what they say. First, I want you to see that *fail-proof* living is not only possible; it is promised. The Greek words that describe "ye shall never fall" are emphatic and active in voice that represents the action as accomplished by the subject of the verb. Another version better amplifies this terminology as "never falling or even stumbling, no not ever, or in no way." This, of course, speaks only to those who have faith in the action Jesus took on their behalf on the cross. The prerequisite here is having "like precious faith." It would seem that the apostle Peter is qualifying all believers into this great promise, for we all have certainly been given the measure of faith according to Romans 12:3. To a person who believes they are falling or failing or are under condemnation and under accusation or are agitated by a fault finding or critical spirit will certainly find this set of verses as food. To me it is as if the Lord is telling us that we won't fall even though we fall. I am quite sure Noah fell down in the ark as the winds moved the ark across the vast waters, but he was *in* the ark, and although he might have fallen down he was able to get up, and he never got wet. I feel it necessary to further clarify or explain the no-fall rule for you. In Galatians 5:4 we read this truth, "Christ is become of none effect unto you, whosoever of you are justified by the law; ye are fallen from grace." It is necessary for us to see this clearly, for if you try to live by the written letter of the law you will fall and fall often. The laws of God were not given to keep us from sin but the rather, to reveal hidden sin in us. This verse clearly shows us that to return to the law, or to return to trying to keep it, is considered a step down, a lesser height or position than that of faith in God's grace toward us. A step into self sufficiency is a step away from Jesus. Our efforts can never match His gracious mercies and kindness and love; in fact, they nullify His grace. We can depend upon Him, but we can also depend upon our inability to not break one of the many commandments of Father God; it is our choice. But if we are under grace we are free from the law. Jesus once said to remember the height from which we have fallen; I believe this is that falling or falling away from faith that works by seeing His love for us and trying to prove our love to Him. Jesus revealed this truth to the angel or pastor at Ephesus—he had forgotten his first love—and who loved who first? Every time we lose focus of this truth we fall—but not out of His hands, for Jesus said that He in fact held the seven stars in His hands. Even if we feel as if we are falling we are still held fast in His hands. This is what Romans 14:4 says, "Who art thou that judgest another man's servant? To his own master he standeth or falleth. Yea, he shall be holden up; for God is able to make him stand." It is not our own strength that will hold us up but our faith in Him and for His own sake. I want to slip in this little truth for us here; it is for life that all of this was done—life is living, is it not? Jesus came that we might have life and life to the overflow, did He not? Can you see this? The Bible teaches us that the just shall *live* by faith. Life then is a result of believing in what the Word says concerning us. This set of verses in 2 Peter 1 also tells us that as we grow in the knowledge "of God and our Savior Jesus Christ" grace and peace will become multiplied, not added, into our lives. This is not by acquisition of something we lack but the rather by a revealing of what is stored already in us. Timothy 1:14 says, "And the grace of our Lord Jesus Christ was exceedingly abundant with faith and love which is in Jesus Christ." This is a releasing of what Jesus is in and through us by faith. Philemon 6 says, "That the communication of thy faith may become effectual by the acknowledgement of every good thing which is in you in Christ Jesus." This is not head knowledge or education but a revelation to us from within us by the Word, knowing of both Father God and of Jesus who indwell us. Only the Holy Spirit can reveal these things! Furthermore, we are told we have already been given all things through this personal, experiential knowledge of Father and Jesus. These are not things we do to get them but to understand that in Jesus in us we already have them. Here we are then instructed that Father has made great and precious promises to us that through these promises we might be partakers—or those who take part in—the divine nature, His nature, having escaped the corruption of this life by no longer lusting after this life. (Remember Hebrews 13:5-6 and Matthew 6:33.) This does not say we should become paupers but that we have spiritual eyes that see our Father as our provision and reward and trusting in Him to move us through this life. The promise to 'never leave us or forsake us' was the prompting to never covet anything in this life- our lack of coveting does not cause Father to not abandon us though- it is exactly the opposite. Isaiah wrote of this in Isaiah 30:22-23:

> Ye shall defile also the covering of thy graven images of silver, and the ornament of thy molten images of gold; thou shalt cast them away as a menstruous cloth; thou shalt say unto it, "Get thee hence." Then shall He give the rain of thy seed, that thou shalt sow the ground withal; and bread of the increase of the earth, and it shall be fat and plenteous: in that day shall thy cattle feed in large pastures.

Once we see the greatness and love of our Father the things of this world grow dim in the light of Him. What once held us here in the lusts of this life are nothing more than waste to us as we began to grow in grace and peace, for they are to be desired above all things, and they are fruits of relationship with Father God and Lord Jesus our Savior by faith, which works by the acknowledging of His love for us. This knowledge of Father's goodness toward His own children replaces our need to be earth focused or fixated.

It is at this time that His blessings begin to flow, and we prosper as His rain causes everything to grow. Romans 8:11 says, "But if the Spirit of Him that raised up Jesus from the dead dwell in you, He that raised up Christ from the dead shall also quicken your mortal bodies by His Spirit that dwelleth in you." In other words what Father has done in Jesus He wishes to do in us. But this hinges strictly upon grace being the foundation and not the law or any blending of grace with the law. Paul once asked the Galatians this question, "This only would I learn of you, Received ye the Spirit by the works of the law or by the hearing of faith?" You cannot operate in the Spiritual realm by your own goodness; it is all by faith that comes from hearing the Word of God. It is a truth seldom understood that faith is not needed in the law but in grace alone. Faith is believing what God has already done for us in Jesus; the law is trusting in our own abilities to perform well enough to earn it. So many people are stymied here by seeing faith as their action—something they must prove or do—in fact, it is a response to what Father has already done! The question is not if this is truth, but will you believe what He has spoken? Without adding our faith to His Word it is nothing more than line upon line and precept upon precept, here a little there a little, but He is the God of more than enough!

The Word then lists seven areas of growth we are to add to the faith Father has given to each of us. We have already looked at the diligence—it is a matter of life or death to the believer—we are to approach this set of verses in, and so these seven qualities are actually already in us in Jesus Christ, but we see them as we release them by faith into our lives. For example, He says, "Add to knowledge temperance or self control." Self control is not done from the outside inward but from the inside outward. In fact, self control is a fruit of the Spirit, which is given to believers. Galatians 5:22-23 says, "But the fruit of the Spirit is love, joy, peace, longsuffering, gentleness, goodness, faith, meekness, temperance: against such there is no law." (Temperance is self-control.) Note that several of the qualities listed in our text are listed here; not as roots but fruits, yielded from the Spirit which indwells the new creation. This teaching is not about what we must do to get these seven qualities but rather what we must do to yield our old ways of thinking to the Spirit and release what Father has placed in us in Himself and in Jesus in us. This, of course, is Colossians 1:27b; "Christ in us, the hope of glory." I read in John where Jesus was praying for us before He left for the cross that we might see His glory, and I truly believe this is what Jesus was speaking of—His glory being revealed in His own. His glory in us and all of these qualities are hidden in us in Christ Jesus.

Second Corinthians 4:7 says, "But we have the treasure in earthen vessels, that the excellency of the power may be of God, and not of us." The Bible is not trying to tell us what we must do but what has already been done in Jesus in us. Right thinking cannot produce right living, but right believing can produce right living. Everything in this teaching is to be built upon the foundation of faith, which of course is simply best defined as believing in what Father has said and done for us. These truths will help you if you will ask Father for a revelation of His love, for this is His love letter to us. And so our journey to the Promised Land has concluded—we are here—these are His great and precious promises to us, His children, heirs and joint heirs of all things with Jesus our Lord and Savior and friend.

As I pondered going through each of these seven qualities and what they mean I have decided that if I tell you everything Father has shown me I am robbing you of your right to discover these truths from Him personally. I have brought you from the promise of God to Abram and from Goshen in Egypt, a place of nearness, all the way across Jordan, past our sins, past what Jesus did in backing them all up until we passed clean and over the river through and past our Gigal, the place of rolling away our shame and reproach in the knowledge of Jesus's finished works on the cross. We have seen the giants as our food, bread to cause us to be stronger and able to fight for our inheritance, and here it lies before us—fail-proof living. And only one thing will cause these qualities to not be in you—look at what the Word tells us—2 Peter 1:9 says, "But he that lacketh these things is blind, and cannot see afar off, and hath forgotten that he was purged from his old sins." The place from where we began we have returned if we ever forget this one thing; we have been cleansed of all sin by the perfect blood of the Lamb. When we forget this truth we become blind and cannot see spiritually or far off. Peter then urges us to make our calling and election sure, for if you do these things, you will never fail. Are you sure beloved? Only in grace can you be sure—Jesus's work on the cross is sure—His grace to us is sure ground; our efforts will always leave us just short, leaving us asking, "What else must I do?"

Remember, Romans 4:16 says, "Therefore it is of faith, that it might be by grace, to the end the promise might be sure..." Only by grace through faith can we have access to what Father has so stored in us in Christ Jesus in us. His promises are ours, and they are sure! Add to faith, goodness, His- and to goodness, knowledge, His, Jesus is become to us wisdom- and to knowledge, self control by the Holy Spirit, a gift- to self control, perseverance; in seeing what Jesus endured for us- to perseverance, godliness- being like our Father who has birthed us by His Spirit in true righteousness and holiness, His DNA and not Adams'- to godliness, brotherly kindness: seeing the kindness of God to us is true repentance, seeing Jesus lay down His life for mine- and to brotherly kindness add love- herein is love, not that we loved God, but that He loved us and sent His Son to be the payment for all our sins.

Of His Fullness

John 1:16-17 says, "And of His fullness have we all received; and grace for grace. For the law was given by Moses but grace and truth came by Jesus Christ." Can you see it? Not *from* His fullness but *of* His fullness have we all received…received what? Grace for grace! This fullness *of* Jesus Christ lies in every believer and awaits the awakening by the Spirit. You lack nothing beloved; everything we need is in us in Him. From a place of nearness to in us; this is a great revelation beloved. Maybe it will be through some words that I have written, maybe through a preacher, maybe through a friend, a family member, but when grace came to us, truth was there in us in Christ Jesus. It is a seed sown into our hearts, Jesus is the seed, and of course He sits waiting for His bride to awaken. For many it is nothing more than your hearts saying yes to the truth you hear or are taught, bearing witness to what you already know somehow. It is freeing, exhilarating, and it is life coming into dry bones. But how do we see this fullness of Jesus in us come alive?

Look at what Paul prayed for those in Ephesus and for us. Ephesians 3:16-21 says,

> That he would grant you, according to the riches of his glory, to be strengthened with might by his Spirit in the inner man; that Christ may dwell in your hearts by faith, that ye, being rooted and grounded in love, may be able to comprehend with all saints, what is the breadth, and length, and depth, and height; and to know the love of Christ, which passeth knowledge, that ye might be filled

with all the fullness of God. Now unto him that is able to do exceedingly abundantly above all that we ask or think, according to the power that worketh in us, unto him be glory in the church by Christ Jesus throughout all ages, world without end, amen.

Can you see it—the fullness of God? Again, it is not *from* His riches of His glory but *according to* simply saying that there is no limit unless you do it! But it is being rooted and grounded in love that enables us to begin to comprehend this amazing love of God for us in Christ Jesus. The verses tell us then that once we know or experience this love we will be filled with the fullness of God. Oh, say, you see now, beloved, can you dare to believe and receive this from Jesus? It was in John that He told us that "of his fullness we all have received," indicating a past-tense experience. It is called salvation, and it came through the cross of Christ. This power that works in us is "faith that works by love," bringing into our lives the abundance above our words and thoughts—and this glory is revealed in the church—in us—not in the buildings or organizations, but in the people who form His body, you and me! Look at this fullness again. Ephesians 1:22-23 says, "And hath put all things under his feet, and gave to him to be the head over all things to the church, which is his body, the fullness of him that filleth all in all." This is given to Jesus to do in us subjecting "all things" to Him because Jesus was raised from the dead, victory completed. But is the church really His fullness? Have we seen this yet? It comes to us though grace but by faith.

Ephesians 4:7 says, "But unto every one of us is given grace according to the measure of the gift of Christ." Not *from* the gift of Christ but *according to* this amazing gift a child was born, but a Son was given. Can you see it yet? Can you see Him now? Can you see His love for you? Ephesians 4:10 says, "He that descended is the same also that ascended up far above all heavens, that he might fill all things." This literally means Jesus fulfilled all things, including you and me, and for a greater purpose. Verses 11 and 12 tell us that Jesus empowered some apostles and prophets, evangelists, and pastors and even teachers to build up the body of Christ to edify and encourage and exhort them to do the work of the ministry, and Jesus gave these until something was to happen.

Verse 13 says, "Till we all come in the unity of the faith, and in the knowledge of the Son of God, unto a perfect man, unto the measure of the stature of the fullness of Christ." It is possible, is it not? But it comes when we see and know and believe and receive His love for us—experience this love for ourselves—and then receive all things that He has for us in this faith, which is simply receiving what He has already done and prepared for us, believing that Jesus truly desires us to be near Him, and He in us. Paul then instructs us to no longer be children moved with words tossed to and fro with every wind of doctrine, being deceived from the truth by cunningness and lies of men seeking to control us. Paul says that His body—the church, that is—is to speak the truth in love, growing up in all things in spiritual truths, being as Jesus is, receiving from Jesus a unity in which all parts work as one, "According to the effectual working in the measure of every part, making increase of the body unto the edifying of itself in love." And what is this "effectual working?"

Philemon 1:6 says, "That the communication of thy faith may become effectual by the acknowledging of every good thing that is in you in Christ Jesus." Faith draws out every good thing if Jesus is in us; Christ in us is the hope of glory. Can you see Him now? Where is this power? Where are the precious promises of God stored? In earthen vessels—us—Jesus in us. He is in you if you are His, and this power works by faith through love. Can you dare to believe this report? Will you? Can you say it now? "As He is so are we in this world." This is our faith beloved; go back and reread 1 John 4:16-18 again. Do it right now and receive this into your life. Be filled with His fullness! Eat of Him and take of Him, for He is life; He is our healing and our health, our prosperity and our wealth, and He is our all in all. Is He yours?

The Secret of Seeing and Hearing

Have you ever awakened and had a song in your heart that you sang all day? It occurred to me that one day as I whistled a tune from a song I knew my wife also began to whistle with me. Zephaniah 3:17 says, "The Lord thy God in the midst of thee is mighty; he will save, he will rejoice over thee with joy, he will rest in his love, he will joy over thee with singing..." The One who loves me sings over me; I hear His voice as He sings in the night watch, and I awake and sing what He has been singing, and where is He who loves me? He is in the midst of me. Christ in us the hope of glory! Here is the secret *code* I have been taught.

I want to shoot down all thoughts that I have found some hidden code in the Bible that others have not yet been able to see; I have not! Yet I will tell you that by simply living out what the Word tells us and believing it, no, believing *Him*, I often find myself being scolded and scorned and rejected by "Christians." I want to give you, and them if they are willing, the secret of seeing what we ask for. Psalm 91:1, says, "He that dwelleth in the secret place of the most High shall abide under the shadow of the Almighty." This Psalm or song of David is a song of victory or praise, and it came to him as he practiced out what he had learned during the long nights and days he spent alone in the fields watching the sheep. He practiced what he believed. David's songs were sung and written down because he was singing to someone—Father God! Maybe he was only repeating songs he had heard as he slept. Who knows for sure? You see, our faith is no more than what we do when we are not around anyone else. Do you think that when David became king and brought the Ark of the Covenant into Jerusalem—His very Presence—this was the first time he had danced almost naked before God? I am sure David danced before Father God many nights as he watched over the sheep. Can't you just close your eyes and see David dancing around the fire, singing his psalms to an unseen Father who delighted in him? Can we dare imagine the same of our heavenly Father? Would He dance and sing over us? David believed this; he so trusted the unseen presence of God that he was able to kill both bear and lion, and he was but a small boy! This is why David always desired the manifest presence of God—always! Are Father God and Jesus and the Holy Spirit a theory or religious thought, or are they real persons? Do they sing songs over you? Especially, *to* you? When you go to the dentist are they invited and remembered by you? If so then everything there will be different than if we forget they are there!

Your worst situations in life can become better—even opportunities—when we acknowledge their presence in our everyday lives. It seems almost as if we welcome fear and dread by not acknowledging their presence in our lives. Here is a key for you; fear cannot remain in the presence of God, for God is love, and perfect love casts out fear! Death cannot remain death in His presence for death is His enemy! Here is the secret place David wrote of; he believed in the presence of God in his life in God's love for him no matter what he had done, including sinning! David feared losing the presence of God more than any punishment he might have had to endure, but we—those chosen to receive grace—have been promised by the Lord Himself, "I will never leave your nor forsake you…" We have seen this over and over from Hebrews 13:5-6, and the response should be this one; "Therefore I will boldly say, the Lord is my helper…. And….I will not fear what any man can do to me." How easily fear is sold on the airwaves of this great land each day, every word denying what Hebrews 13:5-6 just said. Someone is lying; I wonder who it is! Is it Father God, or are those fear mongers liars, selling fear for profit, being blinded to a truth they do not see? He loves us! As I think back over my life I can see a difference in those awful days of fear, and even the days of trials we all often face. Acknowledging the very presence of the Lord makes the things seem to become small in light of who is with me always. I seemed to be small until I remembered Jesus is in me, in us all who believe, and even the storms must respond to His voice. Death could not take Jesus, for He is greater than death, yet He died yielding His Spirit to Father God's care knowing always that Jesus *is* the resurrection and that He *is* the life.

What does Philemon say in verse 6 about faith? "That the communication of thy faith may become effectual by the acknowledging of every good thing which is in you in Christ Jesus." So what is the secret? Practicing what we say we believe! Jesus once showed to a group of people—and many were even Pharisees and non-believers—that the power to heal was present, in that a man who was bed ridden and unable to walk, without any words, without any self efforts, could be healed simply by coming into the presence of Jesus. Another man said that he believed that if Jesus just said the Word, healing would come forth. Another said if I can but touch the hem of His garment I will be healed. And what of Mary and Martha who knew Jesus and said looking backward at what had happened, "If thou had been here he would not have died." Was that an accurate statement of faith? Yes, for no one died in His presence, but Jesus had something more to say and share with them. "Thy brother shall rise again."

Martha, not understanding His presence, said, "I know he shall rise again in the resurrection at the last day..." Was this an accurate statement of faith? Yes, for all who believe in Jesus will be resurrected at the last day, but Jesus had something more to show and say and share with them and us; it was a new revelation of Himself to them who had eyes to see and ears to hear. "I am the resurrection and the life; he that believeth in Me, though he were dead, yet shall he live." It was Jesus revealing Himself in a new and living way. And then Jesus called forth from death Lazarus who had been dead for four days. In His presence there can be no abiding death—ever—for Jesus declared, "I am the life!" Not I *was* life or I *will be* life but I *am* the life—now, right now, right now in your need.

Go with me now to Galatians 1:4. "Who gave Himself for our sins, that He might deliver us from this present evil world according to the will of God and our Father." This is the gospel beloved of God our Father; this is His will. He is an ever-present help in our time of need; what is it you need? Life! And it begins at salvation and grows as we come to know and believe the love Father has for us, as we grow in knowledge of Father and of Jesus who live now in us. As we begin to believe what His Word declares to us, as we acknowledge every good thing already in us in Christ Jesus, we are practicing His presence!

This is what faith does; it speaks, and Father, who is with us always and abides in us cares for His family better than all of us put together as one person would ever do or even think. This is not said to deny the circumstances we often find ourselves in but to declare openly that our Father is bigger than the problems we see with the natural eyes. It is the journey we all must go on, and you have been on one in this book. This has always been His plan—but our choice! Deuteronomy 30:19-20 says,

> I call heaven and earth to record this day against you, that I have set before you life and death- blessing and cursing- therefore choose life, that both thou and thy seed may live...that thou mayest love the Lord thy God, and that thou mayest obey His voice- and that thou mayest cleave unto Him- for He is thy life, and the length of thy days...

He has always been life and length of days to us, but if we do not acknowledge His presence in our lives, even fearing Him because of what we know we have done, we become here-and-now focused and are in need of deliverance by our Deliverer; His name is Jesus! He is our life, and He is the length of our days, not the physical life and the physical world controlling our destinies but Jesus! He is everything we need—and that is right now! He is a present help in our times of troubles, not a distant help we must call down to the earth; He is in us now! This is the secret place of the Most High. I in them and You in Me that we all may be One! (John 17:23). Do you acknowledge this each day and at all times even when we sin or slip up? Instead of acknowledging our sin we should acknowledge His payment for our sins and His presence in our lives for this is the power over all sin; instead of acknowledging our sickness and diseases we should acknowledge His body broken that ours would not be—for this is His presence in us, instead of acknowledging our faithlessness we should acknowledge His faithfulness. Instead of focusing upon our love for Him we should focus upon His love for us. Instead of being fixated upon death we should be fixated upon life, and all of these are in Jesus who lives in us. He is alive forevermore, and He who lives forever in me holds the keys to death and Hades; oh, death where is your sting now?

Do you remember when we began this journey when I wrote of Numbers 5:1-4 and how Father wanted all those lepers and those with issues and those who had touched death to be removed from the camps of Israel so that He could be with them? Can you see His love in this now? His desire is to be with us always—near to us—and now through what Jesus has done on the cross, removing all sin forever for those in faith. Father in Jesus in us is a fact! He has always desired to be with us and now even better He is *in* us always even until the end of the age. This is a truth and not a religion, and the religious and the enemy of Father wants us to ignore and to refocus us back on our old natural self-seeking lives. But because the Lamb of God, Jesus, came and took away all the sin of the world we can enjoy His presence each and every day—even when, especially when, we slip up—until He has become the single focus (the single eye) and His goodness and life and light drive all darkness from around us. No one who really believes that Christ lives in them and Father in Jesus in us could believe His perfection could be in sinful flesh if Jesus did not really do what the Bible says—we would be burnt alive—but we live! I was angry once for what I thought I knew, but now I see how much He yearned to be with us, close to us, and even more so, sending Jesus in for us to free us that He might commune with us now and forever. Don't let words of unbelief rob you of the eternal presence of Father in you now, for this is the plan and will of Him who created all of this for us to be with Him and walk and talk with Him in the cool of the day. This is even better than in the beginning, for we are secured by a work we did not do and could not do—freed from all self efforts to attain and freed from a cross we could not carry and for sins we could never pay enough for, seeing a love beyond human understanding, the love of God for us in Christ Jesus. Do you know Him? If you do not know this Savior, ask Him into your heart now and live forever. There is no death in the presence of Father God, for He is life, and He is the Resurrection for us who have died to ourselves. Even now come—come up thither—to the higher place, risen in Christ Jesus, a place many have fallen from—grace! The highest calling for all, a place we can only receive!

Practice being in His Presence- for in Him is everything we will ever need. Grow in grace, be established in grace, for in grace is all truth revealed, fully showing us all that Father has done for us in Jesus Christ on the cross; He is our sufficiency. Don't confuse our needs with things He has already set aside for us. We need His presence, and you already have it in Jesus our Lord, amen! But you still must choose life, and length of days is assured to us by faith in who is in us to His glory. Amen! Can you hear Him singing now?

Epilogue

Jesus once told John in a revelation from heaven to take the "little book" and to eat it; it would be sweet in his mouth, but it would make his belly bitter. I have often thought about that statement as it was also given to me one day by the Lord through the Holy Spirit. It makes a lot of sense to me now as I come to the end of this writing. Jesus has filled me over and over, and I have discharged the same to you; it makes me sick to my stomach to think that what was sweet to me in my mouth was written out and few will receive it. I am not bitter at anyone but saddened—sick—at the spirit of the world that has hardened all of our hearts, wounded us, and blamed it upon our Father in heaven, left us slow to believe and dull, blinded by the law and legalism and religion, never receiving the truth from the Word. Jesus knew this sadness, as well. He wept over Jerusalem even as they rejected Him. In John 6:36 Jesus spoke these words, "But I said unto you, that ye also have seen me, and believe not." Can you feel His pain in these words?

People only wanted Jesus to do for them earthly or natural things, feed them, make it easier for them, and show them signs and wonders, which would never satisfy their need for more. But His peace was not removed from Him as He spoke the Words that have healed my heart. John 6:37 says, "All that the Father giveth me shall come to me; and him that cometh to me I will in no wise cast out." Jesus returned His focus upon the plan of Father God. John 6:39 says, "And this is the Father's will which hath sent me, that of all which he hath given me I should lose nothing, but should raise it up again at the last day." If Father has so spoken to your hearts in this writing I have done His will; it is not for nothing. In fact, it is the purpose of this writing—you! Oh, I have and often still do try to make it about me; it is a failing common to us on this earth, but I won't allow my peace to be robbed by those who have not heard the call of the Lord. It is a call to life. It is why Jesus came down, to give us life and hope and peace in abundance. The law cannot bring forth life; it is the minister of death, and only in Jesus can you be raised up alive forevermore.

But as I wonder at this I know many have already rejected this; it is their choice. But for you who have been spoken to by the Lord through this teaching, don't stop here; there is always more, keep on climbing, keep on seeking, ask Him for even more, and expect Him to show up. Jesus is still revealing Himself to those who seek Him. Set your anchor of hope in the Holy of Holies, a place where grace is established, where hope may be challenged but never is removed, where His peace remains even in the storm in the seat of you, your heart of hearts. Never quit, don't stop, let the troubles fall away, embrace them, thank Father in them, and learn from them, for this is His will for you and for me and move ever upward toward the higher calling. Don't' be dismayed or despaired; this is His will—to be made more like Jesus every day. Grow in grace, stay in peace, and trust in Him to change those who will not be changed, to change those things and circumstances about us, and allow them the free choice, for this is the will of God our Father for all. But for you who have an ear, it is the call of Jesus to us. "Come up thither…"